IMAGES
*of America*

# UPLAND

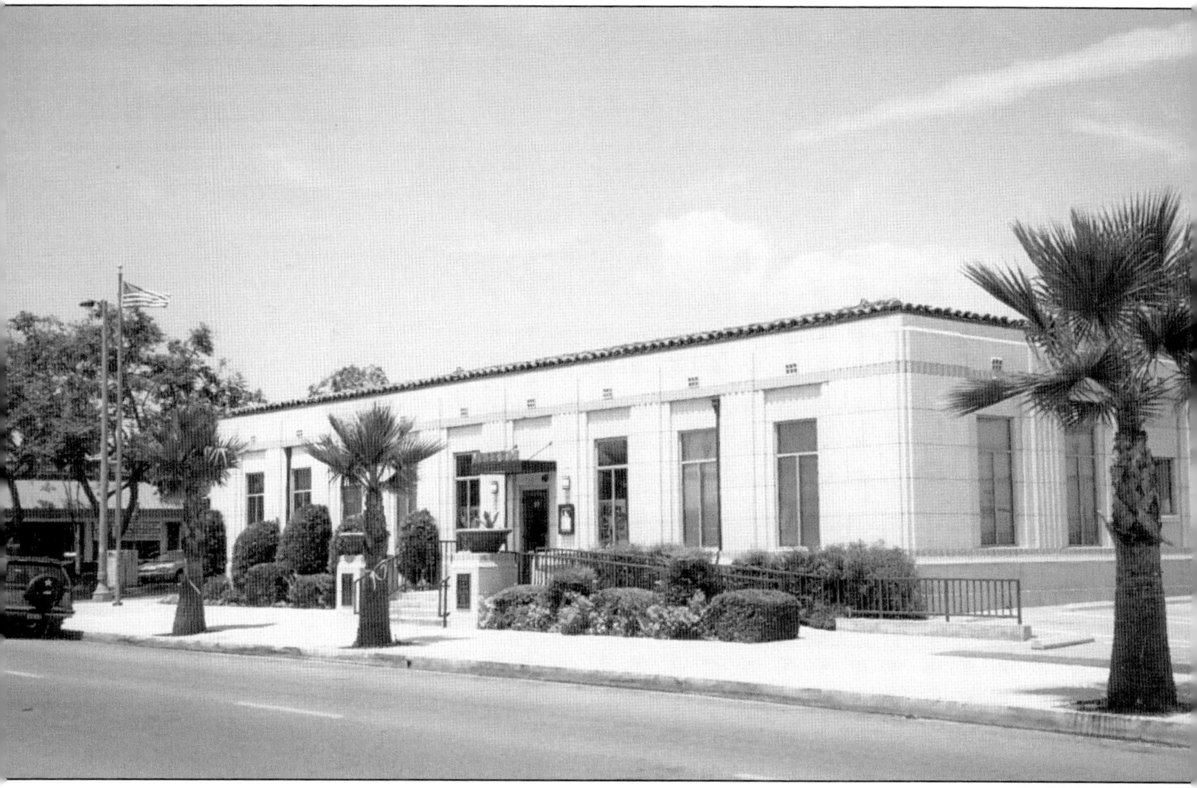

The Cooper Regional History Museum is located in the former Ontario-Cucamonga (O.K.) Fruit Exchange building, which was erected in 1937 at the northeast corner of Second Avenue and A Street. The acquisition and partial renovation of the building was made possible by funds from the estate of Ada Cooper following her death in 1993. (Courtesy Cooper Regional History Museum.)

**ON THE COVER:** "Boys will be boys!" In 1915, the Upland Volunteer Fire Department was on the receiving end of this shiny new fire truck. The lucky driver in the photograph is Mayor T. R. Woodbridge. (Courtesy Cooper Regional History Museum.)

IMAGES
*of America*

# UPLAND

Donald Laine Clucas with
Marilyn Anderson and the Cooper Museum

ARCADIA
PUBLISHING

ISBN 978-0-7385-6984-0

Published by Arcadia Publishing
Charleston, South Carolina

Printed in the United States of America

Library of Congress Catalog Card Number: 2008933394

For all general information contact Arcadia Publishing at:
Telephone 843-853-2070
Fax 843-853-0044
E-mail sales@arcadiapublishing.com
For customer service and orders:
Toll-Free 1-888-313-2665

Visit us on the Internet at www.arcadiapublishing.com

*To Avery Grace and Peyton Alison from Grandpops.*
*I hope you love the places you live in as much as I have loved mine.*

# Contents

# ACKNOWLEDGMENTS

I am grateful to several people for their help on this project. First, thanks to Marilyn Anderson, museum director of the Cooper Museum in Upland, for allowing me to spend a great amount of time in the vault of the museum in order to find the majority of the photographs presented in this book. Also thanks to Lola Lowe of the Cooper Museum for her help in gathering photographs. Thanks to Gena Sizoo, senior library assistant for the Upland Public Library, who helped me not only with this project, but also with others before. My thanks to Bob Dexter, Rick Hess, Cora Rietkerk and her daughter Helen Rietkerk Esh, Michael Stewart, and Dwight Bert for allowing me the use of personal photographs. Thanks also to Wendy Polley, web and graphics director for the San Antonio Community Hospital, and Kelly Zackmann, local history librarian at the Ontario City Library, for assistance with photographs from the institutions they represent. My gratitude also goes to Debbie Seracini of Arcadia Publishing for her incredible guidance and to Scott Davis of Arcadia for his help in making certain I got the photographs done the right way. And, as always, thanks to my wife, Joanie, also an author, who helped with the editing of this book and has continually given me her support through every project I have taken on.

Unless otherwise noted, all images appear courtesy of the Cooper Regional Historical Museum. Other images appear courtesy Upland Public Library (UPL), Robert Dexter (RDX), Rick Hess (RHS), Michael Stewart (MST), the Rietkerk family (RKT), Dwight Bert (DBT), Ontario City Library (OCL), and San Antonio Community Hospital (SACH).

# INTRODUCTION

The roots of Upland lie intertwined with her neighbors to the east and south: Rancho Cucamonga and Ontario. The original inhabitants were Native Americans who called themselves Tongva. The modern history of the area (that period following the Native American era) finds its beginnings with the arrival of Franciscan priests and Spanish soldiers. The first expedition through the region was led by Capt. Juan Bautista de Anza.

Following the secularization of the Spanish missions in California, a wealthy Los Angeles businessman by the name of Tiburcio Tapia became the grantee of a 12,000-acre parcel of land he called the Rancho Cucamonga. In later years, the rancho would be divided into smaller portions and sold to others who were interested in either acquiring small ranch and farm land for themselves or land which they could resell for a profit. One of those men was retired Portuguese sailor Capt. Joseph S. García.

On a fall day in 1882, George Chaffey stood on a mesa in what is now San Antonio Heights north of Upland gazing out into the valley that lay in front of him. He would later reflect, "From the plateau at the foot of the mountain, I obtained a bird's-eye view of the whole area I proposed to acquire, and while I was standing there looking at it, I saw what Ontario was to, and did become." It had been almost exactly a year since he, along with his brother, William, and J. C. Dunlap, had made what would be remembered as his notable "Thanksgiving Day Ride" and purchased some property from García. The property he had bought from García became part of the neighboring colony of Etiwanda, and those lands had sold well to the public. It was now time, Chaffey thought, to take the financial gains from the Etiwanda venture and plan a second settlement.

In May 1882, the Chaffey brothers had purchased more than 6,000 acres of property from the Cucamonga Company for a reported $60,000. The transaction included water rights for San Antonio Canyon and wastewater from Cucamonga Creek.

Along with this land, the Chaffeys purchased the 4,000-acre Kincaid Ranch at the mouth of San Antonio Canyon, comprising what would be the original Ontario settlement.

It was George Chaffey's plan to develop a water system that depended upon gravitational flow from the canyons to the valley below. At the outset, Chaffey had a struggle obtaining use of the water in San Antonio Canyon because the town of Pomona had laid claim to that region.

The initial battle for water rights was short but heated. Settlers at Pomona, believing they had rights to the water, sent an armed guard to protect the canyon from outsiders. George Chaffey sent his foreman into the canyon with orders to fence it off. This brought about an altercation between the guard and the foreman, with Chaffey's man coming out the better. The man from Pomona quickly packed his rifle and left the canyon.

There would be future disagreements and claims concerning the water, but for all practical purposes, the Chaffeys had their land and their water. What they did not yet have was a settlement.

With what would be later described by Southern California historian L. A. Ingersoll as "the most perfect plan then formulated," the Chaffeys were finally able to develop their settlement. The development of Ontario was so well established that a group of Australians visiting the area in 1885 dubbed it the "model colony."

Word spread so quickly concerning the beautiful town site and its surrounding area that settlers began coming in droves to see if they, too, could be a part of the growing enterprise. Among the colonists were those whose interests were aroused in the area of Ontario that lay north of Seventh Street.

In 1886, Nathan Stowell, a pipe maker who had been an employee of the Chaffey brothers, purchased 60 acres of land lying on the east side of Euclid Avenue between Seventh and Eighth Streets. This was the beginning of the new colony of North Ontario. Although Stowell's primary objective was to lay cement pipe for the colony, he first had to lay several feet of wooden pipe, which was used for a turbine wheel that ran the machine that produced the cement pipe. Stowell ultimately laid his cement pipe from the mountains to the colony.

Probably the most significant enterprise in North Ontario following Stowell was that of the Bedford brothers. Alfred, Lyman, Edmund, and Daniel had moved, one by one, from Pennsylvania to California between 1883 and 1887. The brothers were called the "Iowa Syndicate" by the *Ontario Record* newspaper because some of them had done business in Sioux City, Iowa, before coming west.

In 1887, the Bedfords purchased 200 acres of North Ontario. The tract of land was bounded by Euclid and Campus Avenues on the west and east and by Eleventh and A Streets on the north and south.

The Bedford brothers turned the barren 200 acres into a thriving community they called Magnolia. It contained everything a town destined to become a city needed, including the Atchison, Topeka, and Santa Fe Railroad. To the Bedfords' dismay, however, the railroad gave the name of North Ontario to the depot, and the town took on the same name, rather than Magnolia.

The township continued to grow with not only grand homes being built, but also churches, business blocks, a massive hotel, and a mule-drawn railroad along the beautiful tree-lined median of Euclid Avenue beginning in the town of Ontario and traveling to San Antonio Heights above North Ontario.

November 1887, however, brought a devastating blow to the Bedfords' plans. A huge windstorm struck the area, and their hotel, the Magnolia Villa, suffered a tremendous amount of damage. Financial problems began to hit hard, and the brothers eventually had to call it quits. In May 1888, foreclosure proceedings were filed against the brothers and all those associated with them in their business venture. By September, the Bedfords had moved out of the Magnolia Villa, and at the end of October, the furniture was auctioned and the hotel doors were closed.

The same year as the demise of the Bedford venture, North Ontario became quiet but not silent. Life still went on, and there were those who would see that the town site became an important part of San Bernardino County. The sleepy village continued to maintain a post office, and a new group of entrepreneurs arrived on the scene to try their hand at developing a community.

The Ontario Land and Improvement Company was made up of men such as Charles Harwood, Hugh Macneil, Charles Frankish, Daniel McFarland, Lyman Stewart, Oliver S. Picher, Godfrey Stamm, Frederick Gissing, and Milton Stewart.

Through various sheriffs' sales, Charles Harwood and his brother Alfred bought up land that had at one time been a part of the Magnolia tract. One purchase also included the Magnolia Villa. The Harwoods immediately set the eastern 100 acres of the newly acquired land to oranges and re-landscaped the hotel property.

The newly revitalized town of North Ontario began to flourish, and by 1897, it boasted two newspapers. This was a true indication that the town was here to stay.

Another sign of its growth was the economic independence North Ontario was developing through its rapidly expanding citrus industry. In 1897, Charles D. Adams and a group of his friends decided to establish a new citrus packing association. Adams was manager of the Ontario Fruit Exchange, which was already in existence. He was a knowledgeable man in the field of agriculture, and he knew that fruit produced at higher altitudes was usually of better quality. Therefore he suggested the new exchange be called the Upland Citrus Association, reflecting the fact the fruit was raised in the higher ground.

Because Adams suggested the name Upland by making it part of the association's name, he is given credit for originating the name of the city. The citizens liked the name, and in 1902, they persuaded the San Bernardino County Board of Supervisors to rename the community.

Incorporation had not yet come for Upland, however, and the city of Ontario made moves to push its boundaries northward. One of areas Ontario was attempting to annex was land that included the Atchison, Topeka, and Santa Fe Railroad along A Street as well as the Upland depot. Upland residents could not bear to think of their railroad station and the post office it included being located within another city's boundaries. Therefore citizens of Upland called for a meeting concerning the problem. Gathering together at the International Order of Odd Fellows Hall on the west side of Second Avenue, the residents met with county supervisor Dr. E. W. Reid. This caucus took a vote, and it was decided incorporation would be the desired course of action. On May 5, 1906, Upland held an election to decide the matter. The people of the town decided in favor of incorporation with a vote of 183 to 19. The city of Upland had been born.

Since that time, Upland has, like any city across the United States, gone through good and bad times as it has grown. Some of the times have been difficult, such as suffering the grief of the Spanish influenza and two world wars along with the rest of the nation. Sometimes it has struggled along with neighboring cities through earthquakes, floods, windstorms, and brush fires. At other times, it has been left to suffer alone, as when a peace officer has been wounded or lost his life in the line of duty protecting his city.

For the greatest part, however, Upland's history has been a truly happy one. It has been one of everyday people doing everyday things but doing them in a way that has made Upland one of the most wonderful places to live. Perhaps that is why someone, although his or her name has been lost to history, chose to call Upland "the City of Gracious Living."

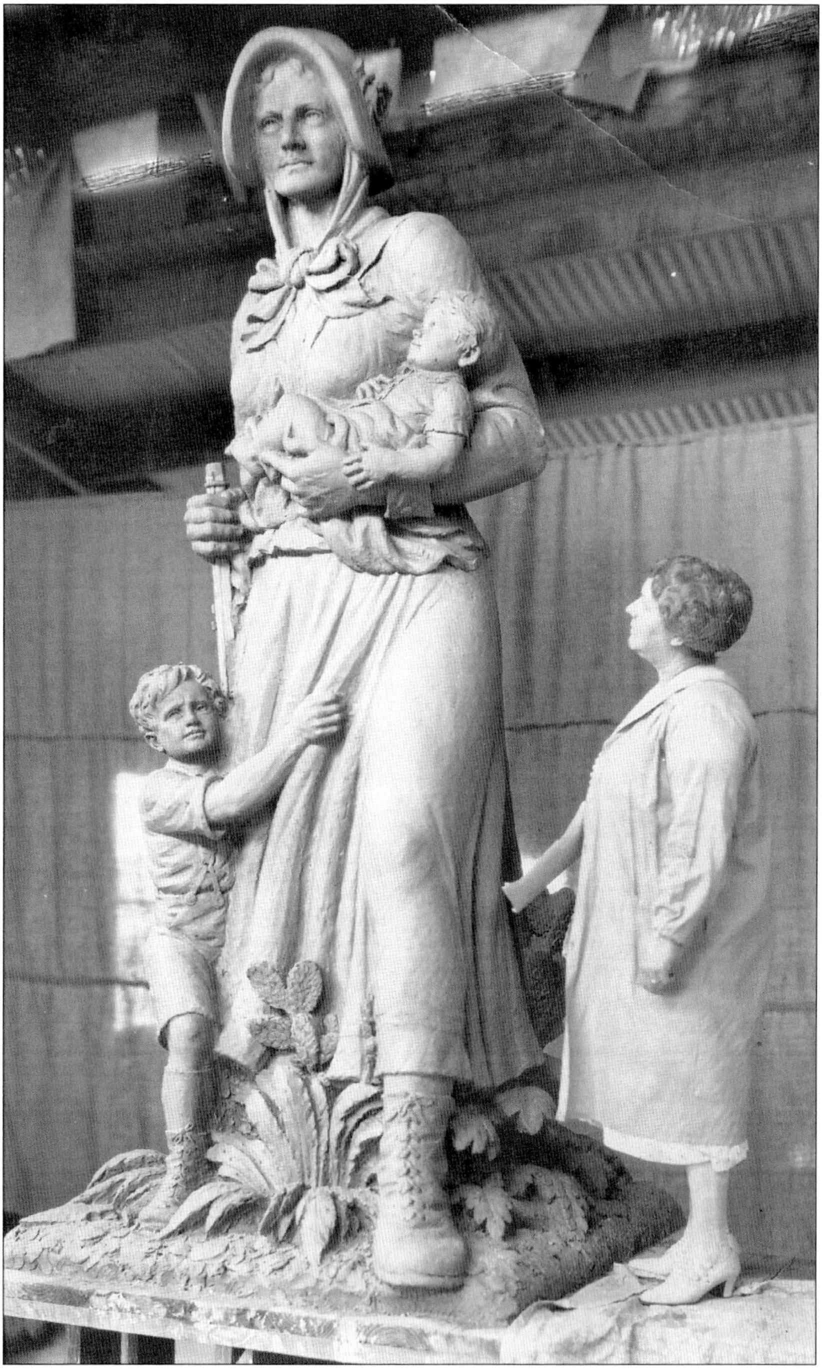

If an Uplander were to be asked the question, "What is the symbol that most represents your city?," the answer would likely be, "the Madonna of the Trail, of course." Beginning in 1928, the National Society of Daughters of the American Revolution erected the monuments at 12 sites along the National Old Trails Highway from Bethesda, Maryland, to Upland. In this 1927 photograph, Mrs. John Trigg (Arline) Moss, national chairman of the National Old Trails Roads and Daughters of the American Revolution, is seen admiring the prototype for the monuments.

# *One*

# Men, Women, and Kids

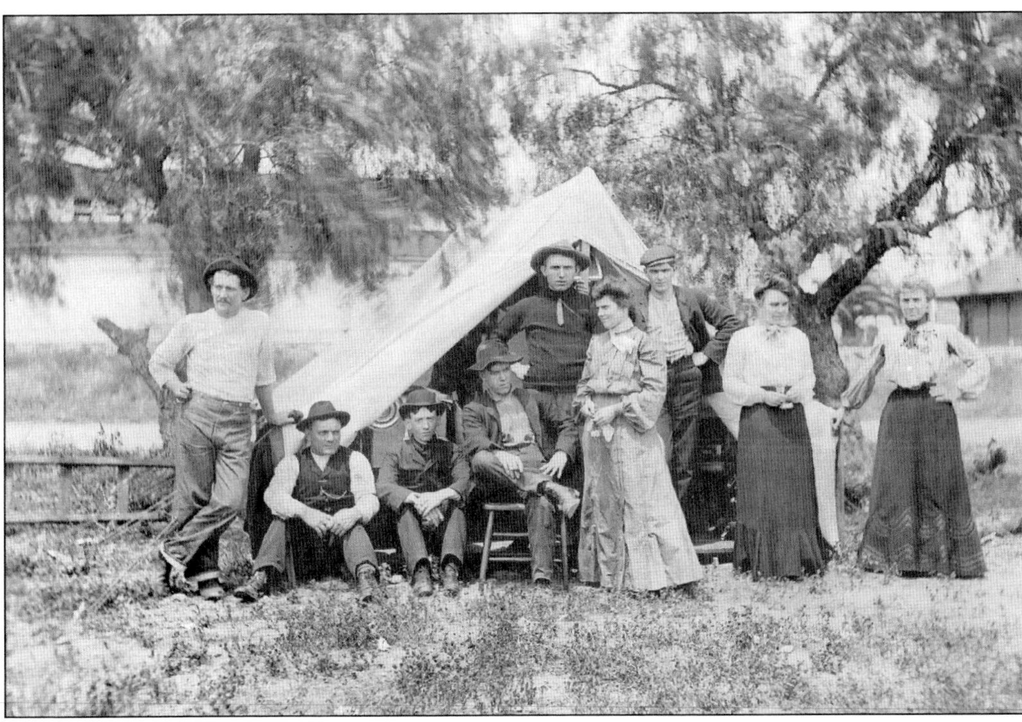

Taken some time during the 1890s, this photograph shows the William Bowden family. Before moving into the home they built on Twelfth Street (Arrow Highway), the Bowdens made their residence in this tent.

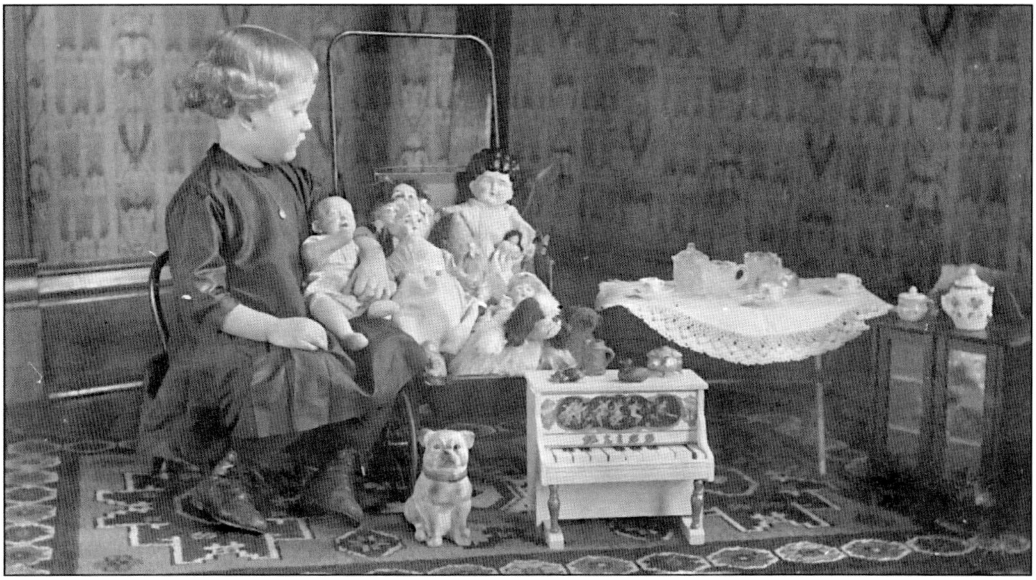

As with children in any town or city, the youngsters in Upland were adept at using their imaginations during playtime. Thelma Marie Couch was three years old when this photograph of her playing house was taken around 1900.

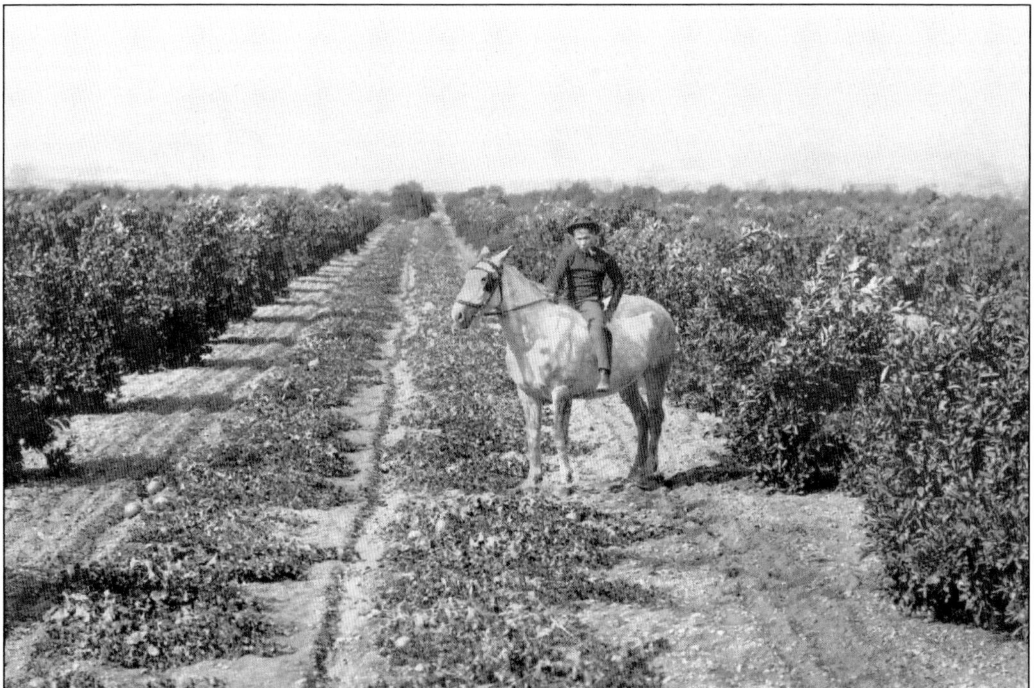

This young boy riding bareback on his horse does not appear to be extremely pleased as he is having his photograph taken in an Upland citrus grove, also about the year 1900. (UPL.)

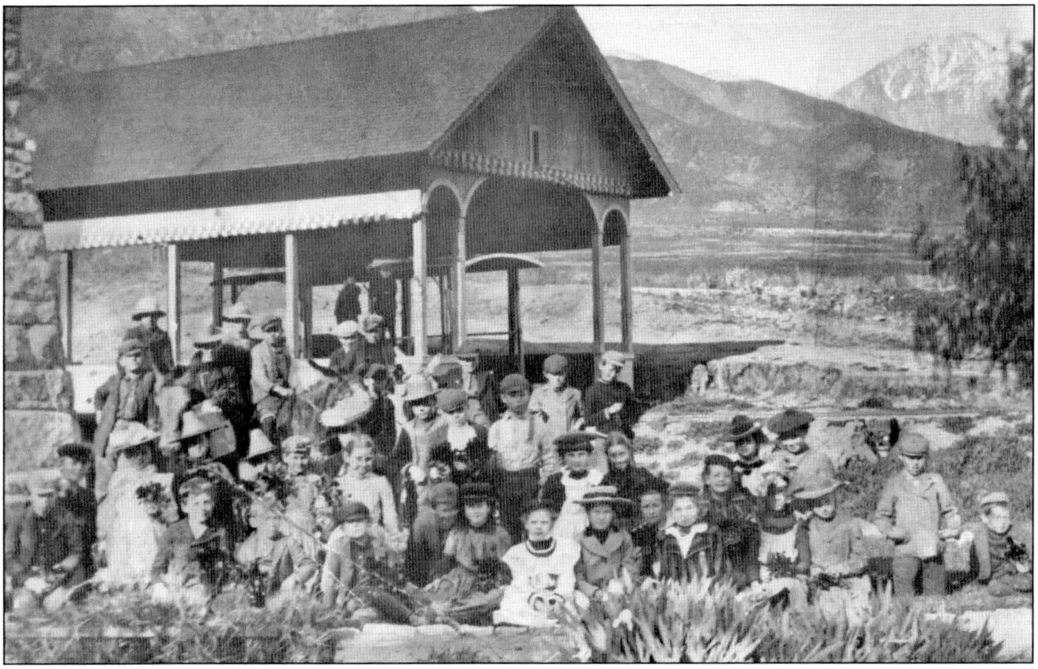

A group of school children is patiently waiting next to the old "stone castle" power station for the streetcar to take them back to school following an excursion to the foothills above Upland. The date is sometime in the 1890s.

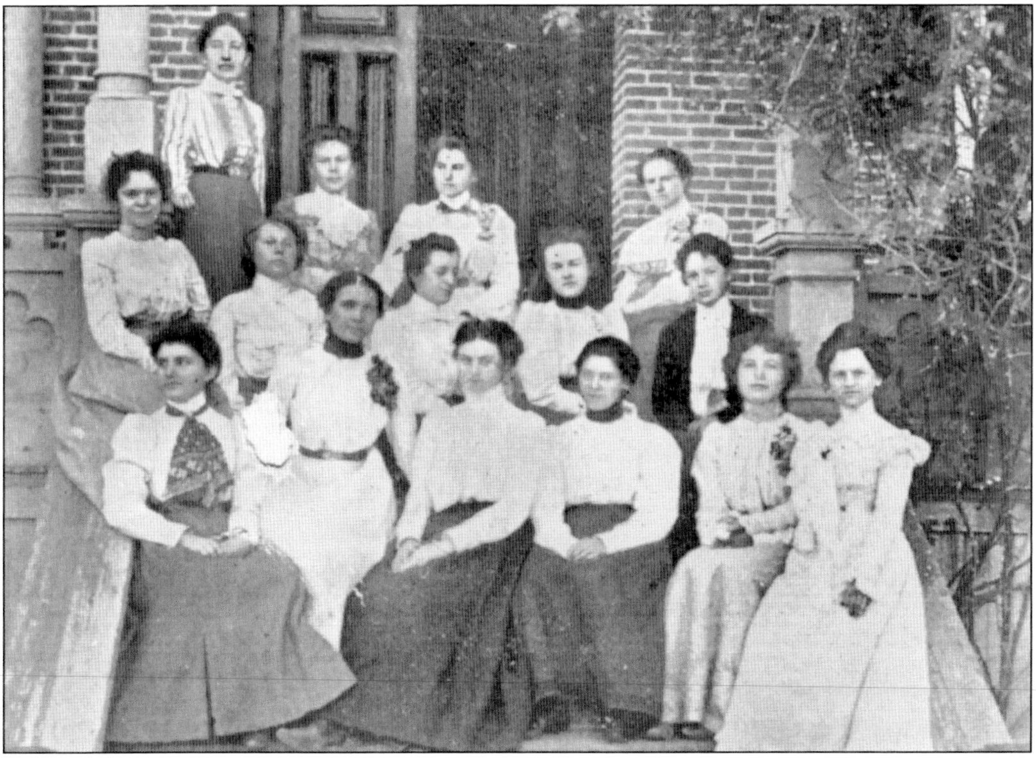

In 1890, this group of young ladies gathered together to form the Upland Girls Glee Club.

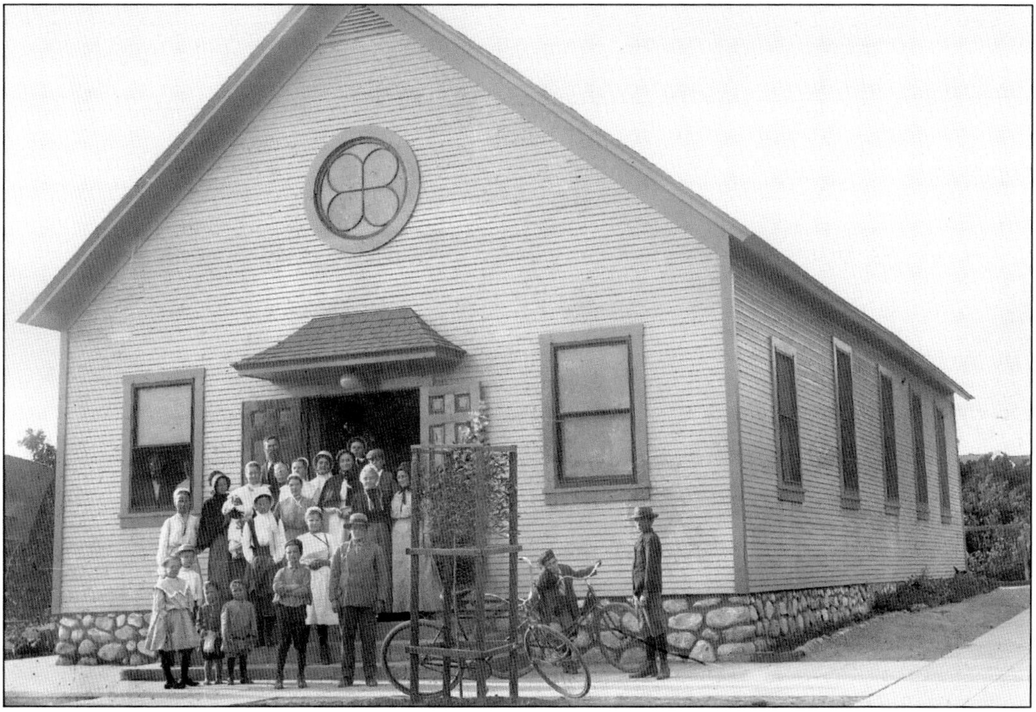

The Upland Brethren in Christ Church was founded by Christian C. Burkholder and his wife, Fannie, in 1903. Early parishioners stand in front of the original church building, which was erected at the northwest corner of Third Avenue and F Street. Following many changes and additions, the structure was torn down in 1919 and was replaced with another, which stands to this day. (UPL.)

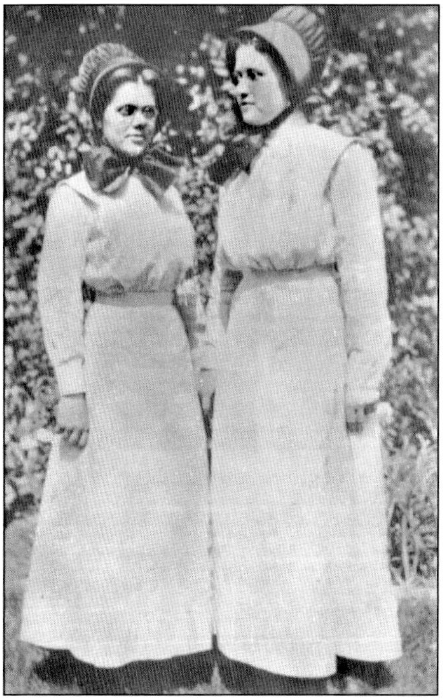

Adeline Burkholder (left) and Jenny Plum are pictured in typical Brethren in Christ Church daily wear in 1904. (UPL.)

Jenny Plum's parents, Wesley (left) and his wife, are with some friends in 1904. (UPL.)

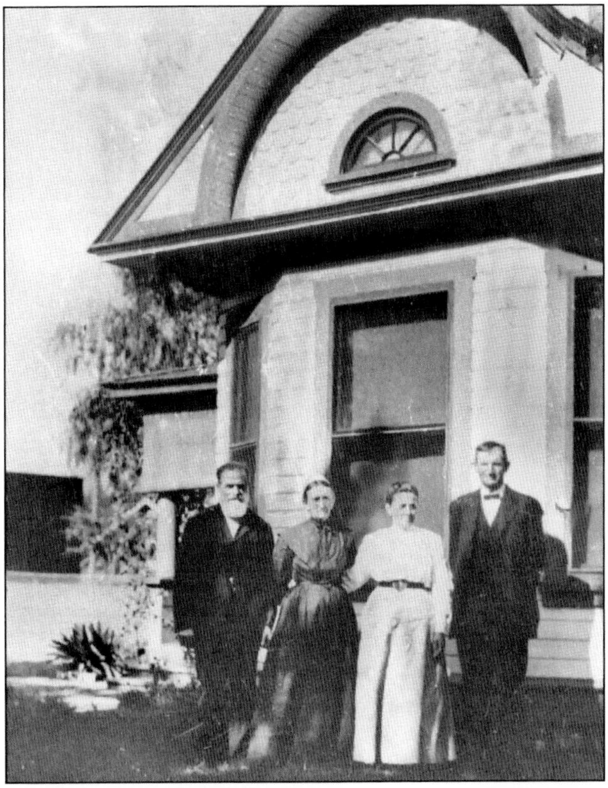

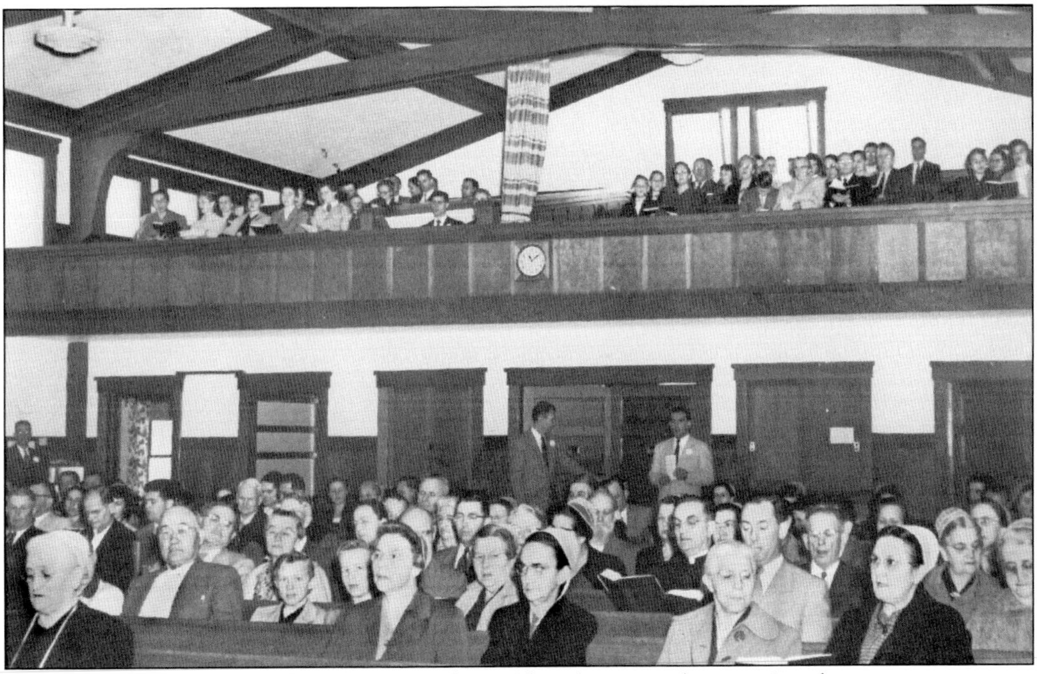

The interior of the Upland Brethren in Christ Church is seen during a Sunday morning service. Upland Brethren in Christ was the home church for Upland College. Note the women still wearing bonnets in this 1956 photograph. (RDX.)

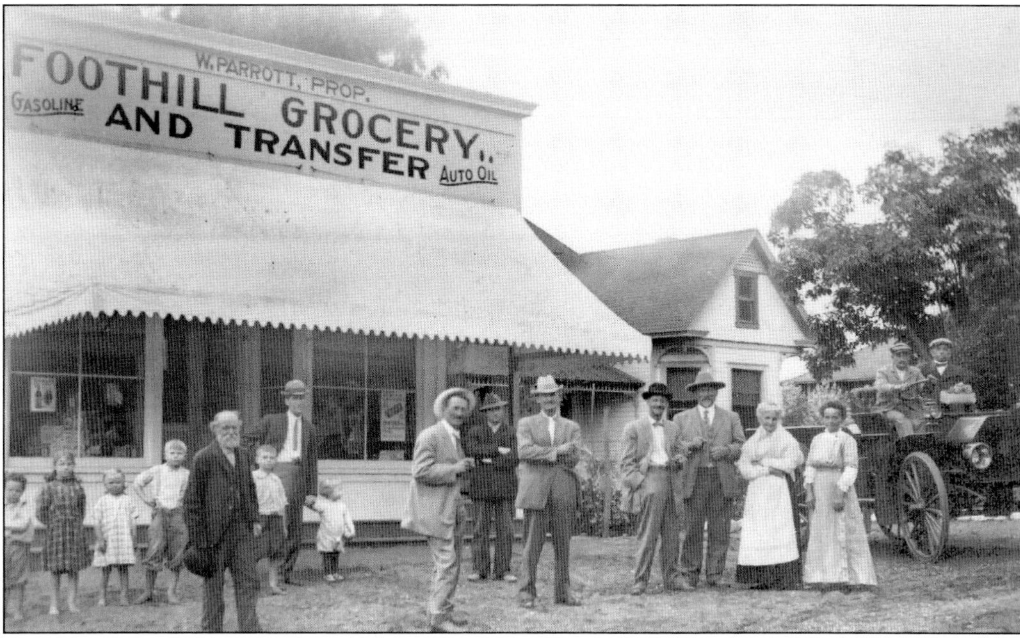


This group has gathered in front of the Foothill Grocery and Transfer, which was located in San Antonio Heights during the early 1900s. (OCL.)

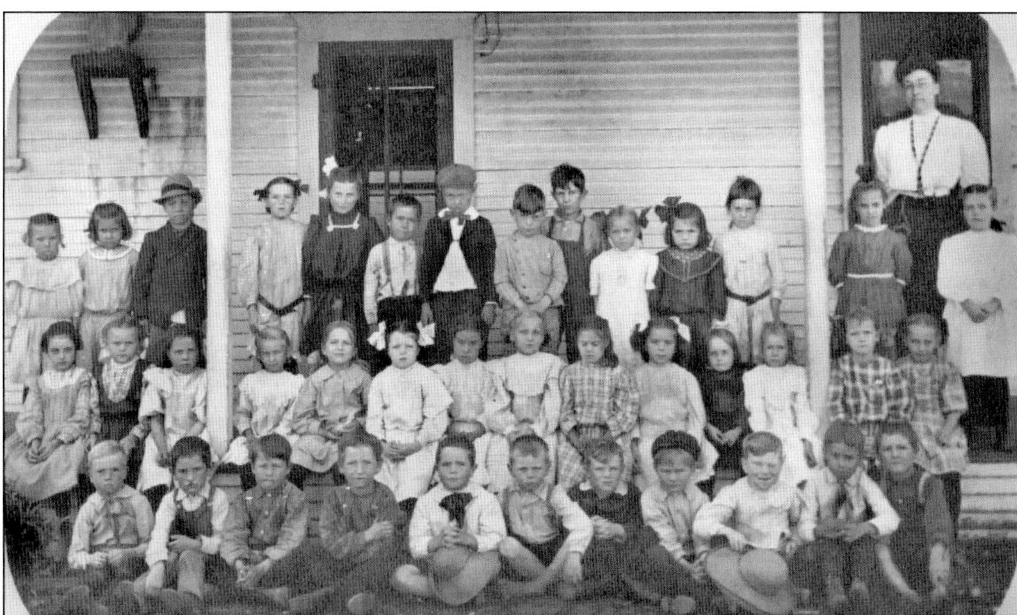

This group of first graders and their teacher, a Miss Brown, pose in 1907 outside a private school operated by Ella Schmidt. The first grade was the only one housed in the building located at the north end of the 200 block of North Second Avenue. All other grades were taught at Schmidt's school at Euclid Avenue and Ninth Street. In 1908, all classes were combined and moved to Upland Grammar School.

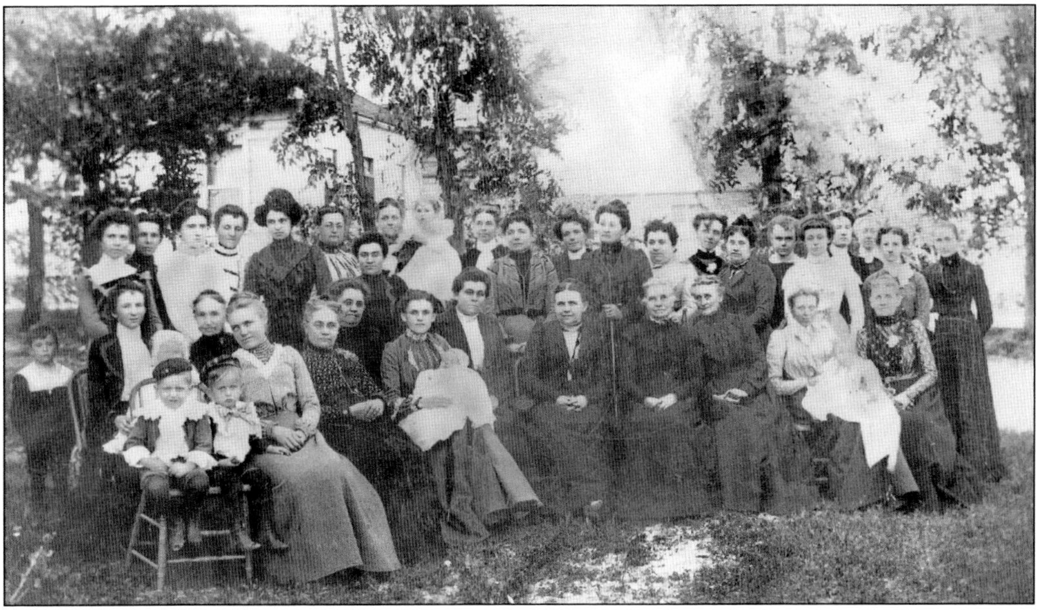

Ladies aid societies were formed throughout the United States to help promote the welfare of their local communities in whatever ways necessary. The North Ontario women pictured here in 1902 were dedicated to the same cause.

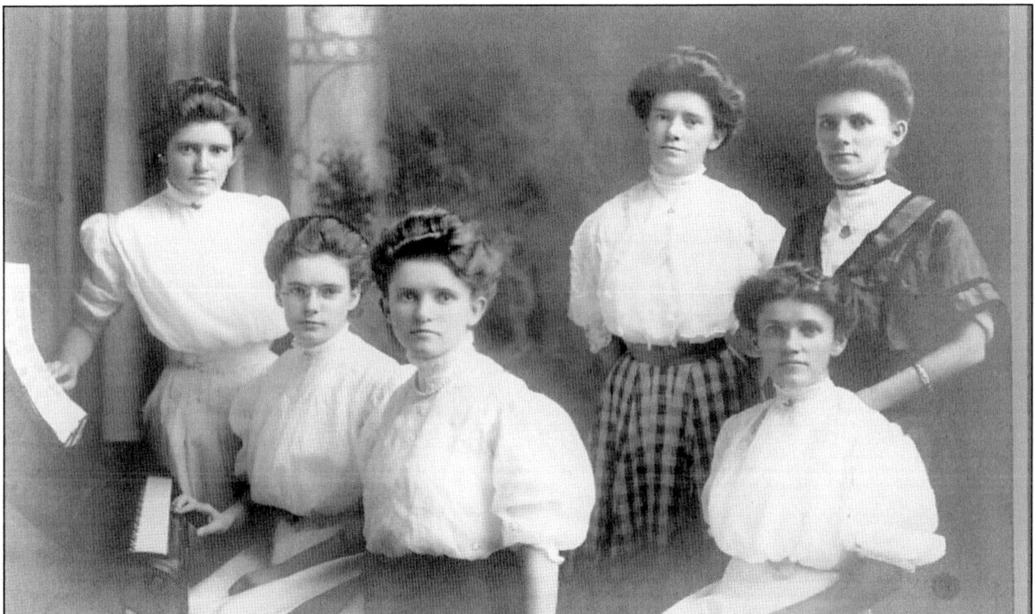

The Gerry sisters are pictured in 1907. From left to right are (seated) Maude, Beatrice, and Eliza; (standing) Eva, Amanda, and Alma. They were daughters of John Gerry, a noted contractor and builder during the 1880s in what was to become Upland. In 1887, Upland was hit by one of its frequent, terrible northern winds. Having lost part of their home to the storm, the Gerrys raced to seek shelter in a ditch a short distance from the house. After some time had passed, it was realized that little Eva was not with the group. One of the sons, Jack, raced back to the partially destroyed building only to find his little sister asleep in a rocking chair.

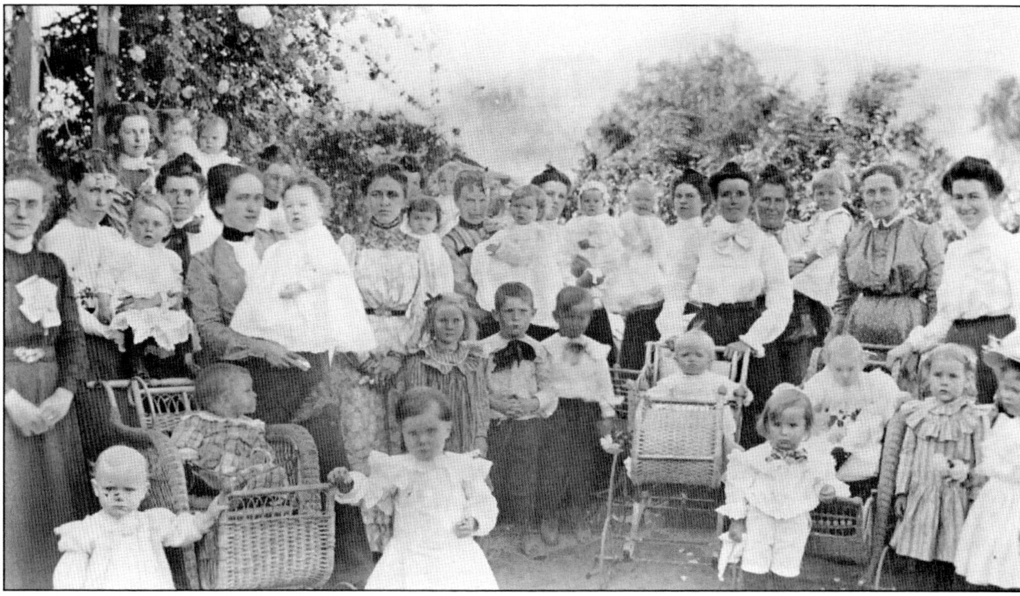

Ladies and children are pictured in front of the Kouts family home on First Street around 1900.

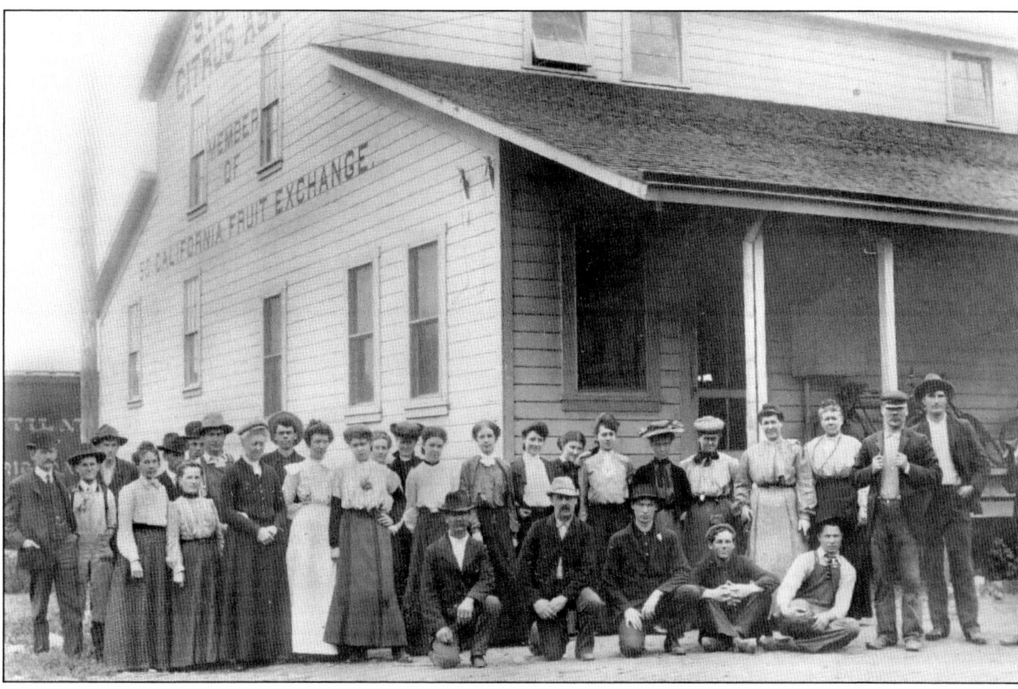


This crew of workers at the Stewart Citrus Association gathered for this photograph outside the main packinghouse located on East A Street in 1901. Many of the citizens in and around Upland were employed by the citrus industry, which contributed immensely to the economy of the area for several decades.

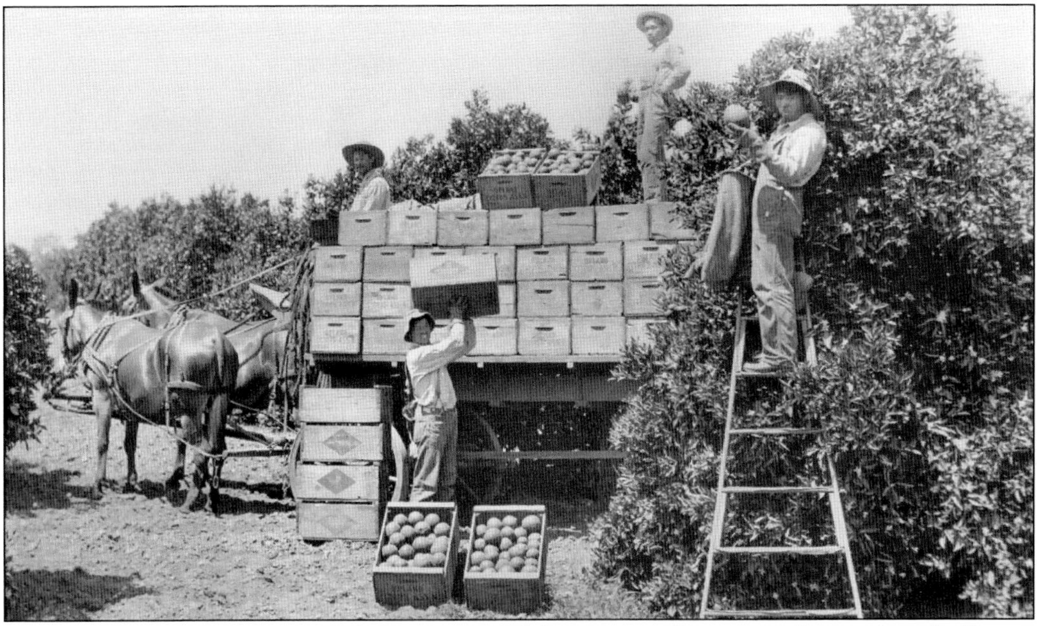

One of the many tasks vital to the operation of the citrus industry was the quick and efficient harvesting of the fruit. This 1915 photograph shows a crew from the Upland Citrus Association posing while at work.

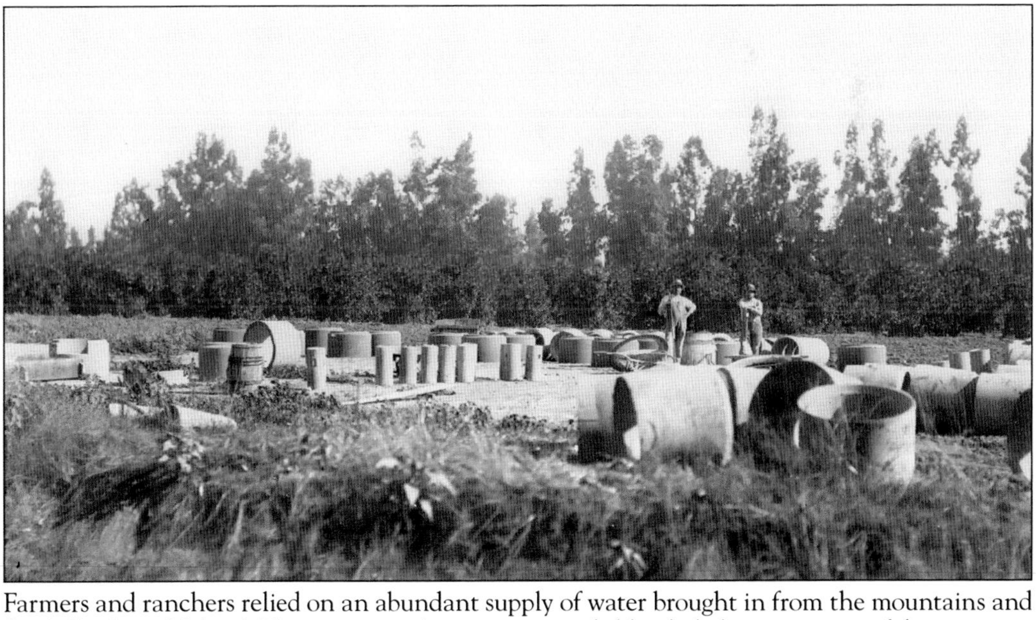

Farmers and ranchers relied on an abundant supply of water brought in from the mountains and foothills above Upland. These men are laying pipe in a field to help bring in some of that precious commodity around 1900. (UPL.)

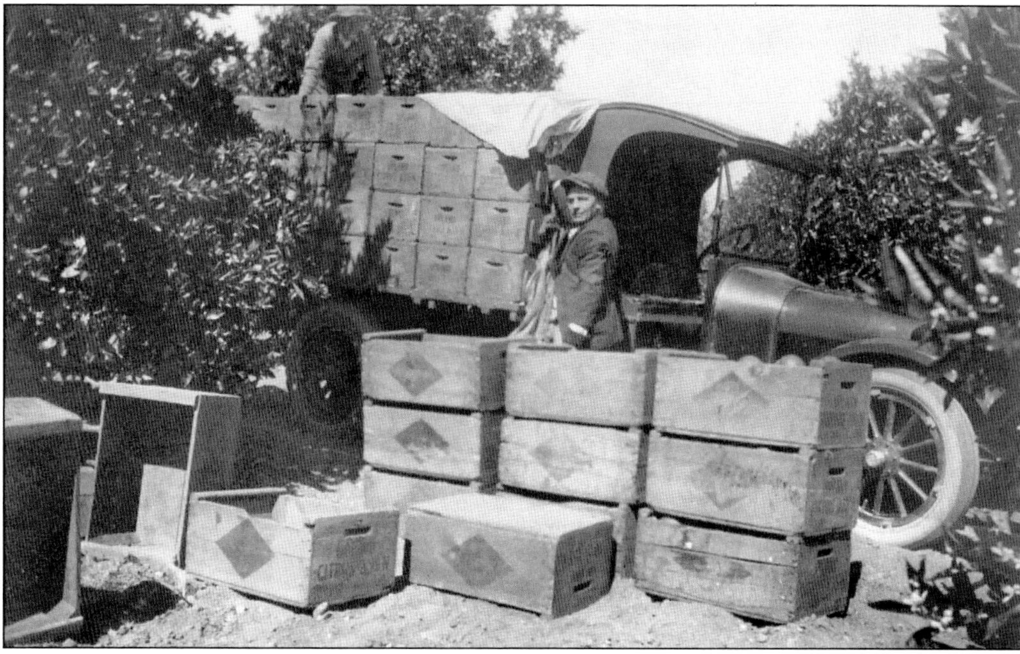

One man from the Upland Citrus Association proudly poses as the photographer takes a picture of him and another worker on top of the loaded citrus truck somewhere in an Upland grove in 1925.

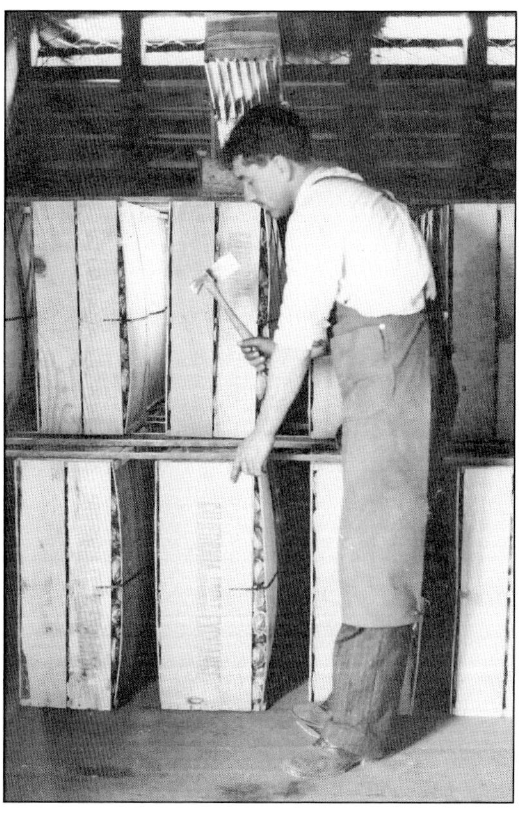

It was also important for the packinghouses to be supplied with a sufficient quantity of shipping crates. Harry Fries demonstrates his ability at making wooden boxes for the cameraman.

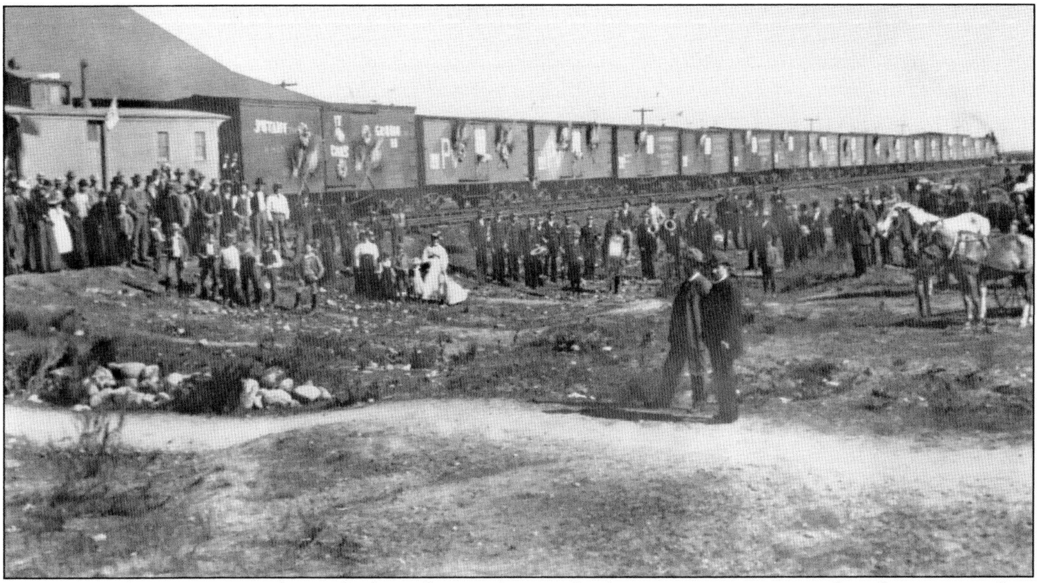

Several of the townspeople, including those who worked at various citrus packinghouses, gather to watch the railroad cars being loaded with fruit they have processed. It was then shipped to points east in the United States. (UPL.)

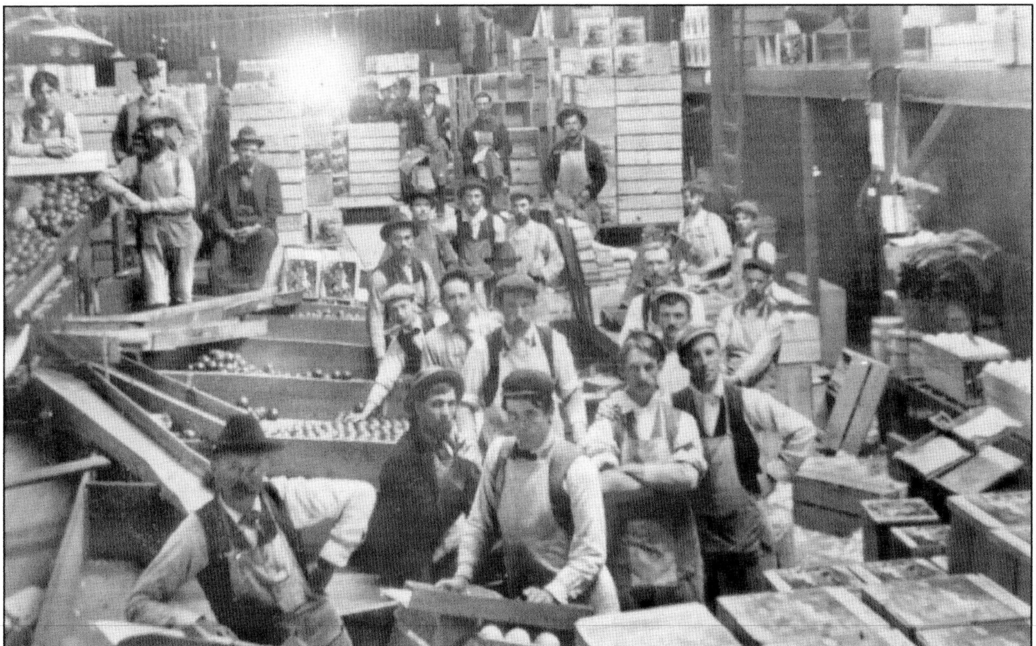

This interior view of the Upland Citrus Association packinghouse gives a good idea of the number of employees it took to operate the facility around 1900. (UPL.)

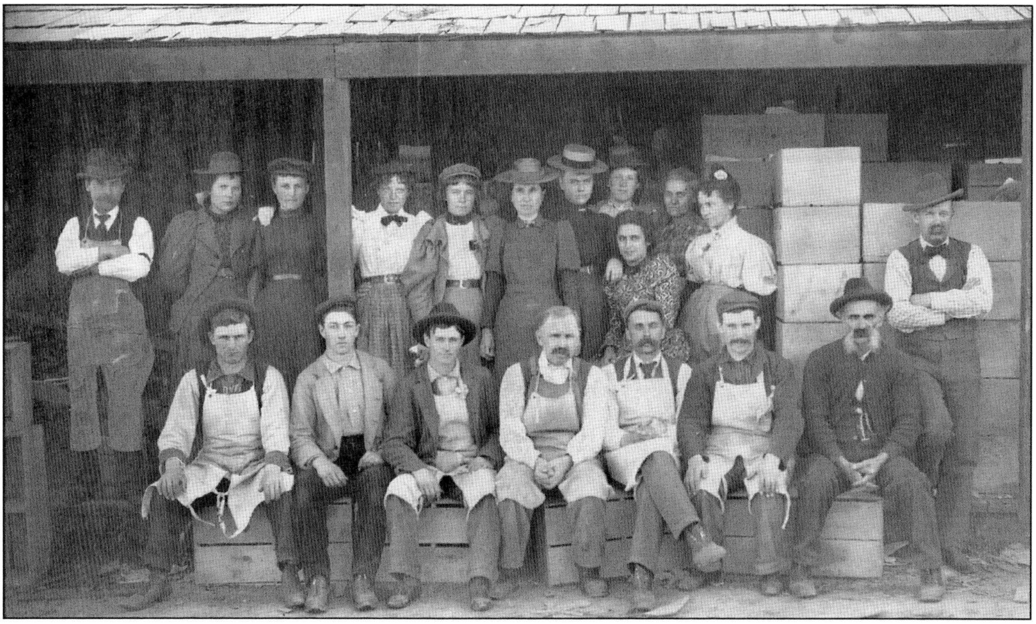

The employees of the Upland Citrus Association gather for this photograph some time during the 1890s. (UPL.)

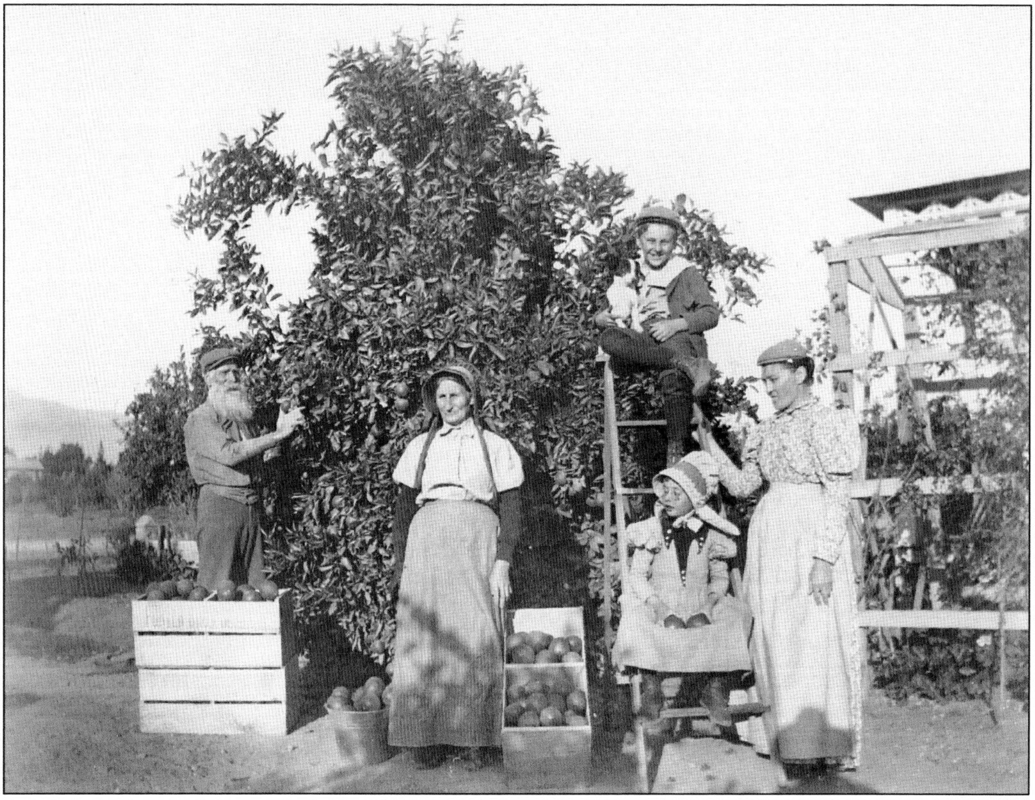

Citrus was important not only as a business in Upland, but also to individuals themselves, as is seen in this 1900 photograph of a family enjoying oranges from one of their own trees.

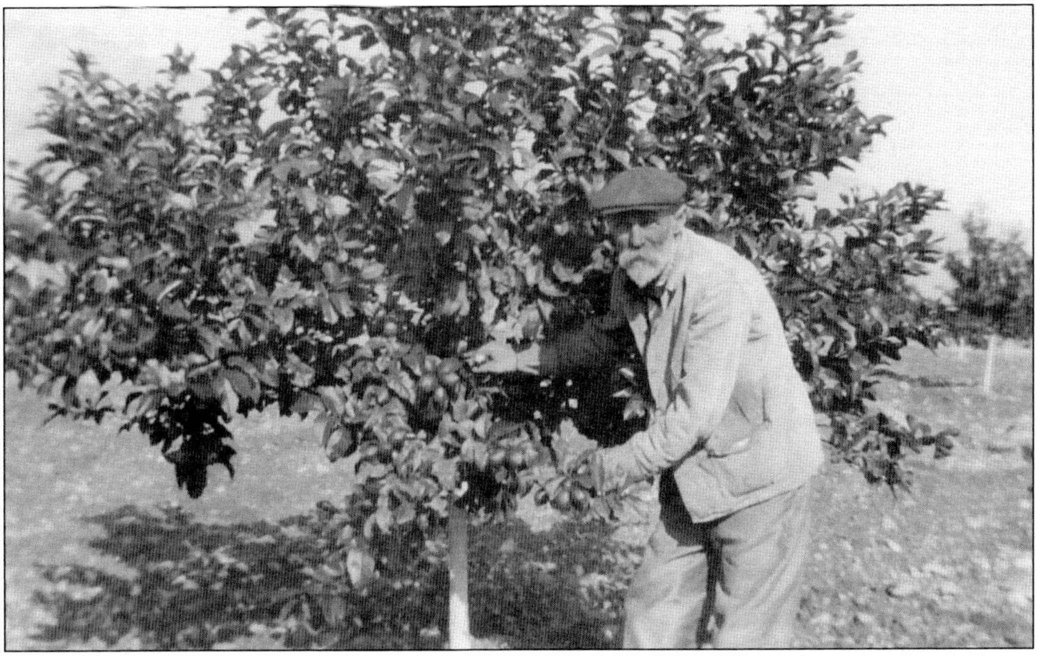

This 1912 photograph shows H. B. Taylor and a eureka lemon tree he had planted on his Bellevue Ranch in 1910. He was demonstrating the typical amount of growth of citrus plants in Upland in just two years. The eureka was the leading variety that boosted Upland's economy during the first half of the 20th century.

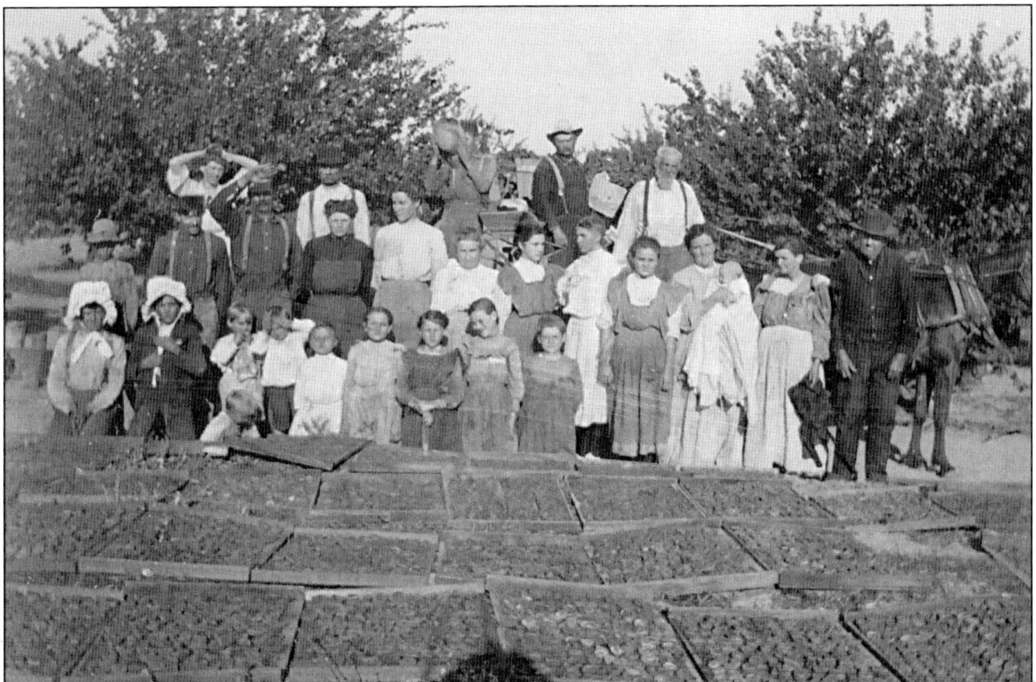

Citrus was not the only agricultural commodity produced in Upland. This photograph shows a group of workers in a stone fruit dry yard in the early 1900s.

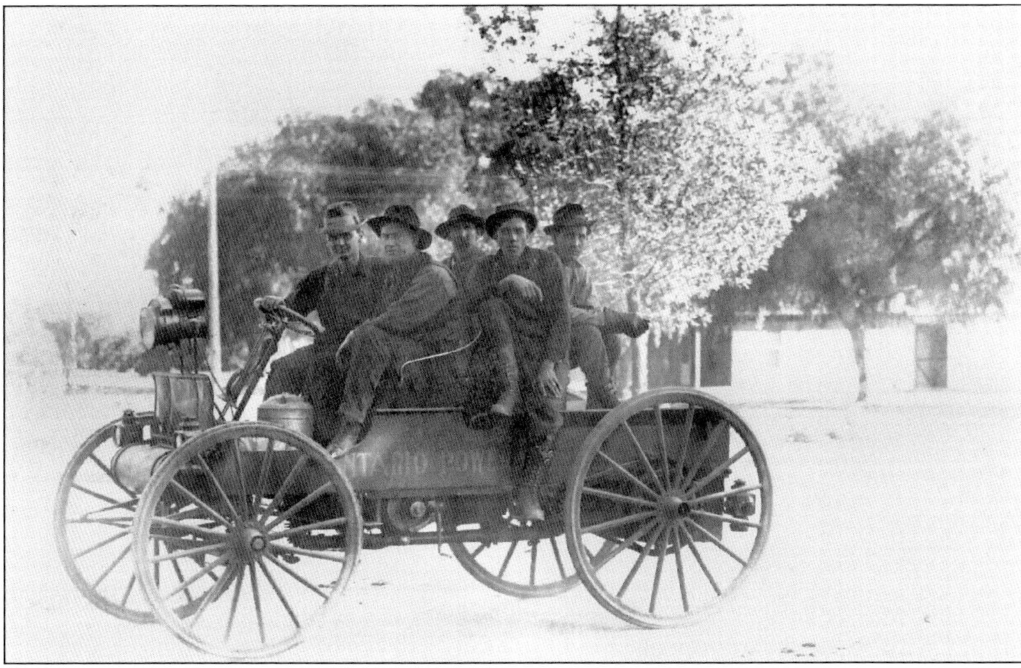

The crew from the Ontario Power Company of Upland proudly shows off their new horseless carriage in the early 1900s.

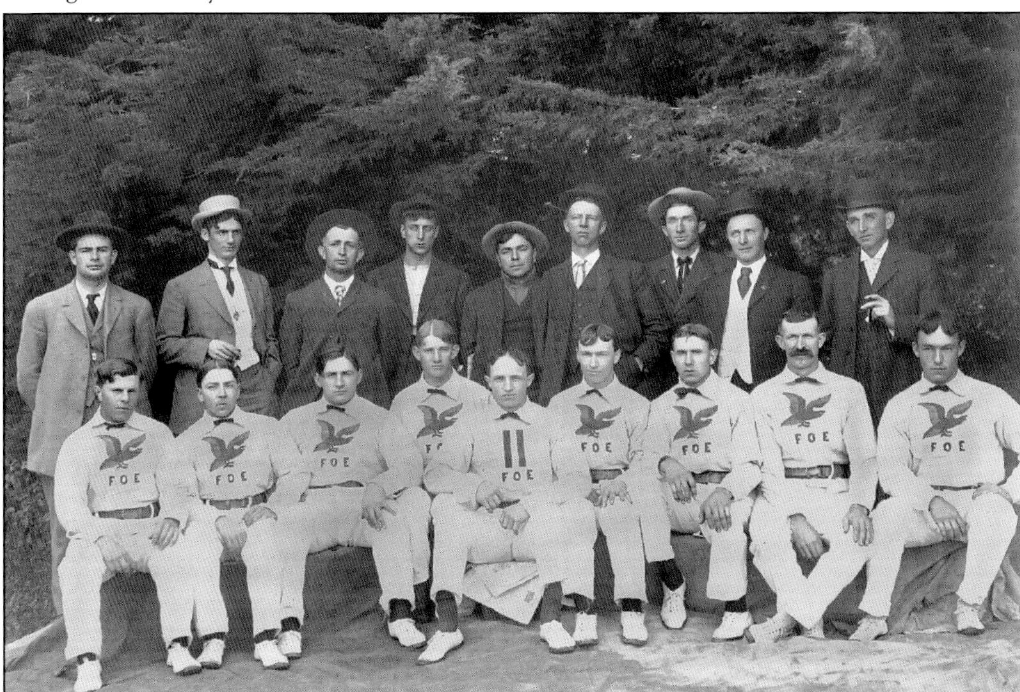


This photograph, taken about 1900, shows a fine looking group of men who were Upland's Fraternal Order of Eagles. Jedd Sawyer, who would become the first chief of police when the city was incorporated in 1906, is standing in the second row, fourth from the right. (UPL.)

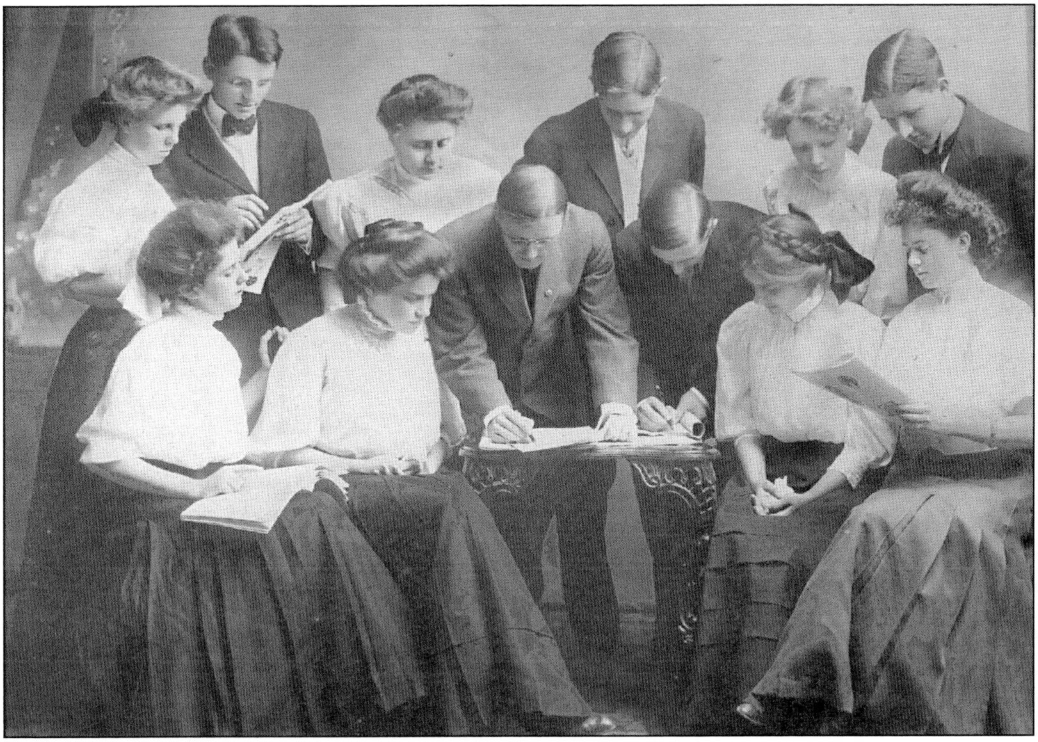

The Chaffey Union High School *Fasti* yearbook staff of 1908 is pictured here.

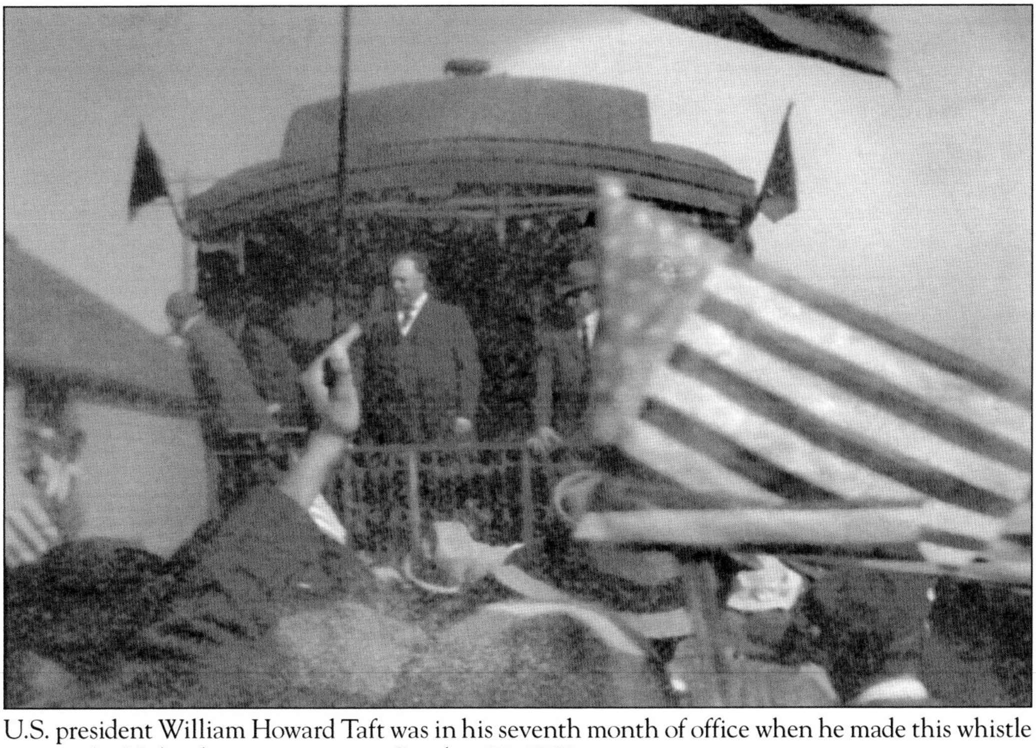

U.S. president William Howard Taft was in his seventh month of office when he made this whistle stop at the Upland train station on October 12, 1909.

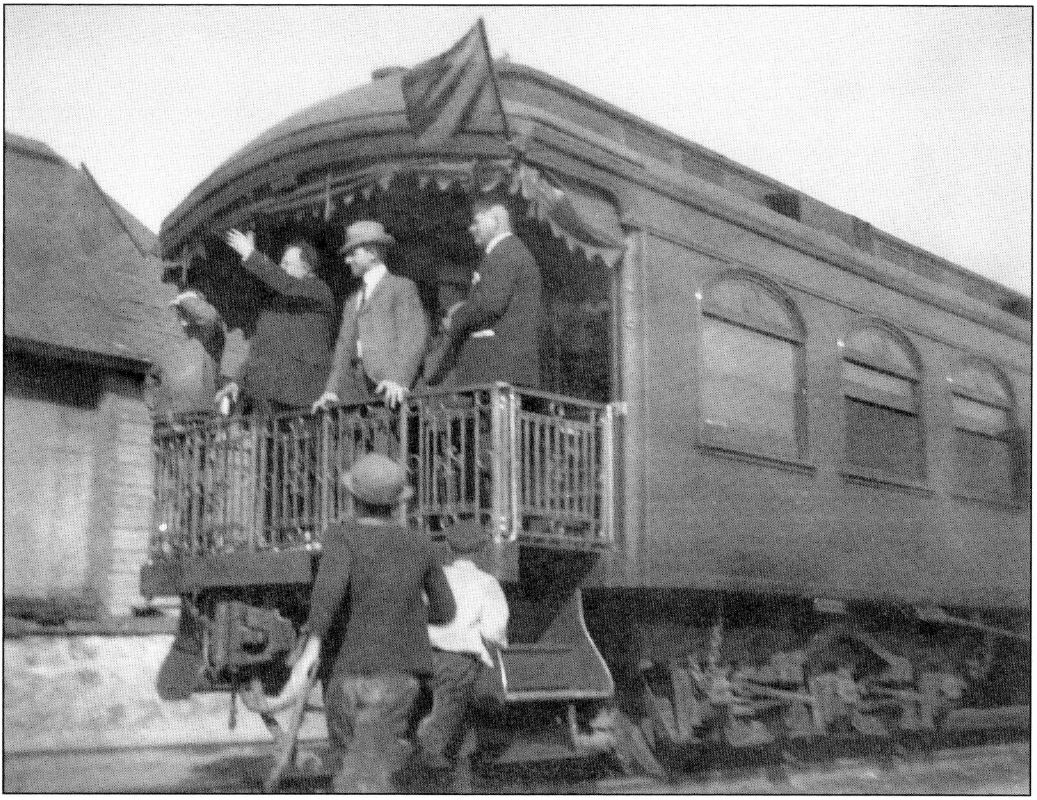

Taft was not the only U.S. president to visit Upland, as is attested by this photograph showing Theodore Roosevelt waving to an Upland crowd from the back of a train in 1910.

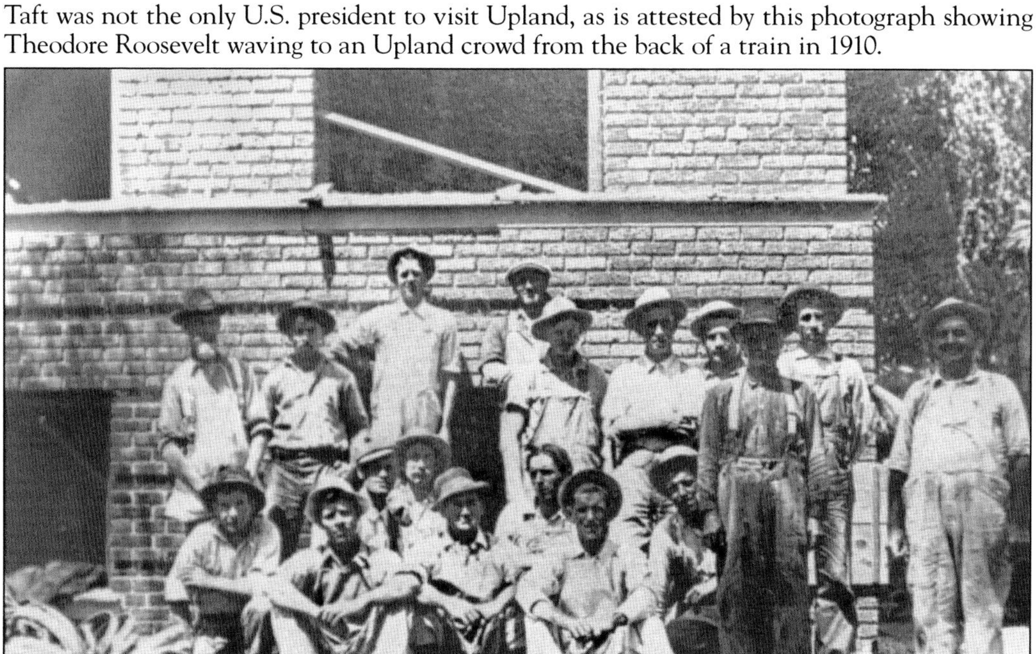

This group of workmen took time out from construction on Upland's beautiful Andrew Carnegie Library building, which opened in 1913, for this photograph. (UPL.)

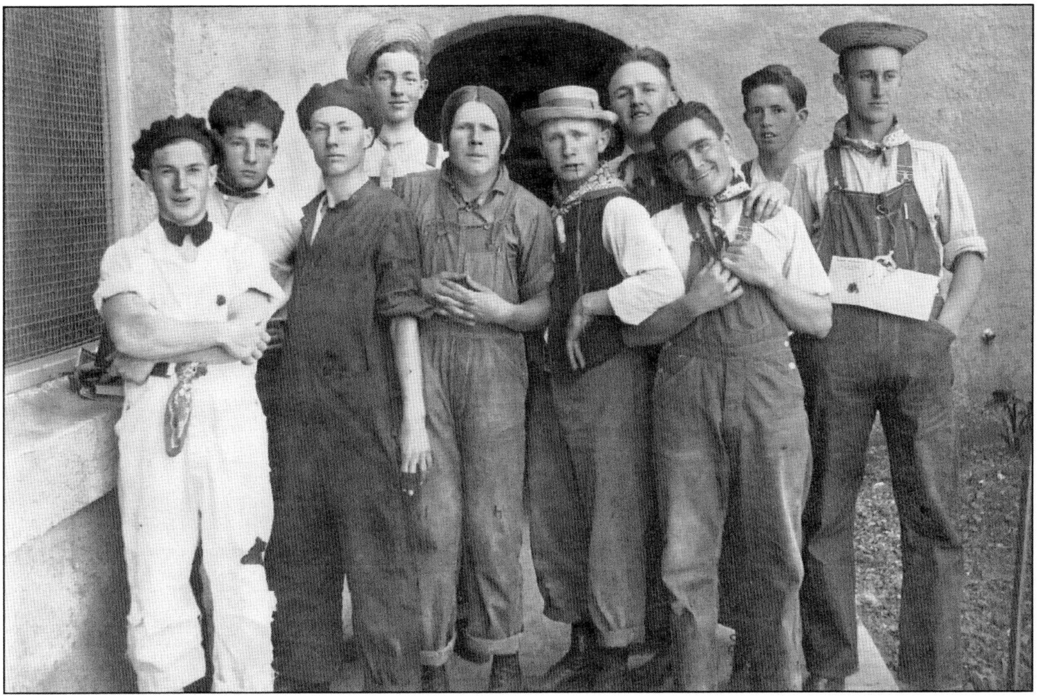

Although Chaffey High School is located to the south of Upland in the city Ontario, students from Upland attended Chaffey because the city of Upland did not construct and open its own high school until 1963. The students pictured above, including some from Upland, took a few minutes from their antics to pose for this "ditch day" photograph in 1915.

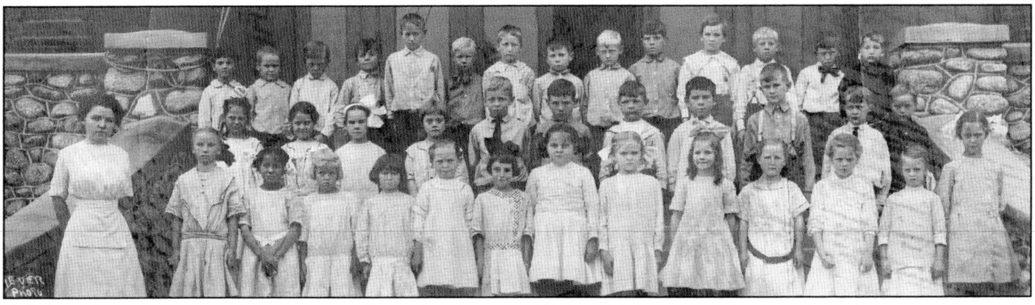

A Miss Roy poses with her second-grade class at Upland Grammar School in 1912.

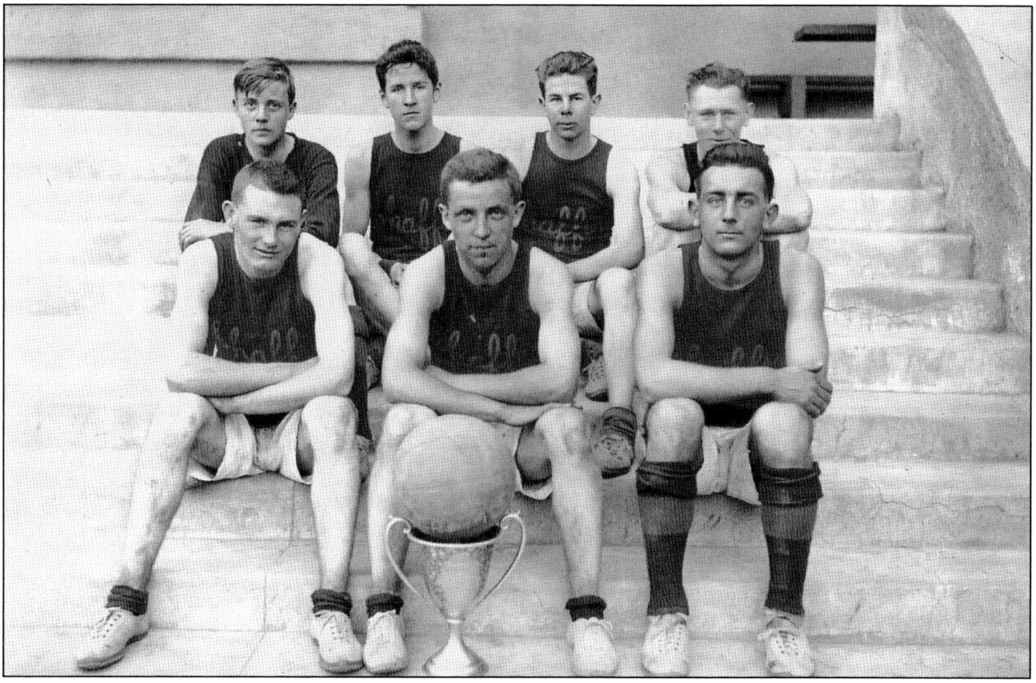

It would appear that the Chaffey Union High School boys' basketball team had only two reserve players in 1910.

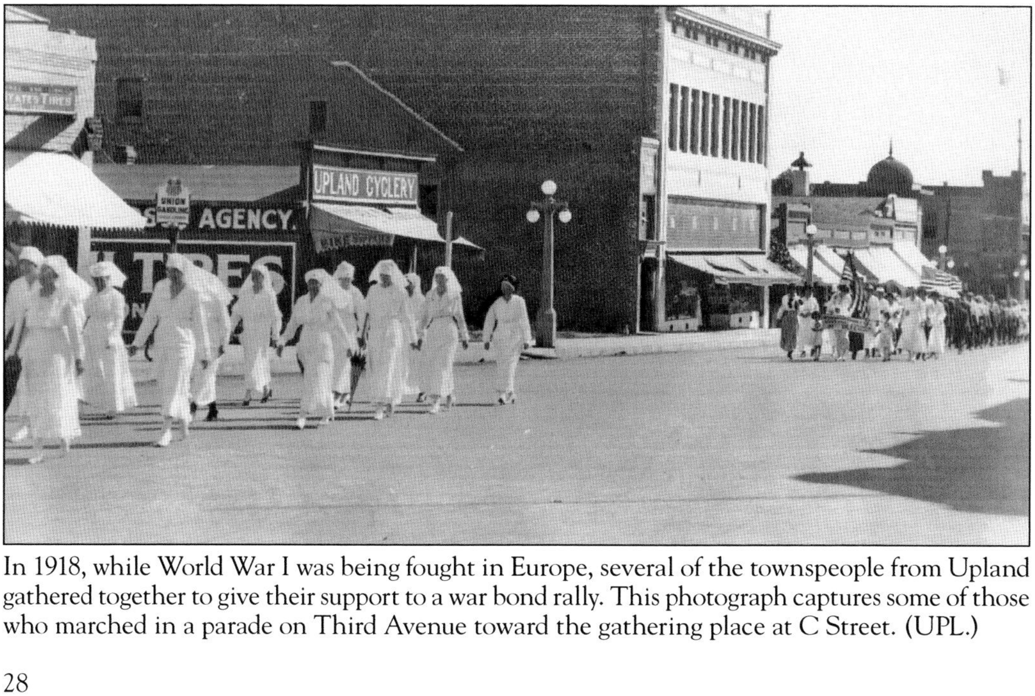


In 1918, while World War I was being fought in Europe, several of the townspeople from Upland gathered together to give their support to a war bond rally. This photograph captures some of those who marched in a parade on Third Avenue toward the gathering place at C Street. (UPL.)

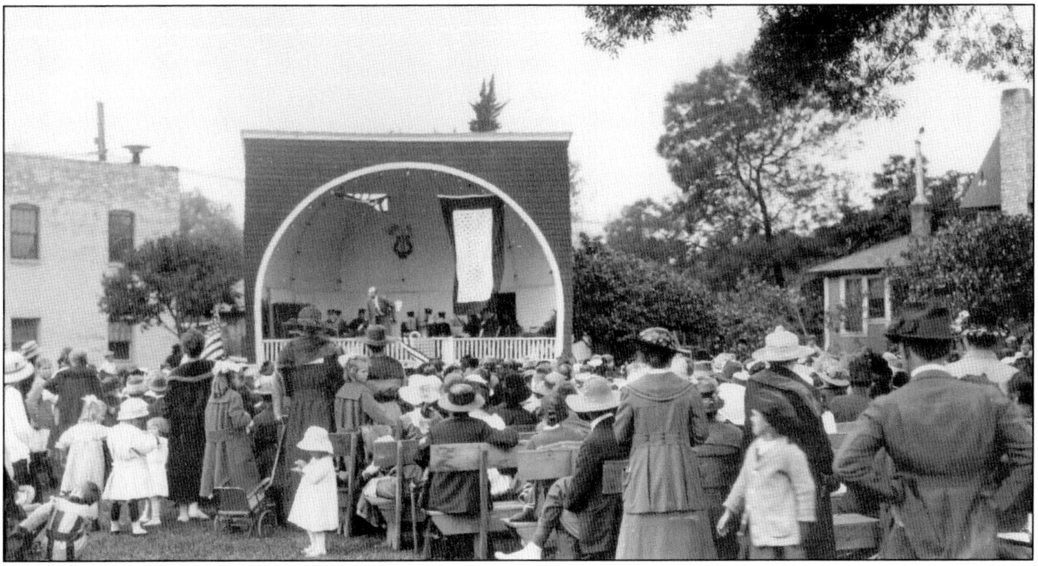

The parade culminated at the town bandstand at the corner of Third Avenue and C Street, where the people gathered.

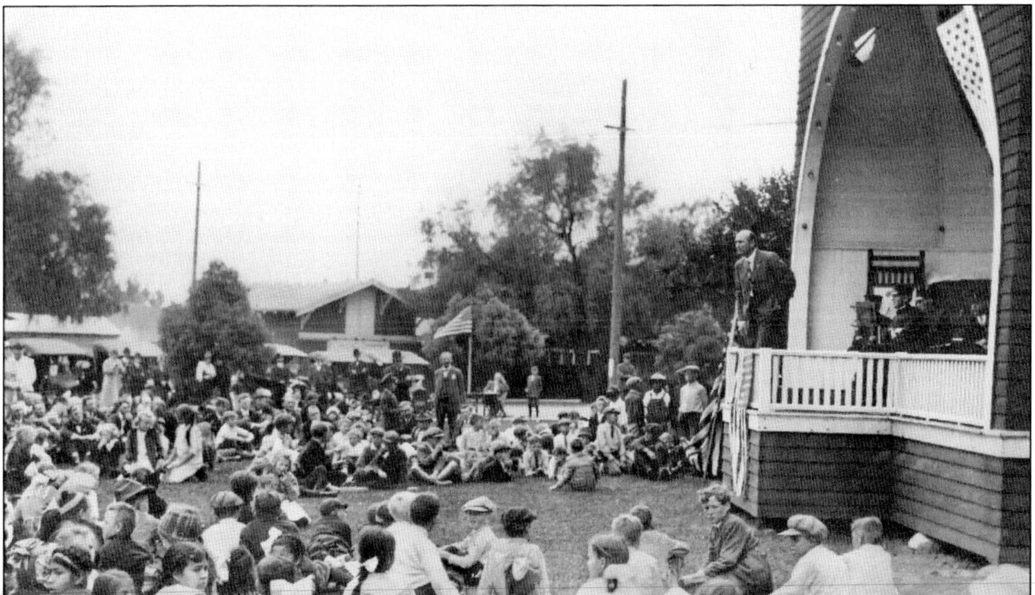

This gathering at the town bandstand was probably held as part of a Fourth of July celebration shortly after the end of World War I.

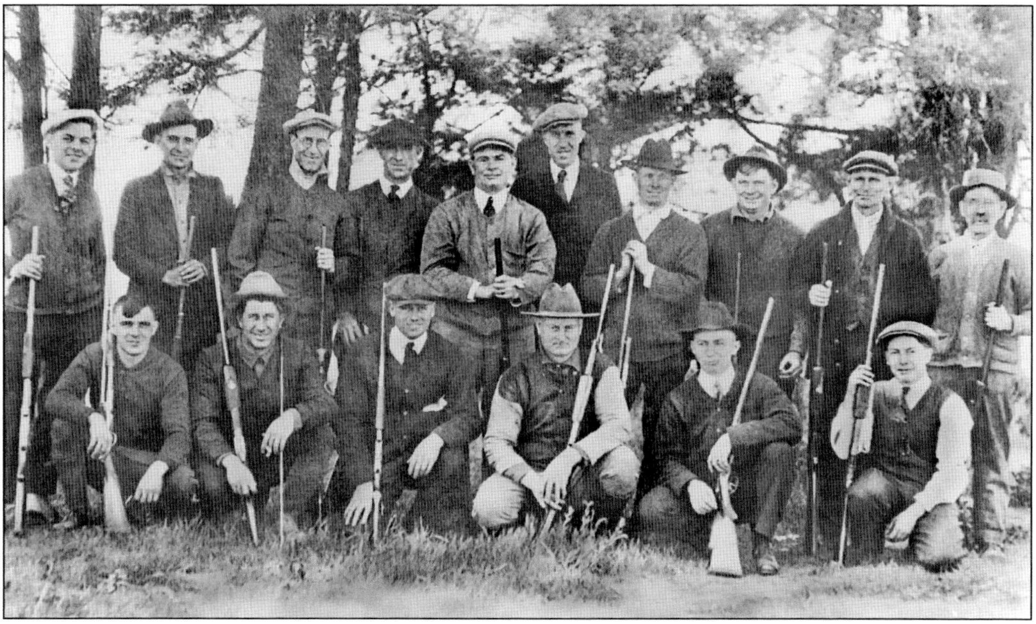

In 1920, these members of the Upland Red Hill Gun Club were photographed carrying shooting gear of a different sort than that which they might have used during the Great War two years earlier.

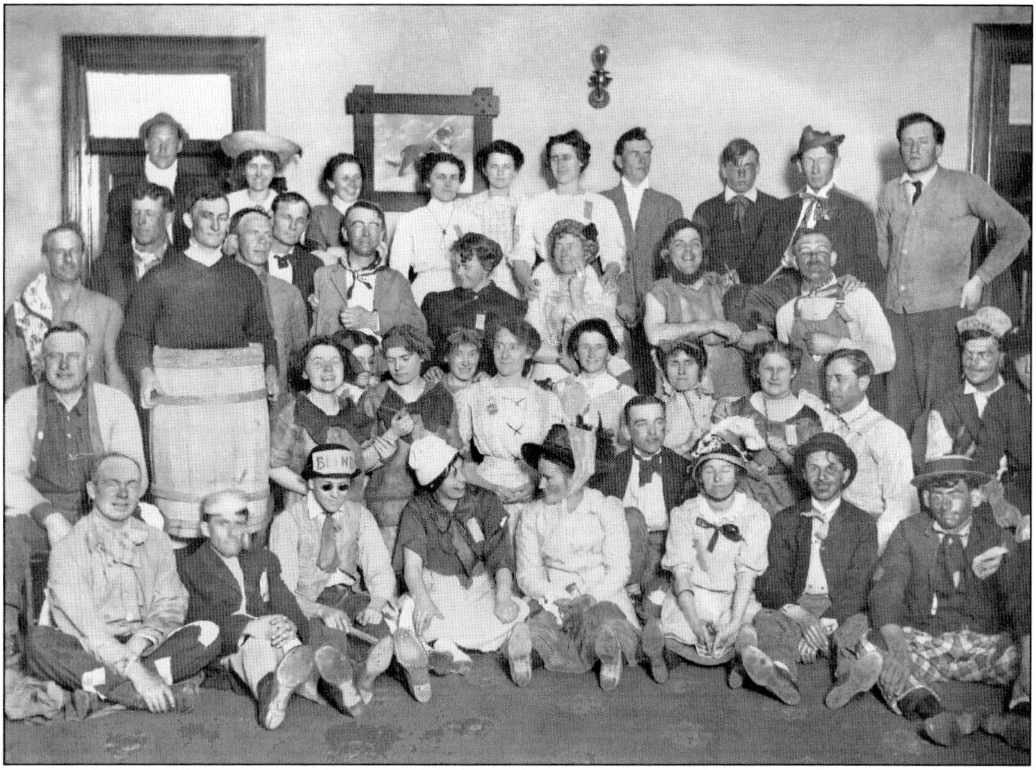

Community theater has been an important part of Upland life for quite a long time. This group of budding actors and actresses are dressed for what appears to be a comedy in 1920.

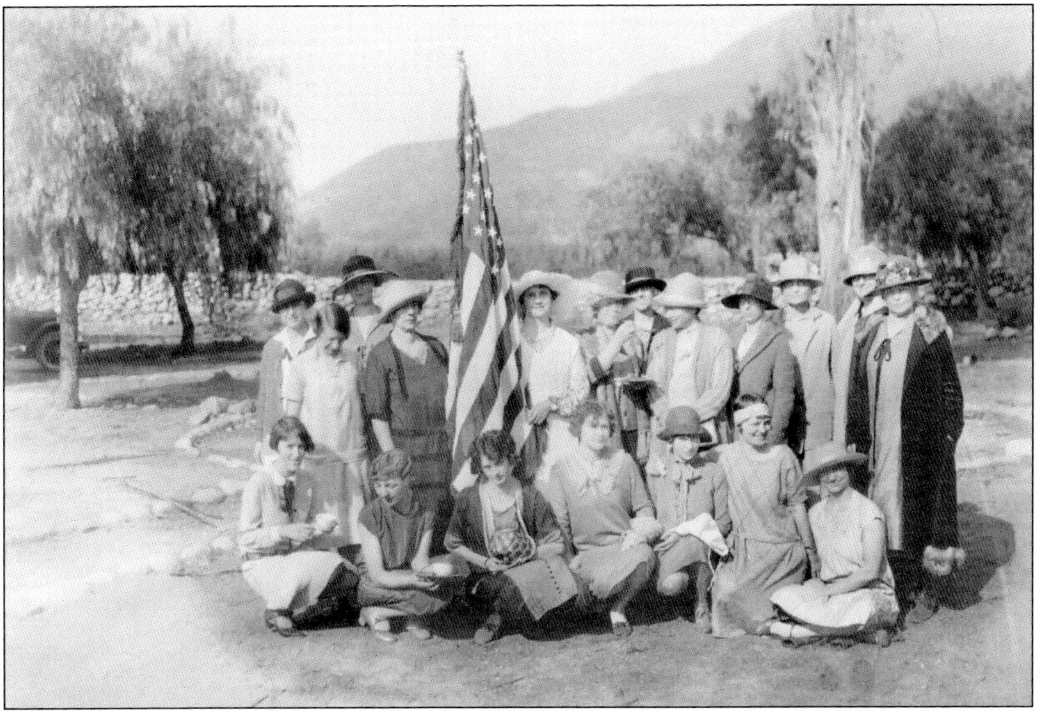

This photograph of the Upland Business and Professional Women's Club was taken in 1926 at San Antonio Park. The ladies had possibly ridden the train up Euclid Avenue to the stone waiting station at the park.

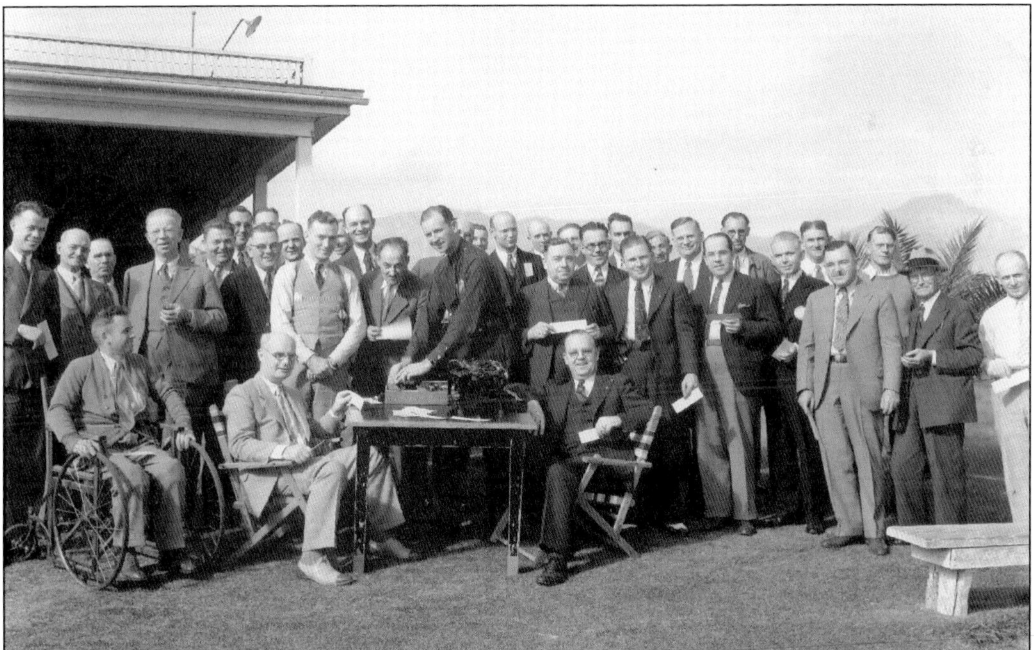

Many of Upland's notable men gathered for this 1940 photograph of the Upland Red Hill Men's Club.

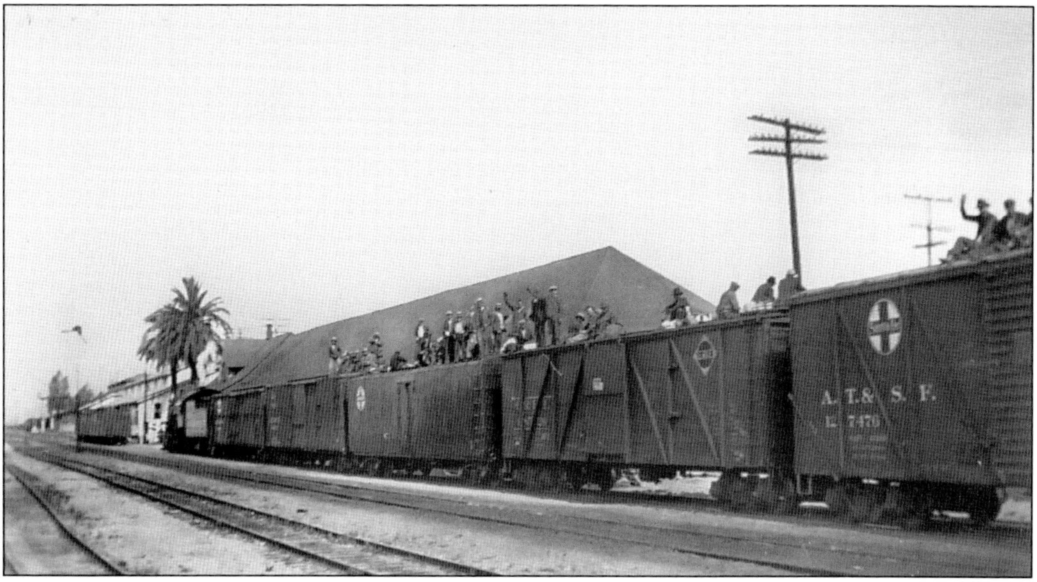

It is not certain if this 1935 photograph shows a crew of railroad construction workers at the Upland depot or men who were riding the rails during the Great Depression.

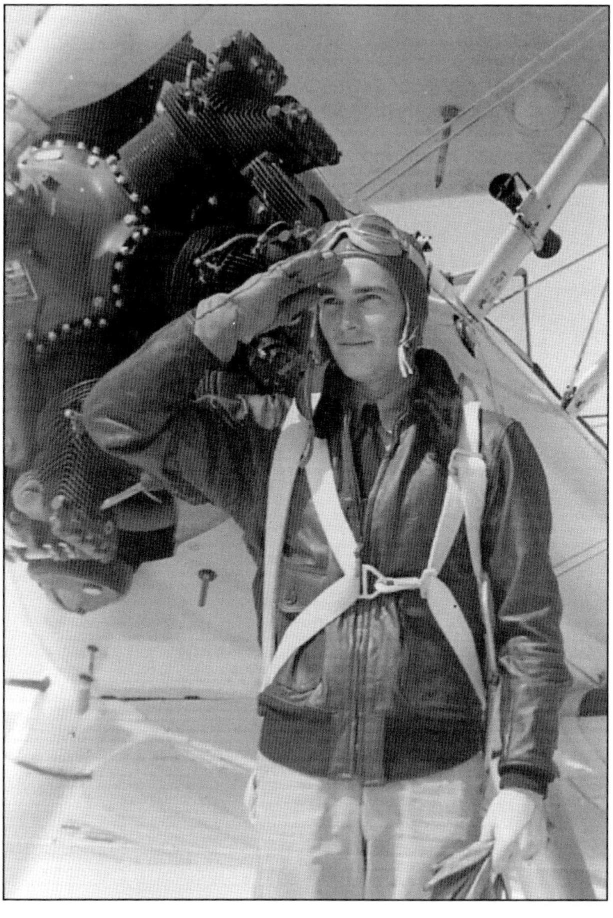

Rahe E. Hargrave strikes a fine pose in the pre–World War II photograph. Hargrave later served as a commander in U.S. Navy.

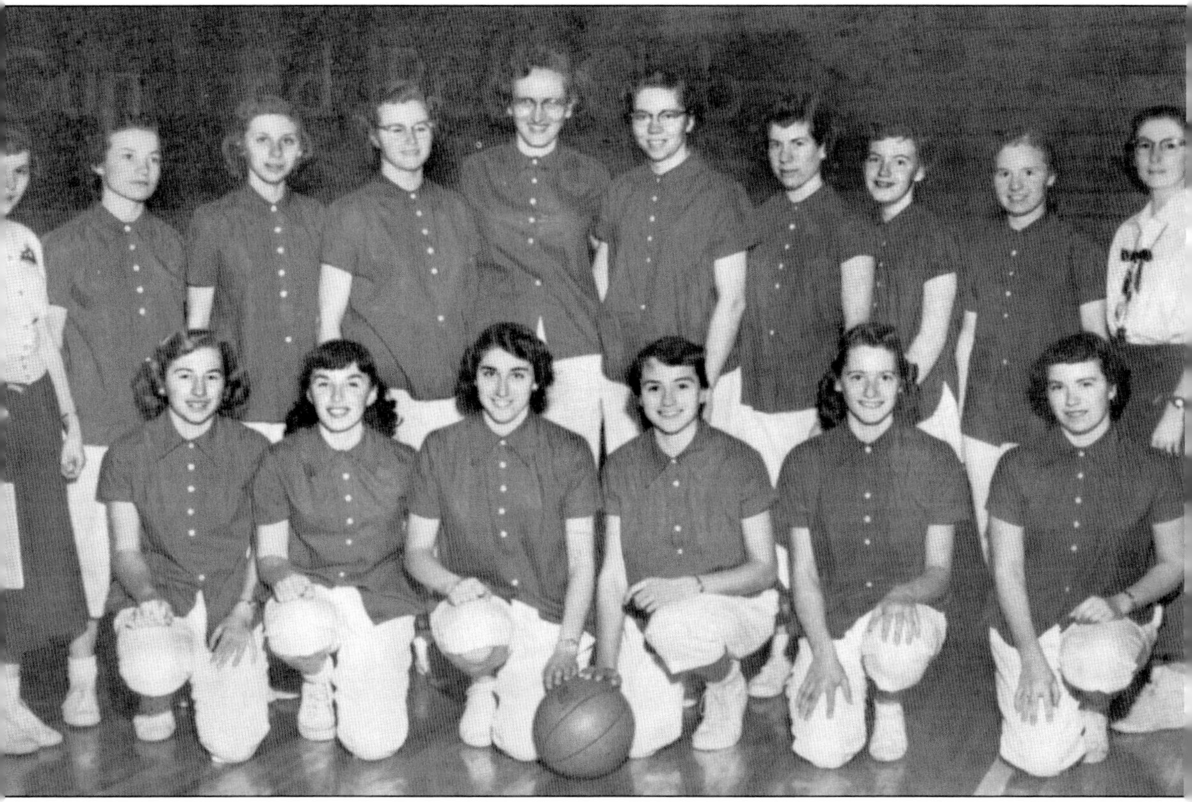

The 1954–1955 Upland Academy Spartanette basketball team is pictured here. Note that modest pedal pushers were part of the uniforms rather than shorts. (RDX.)

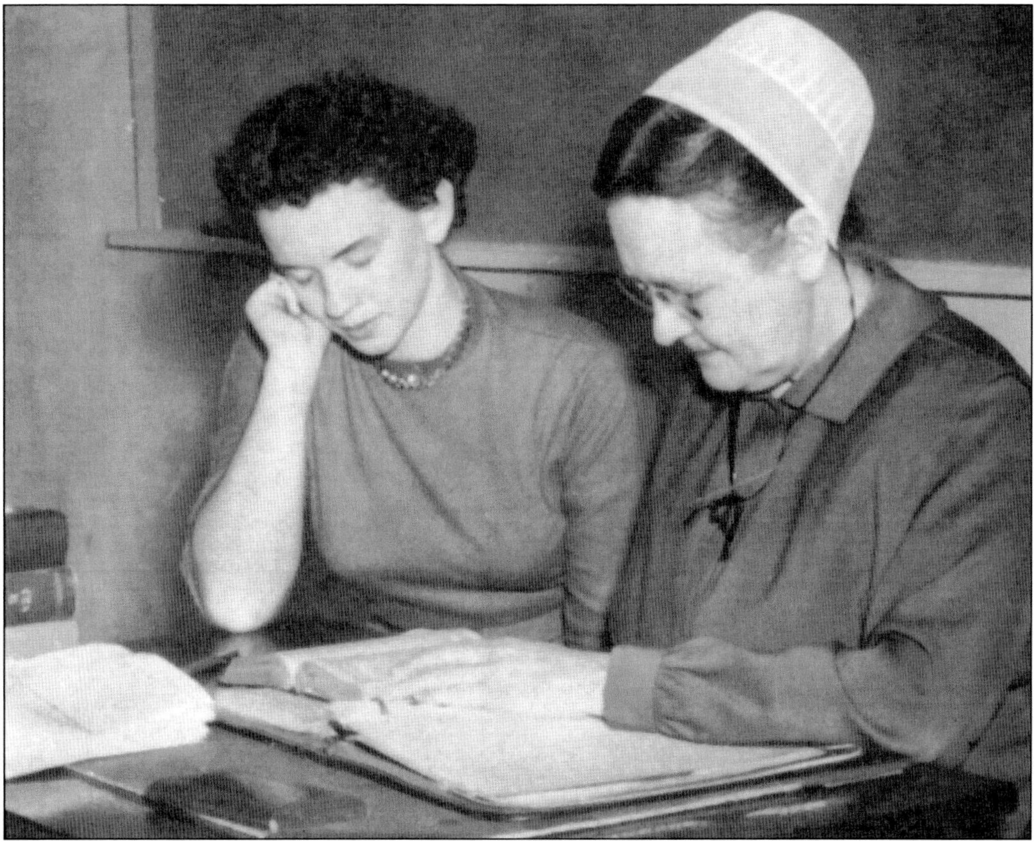

During the 1950s, some of the female students and faculty at Upland College still wore the traditional head coverings of the Brethren in Christ Church. (RDX.)

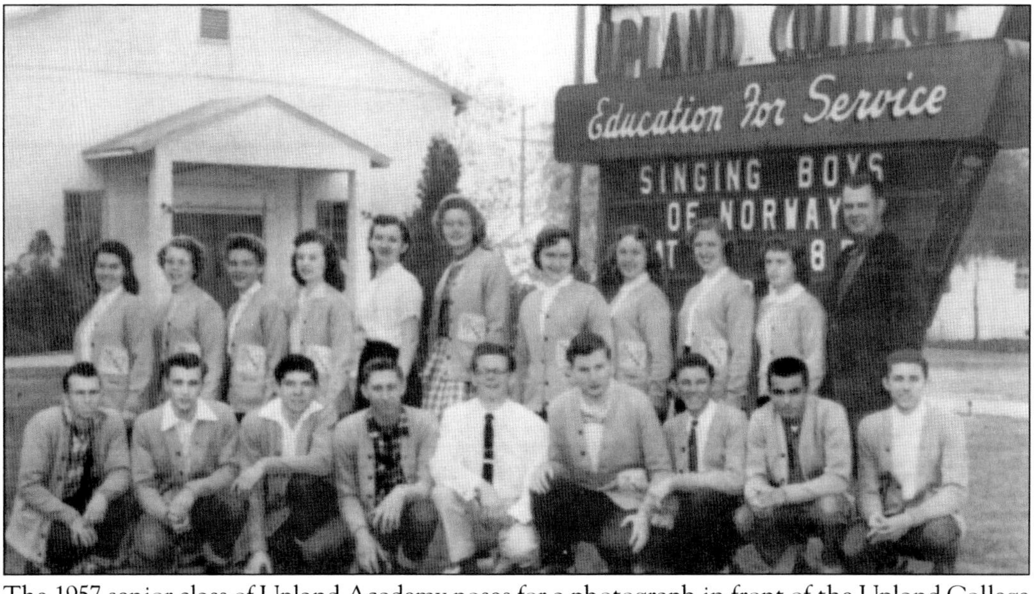


The 1957 senior class of Upland Academy poses for a photograph in front of the Upland College marquee on the campus at San Antonio Avenue and Arrow Highway. (RDX.)

# *Two*

# GOING UP EUCLID

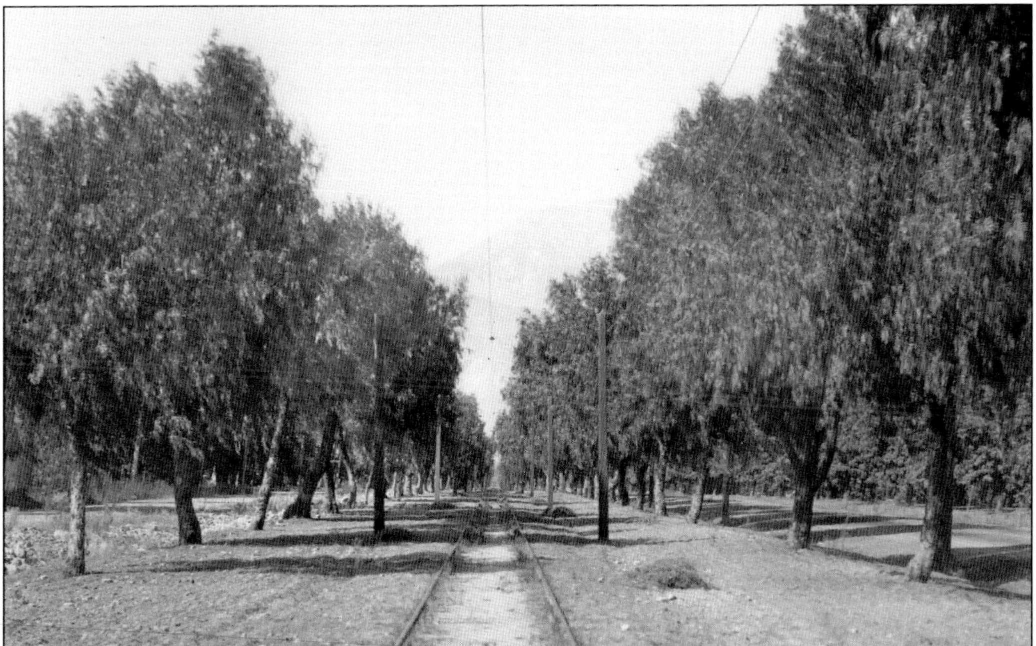

These rails were laid in 1887 by a crew working for Charles Frankish in order to bring about his vision for a rail system that would bring passengers from the valley below to San Antonio Heights above Upland. (UPL.)

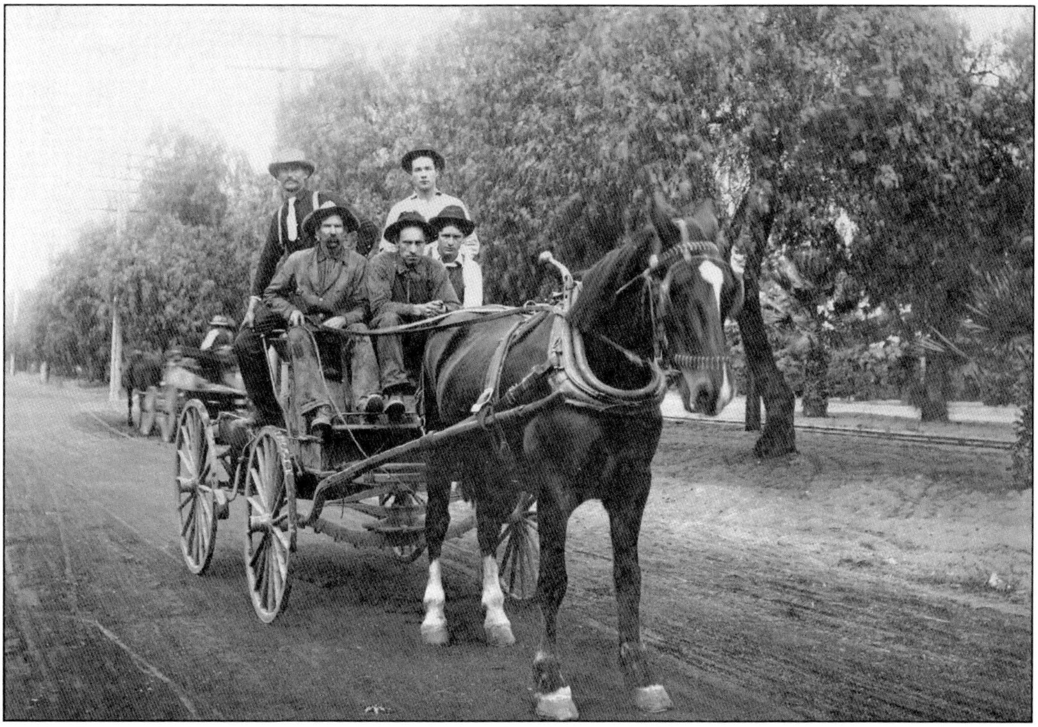

The Ontario Power Company crew is pictured on Euclid Avenue in the 1890s.

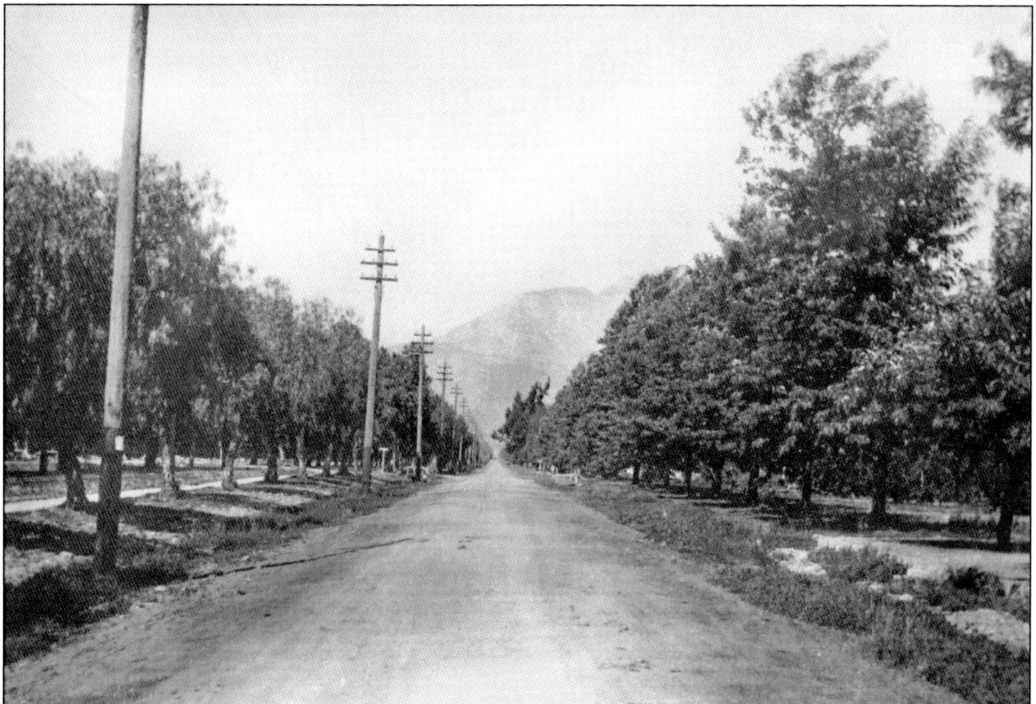

This view looks north on the east side of Euclid Avenue when it was still a dirt road about 1900.

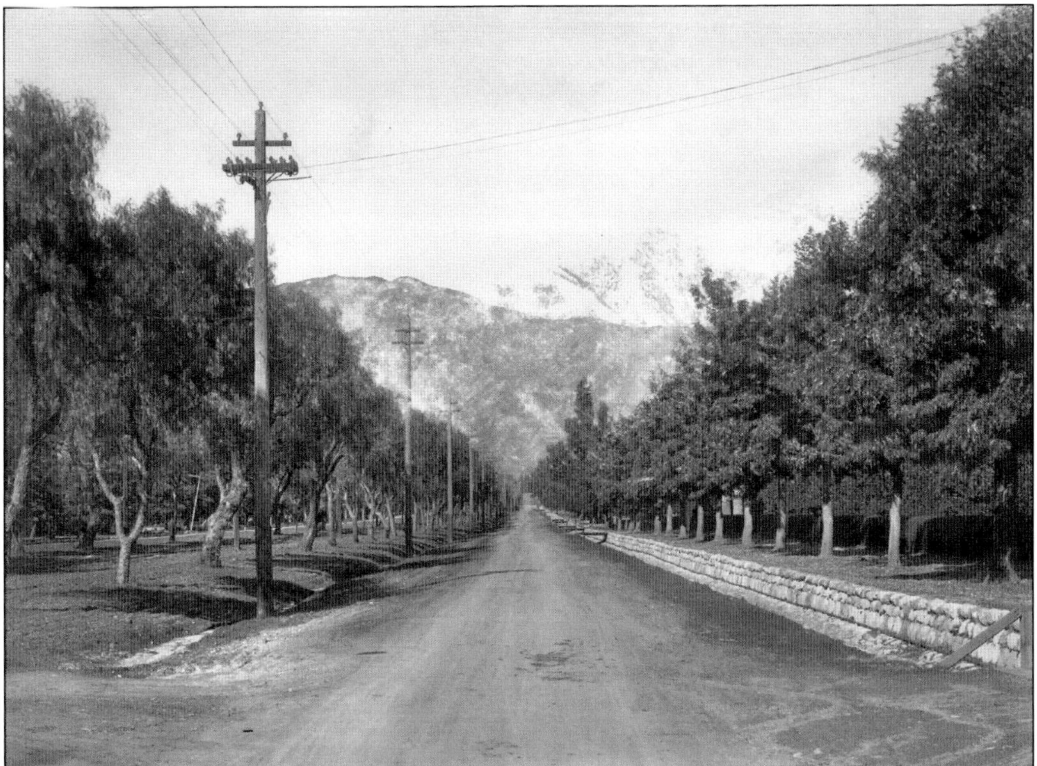

By 1910, more changes would come about, such as stone-reinforced draining ditches to carry rainwater and excess agricultural runoff down Euclid Avenue from the foothills.

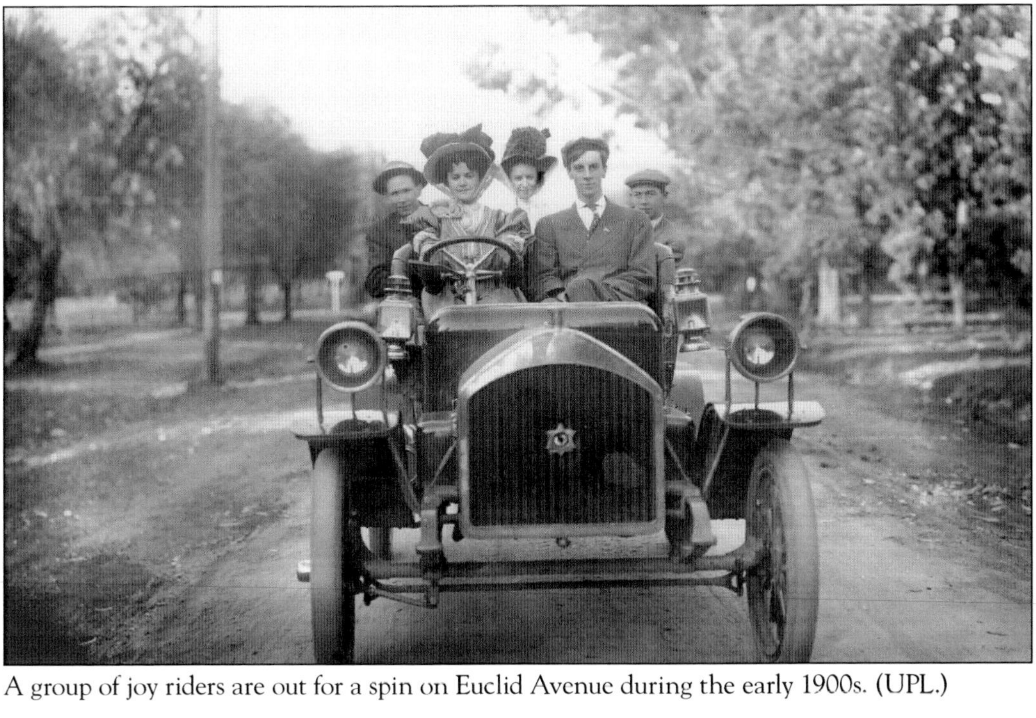

A group of joy riders are out for a spin on Euclid Avenue during the early 1900s. (UPL.)

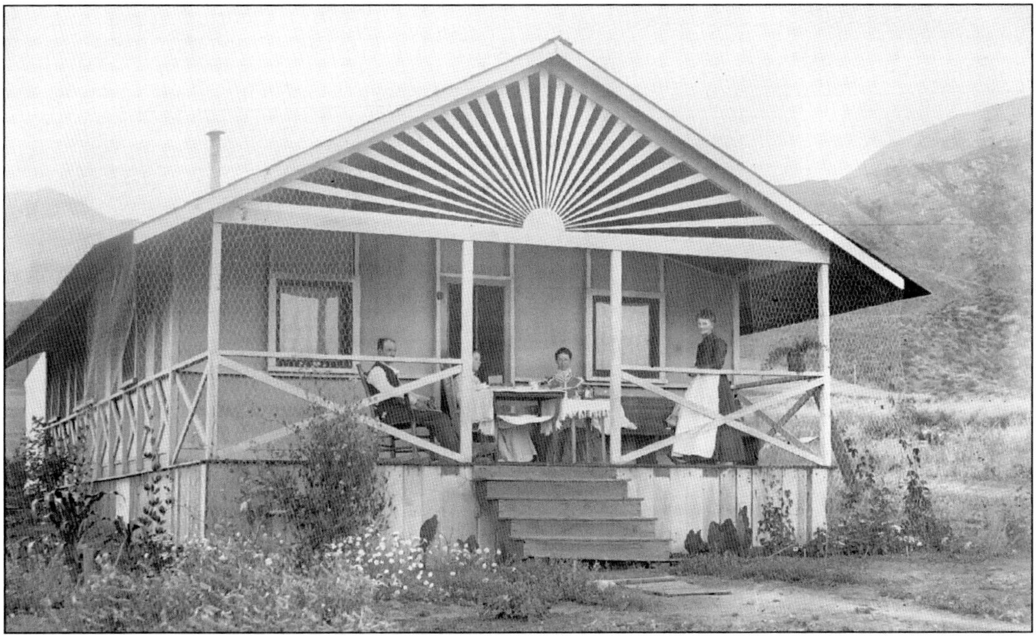

Anyone traveling up Euclid Avenue into San Antonio Heights during the early 1900s could see a few scattered homes with families on the front porches enjoying the cool air and possibly a bite to eat.

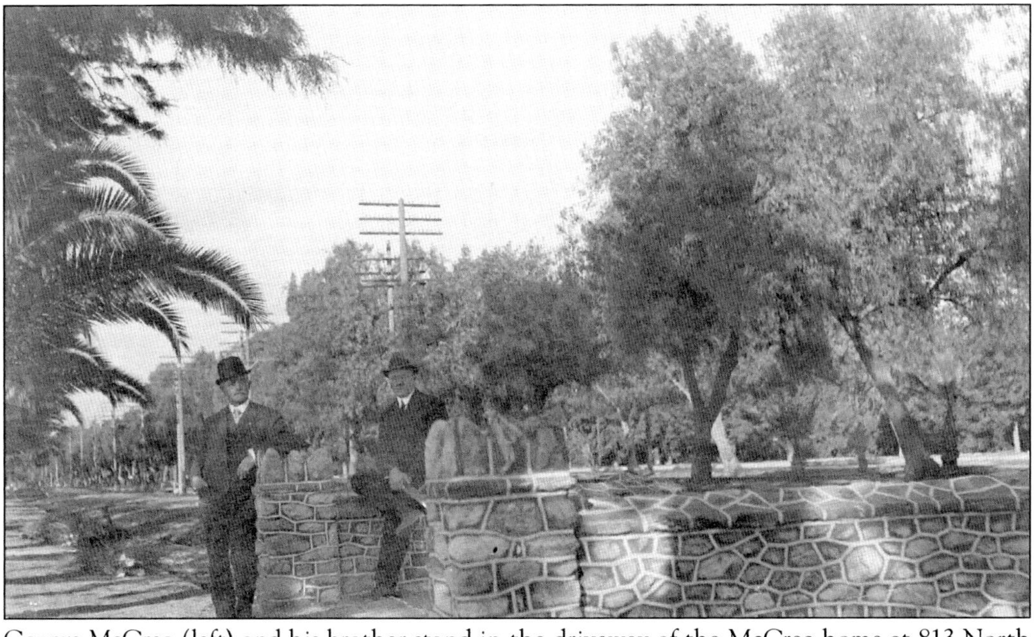

George McCrea (left) and his brother stand in the driveway of the McCrea home at 813 North Euclid Avenue in 1920.

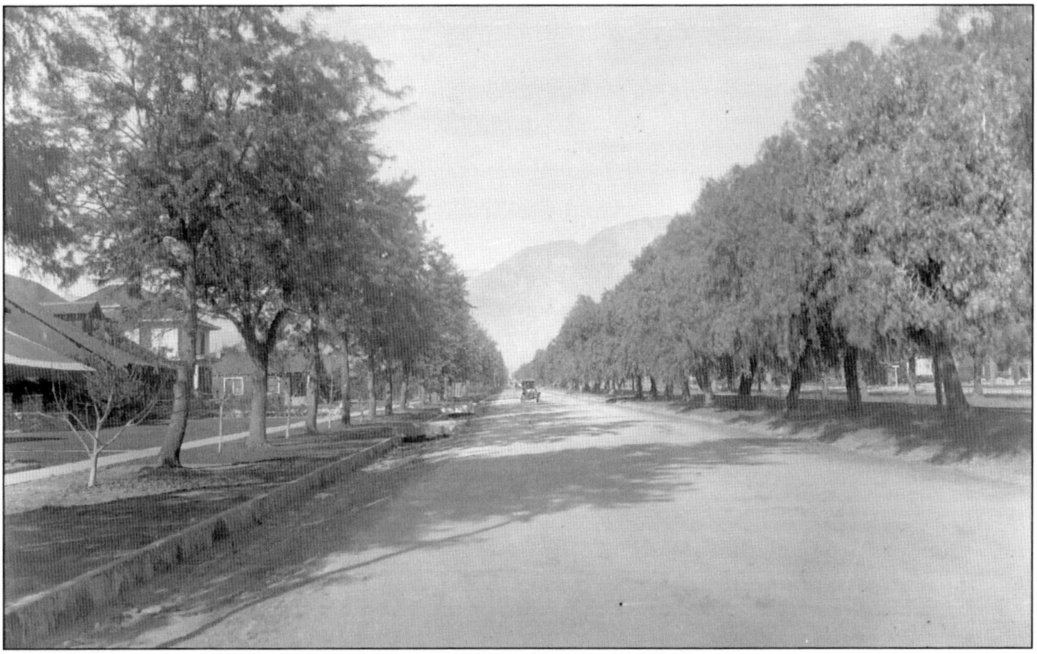

During the 1910s and 1920s, more homes were constructed along Euclid Avenue. Some of these were erected by permanent residents, while others were smaller vacation homes built by people from such far away places as Pasadena and Los Angeles. (UPL.)

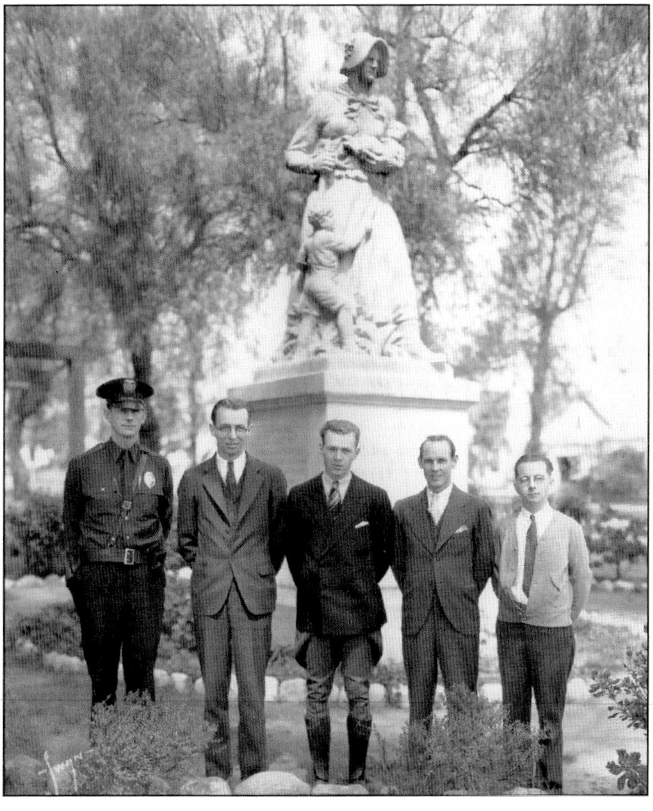

This image was taken at the base of the Madonna of the Trail statue in the 1930s to note five youngsters under the age of 30 who were helping to direct the affairs of the city. From left to right are Cecil Myers, police desk sergeant; Ernest Tweed Stone, president of the chamber of commerce; Ted Combs, city building inspector; Avery Allen, secretary of the chamber of commerce; and Ernest Olson, business men's division of the chamber of commerce.

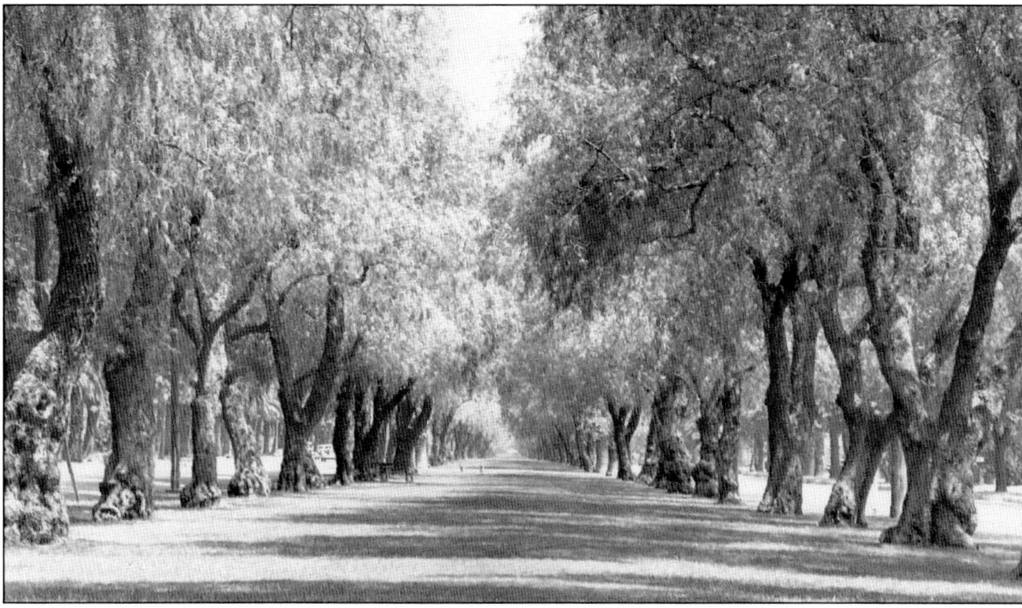

Taken in 1940 by noted floral photographer Clint Bryant, this is a beautiful example of how the pepper trees planted by George Chaffey and Andrew Rubio had grown by that time.

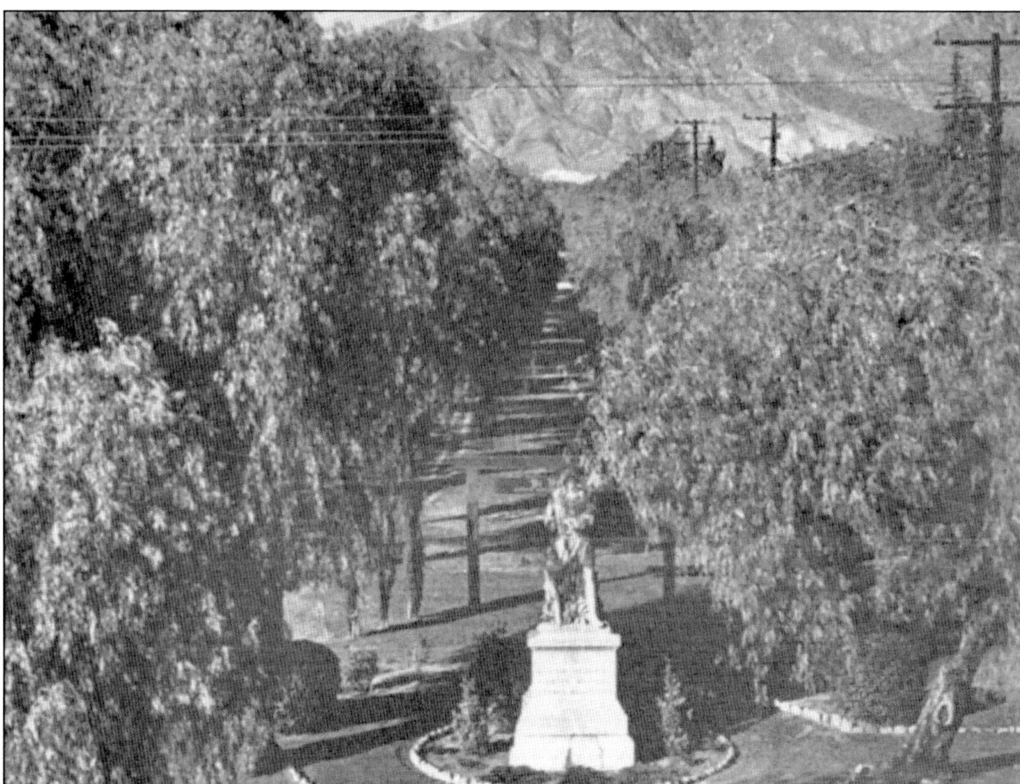

This aerial view of Euclid Avenue and the Madonna of the Trail statue was taken in 1940.

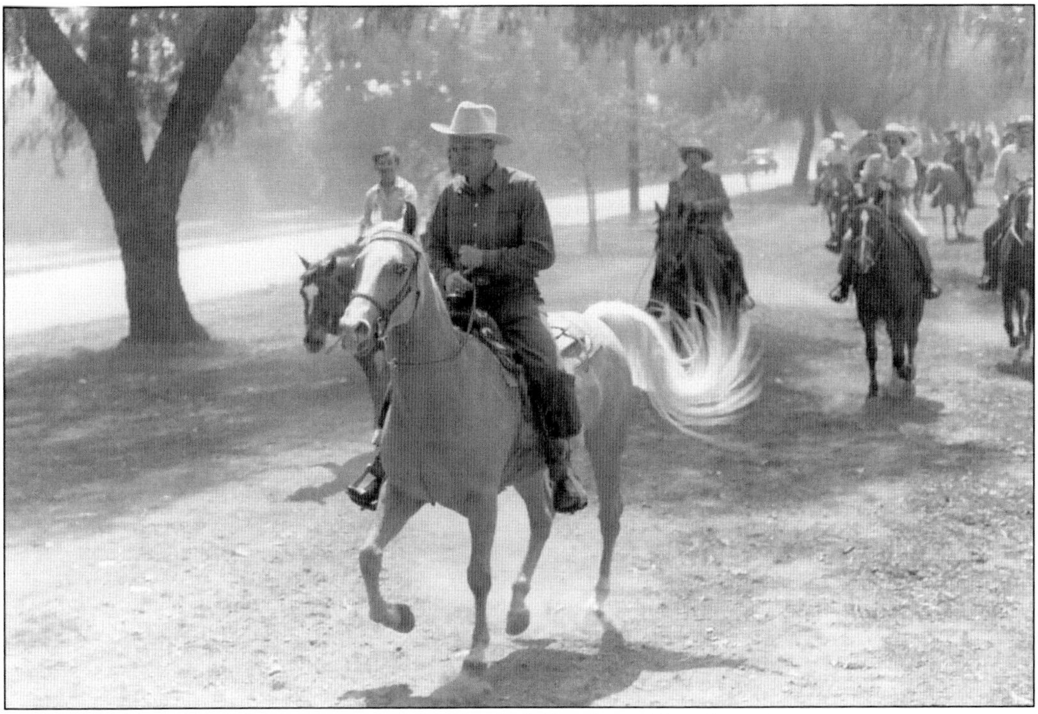

For many years, Euclid Avenue north of Foothill Boulevard has been kept in a more primitive state than the section south of Foothill. This practice has provided a trail for the enjoyment of hikers, joggers, and equestrian riders. (UPL.)

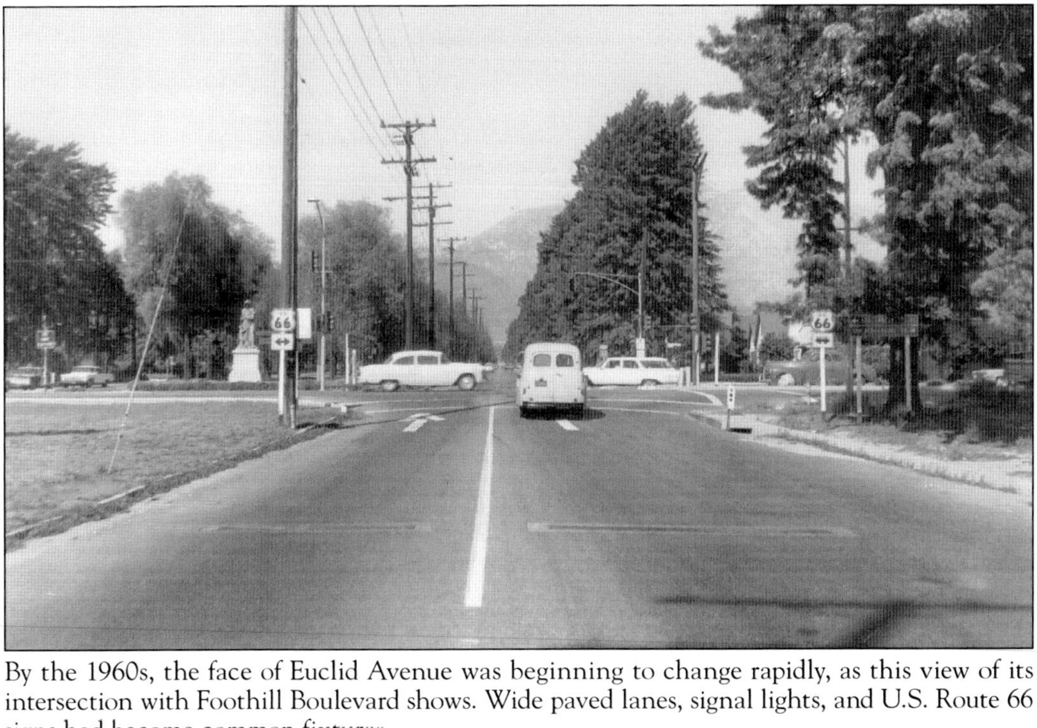


By the 1960s, the face of Euclid Avenue was beginning to change rapidly, as this view of its intersection with Foothill Boulevard shows. Wide paved lanes, signal lights, and U.S. Route 66 signs had become common fixtures.

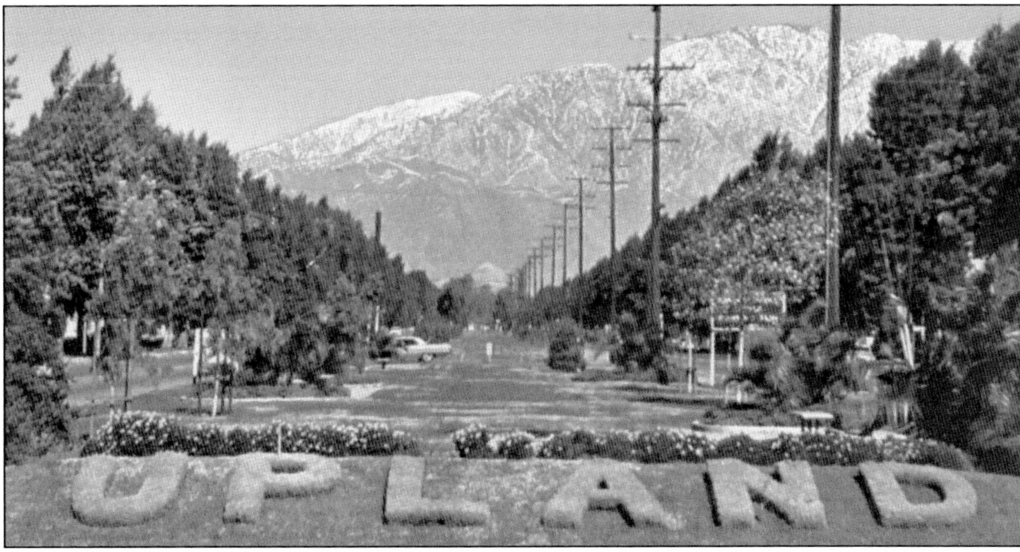


When the Ramona Parkway (later the San Bernardino or I-10 Freeway) made a definitive line between Upland and Ontario to the south, city officials decided to construct this Euclid Avenue sign made of shrubs in order to welcome people to Upland.

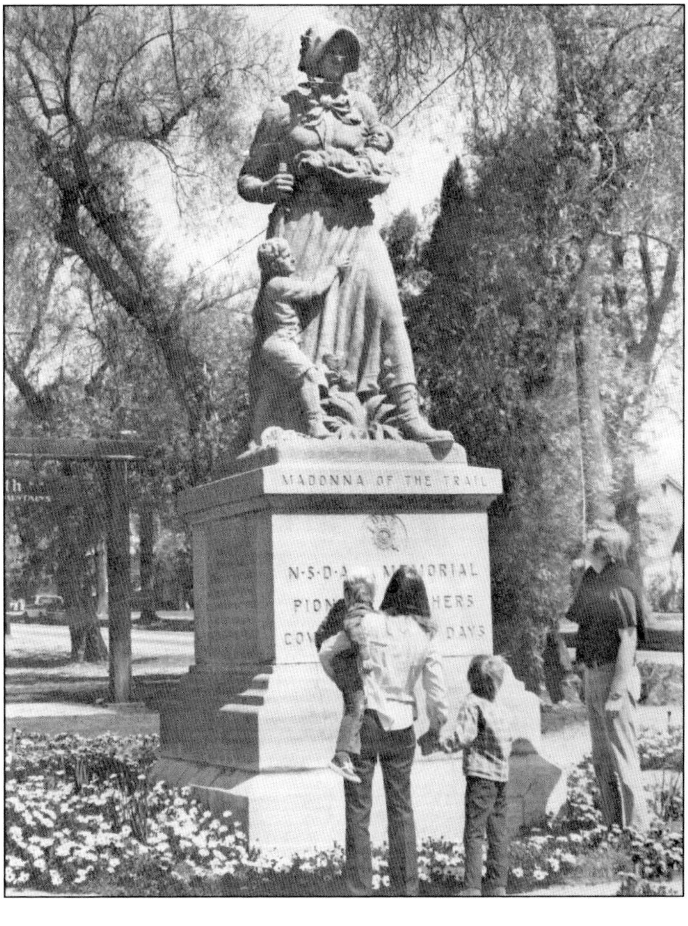


A family in 1970 stops to admire the Upland Madonna of the Trail, which was dedicated in 1929.

# *Three*

# Going Downtown

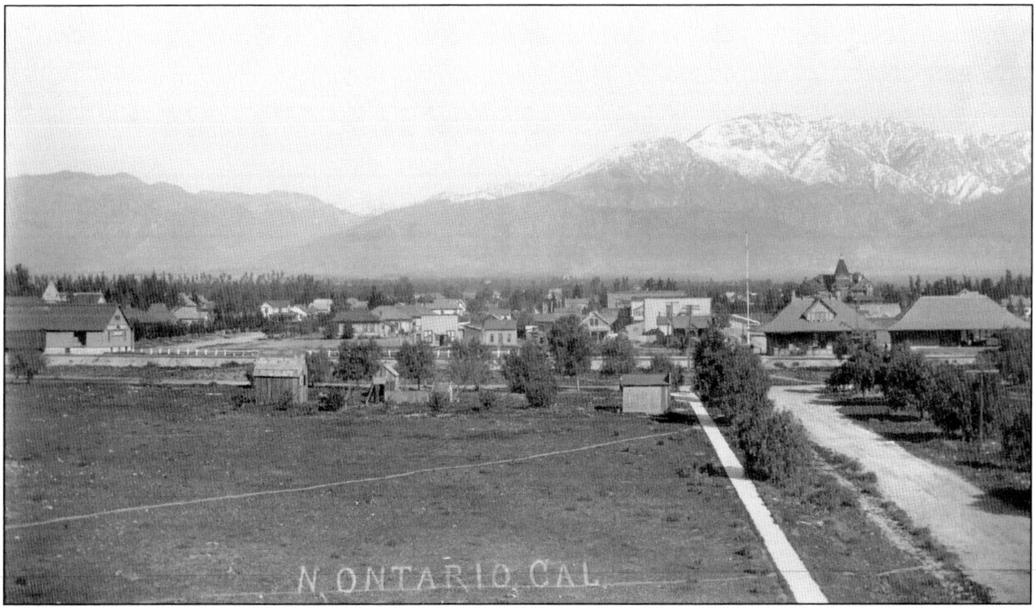


An 1898 view shows North Ontario, which would later become the downtown area of the city of Upland. The Magnolia Villa can be seen in the distance on the far right.

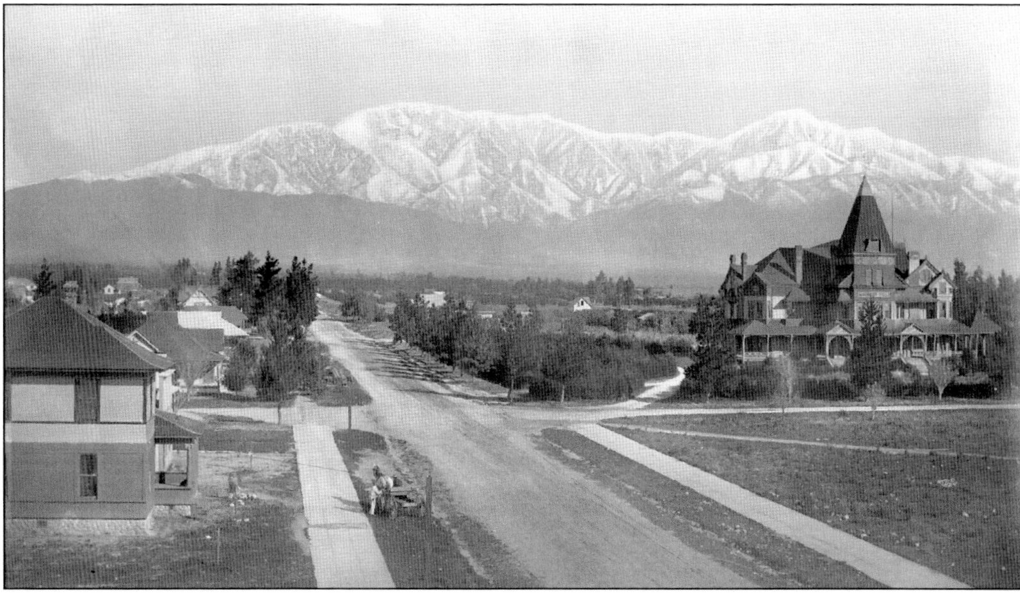

The magnificent Magnolia Villa hotel, seen on the right in 1896, was built by the Bedford brothers in 1887 as part of their real estate venture known as Magnolia. Following financial difficulties, the Bedfords gave up their dream, and Magnolia became part of North Ontario, which was later incorporated as the city of Upland in 1906. The hotel was demolished in 1903. The dirt street in the center of the photograph is Second Avenue.

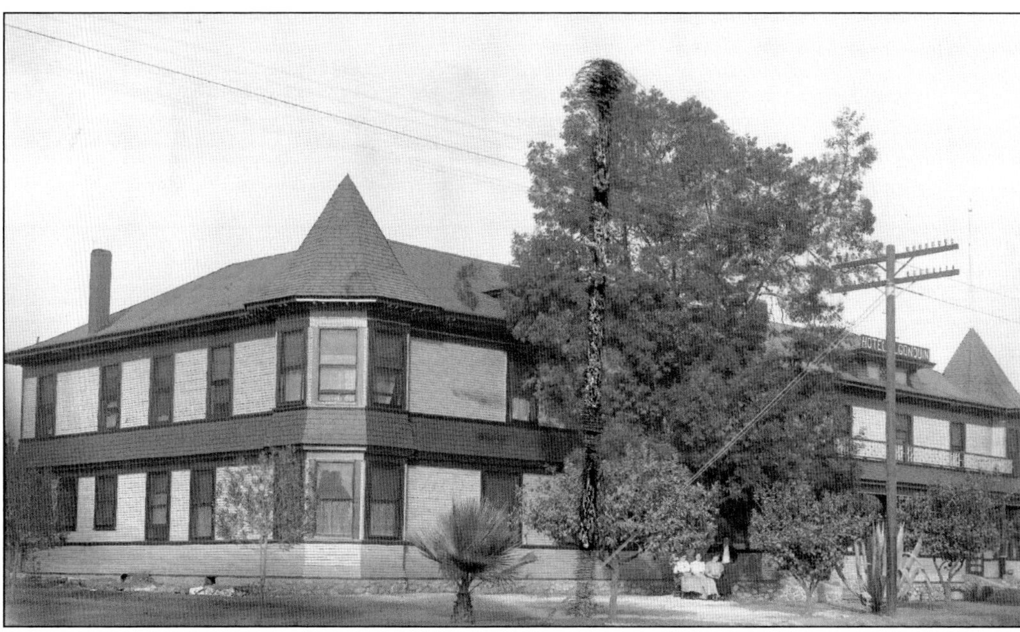

Although not as enormous as the 80-room Magnolia Villa, the Hotel Algonquin was a fine establishment. Built in 1901, it was later renamed the Upland Inn, and it burned in 1976. (UPL.)

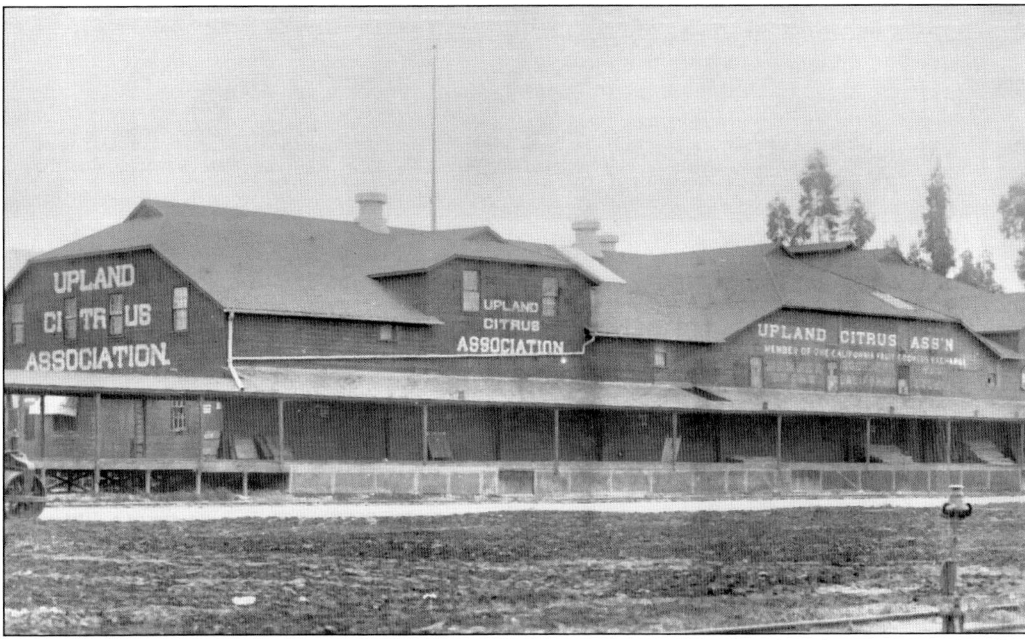


The Upland Citrus Association was organized in 1897. The company packinghouse was a familiar site in downtown Upland until the mid-1920s, when it was torn down in order to make room for a new facility. (UPL.)

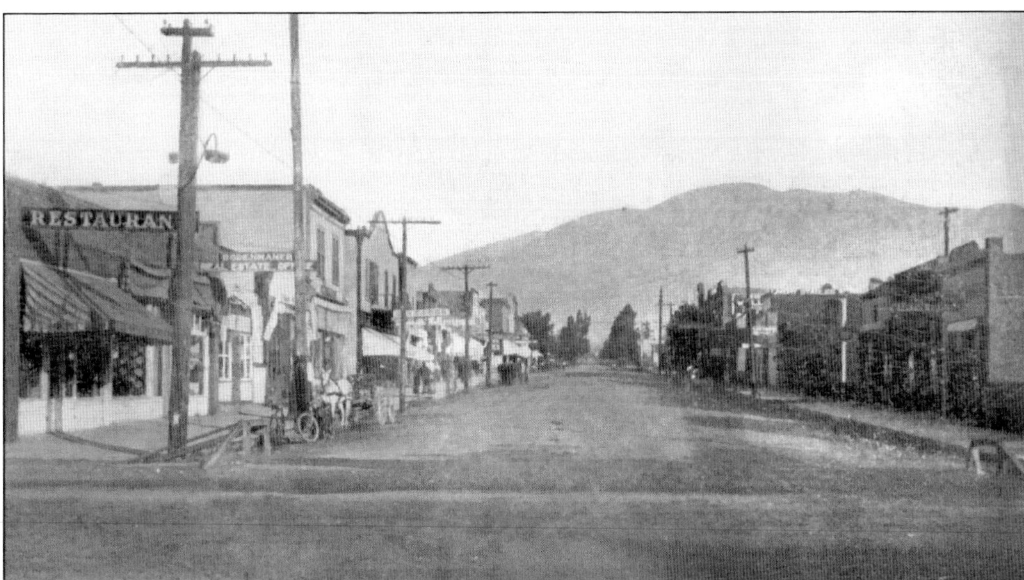


This view looks north on Second Avenue in the downtown area during the 1890s. (UPL.)

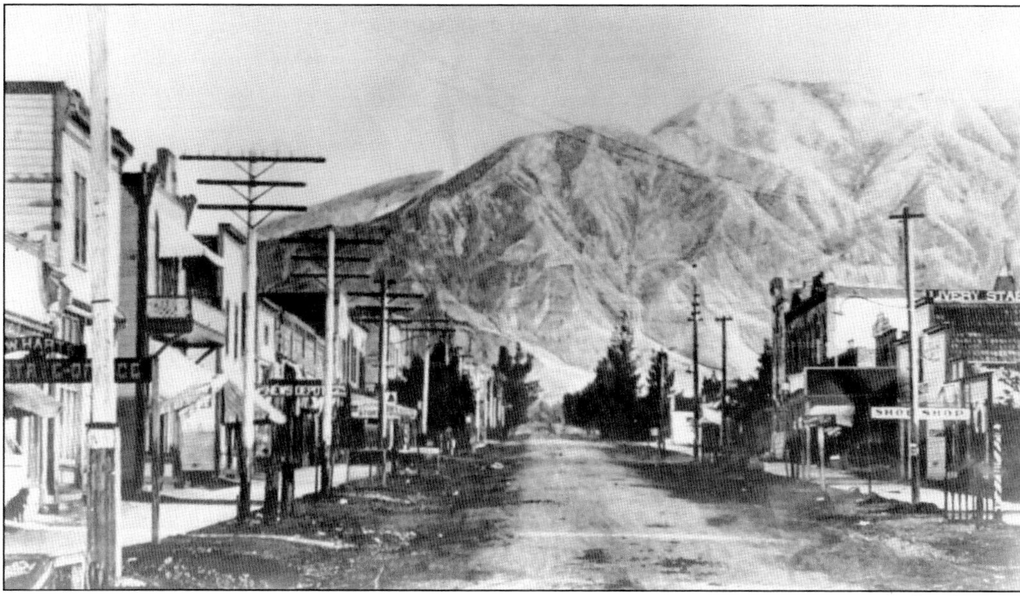


By the early 1900s, the view of Second Avenue had not changed much. (UPL.)

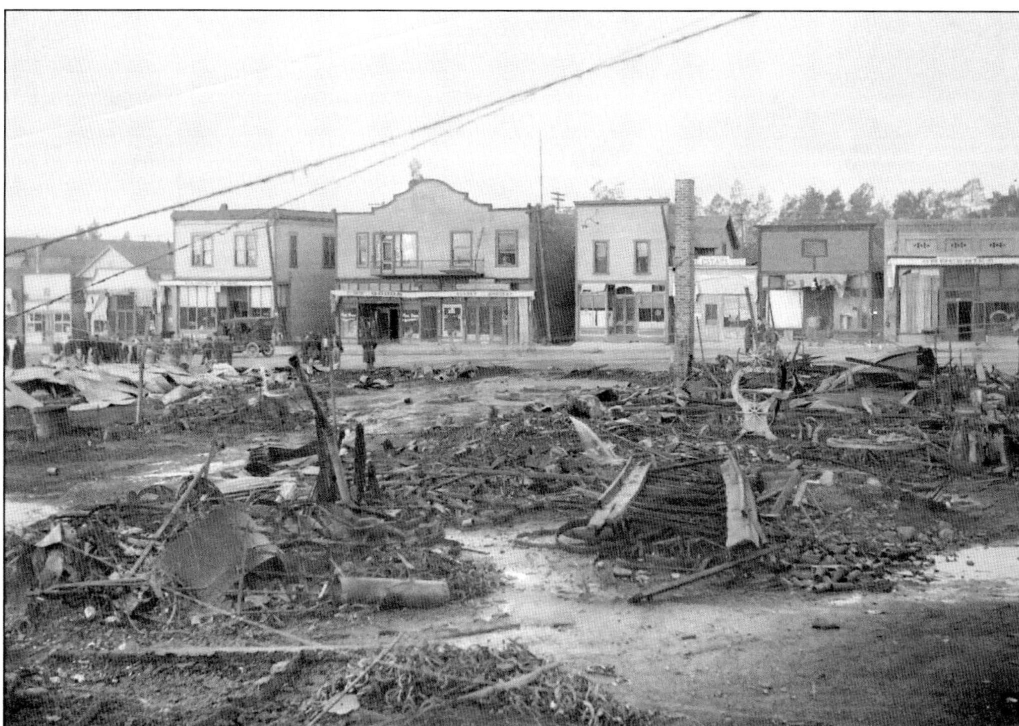

The fire of December 1912 was devastating to the downtown merchants of Upland. What was then called the "Big Fire" began in Roy Creighton's garage, burning several vehicles inside the building. The inferno spread until it destroyed the entire area from Second Avenue east to Third Avenue and from Ninth Street south to A Street.

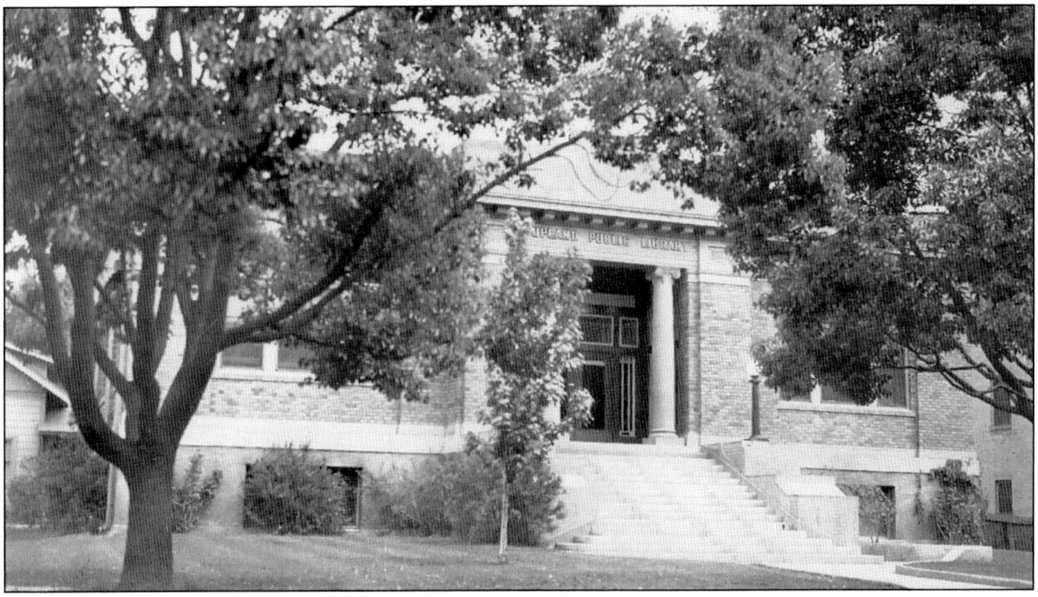

The burned section of Second Avenue was rebuilt, and other areas of the downtown began to be razed and rebuilt as the years passed. Construction of beautiful buildings in other parts of the downtown area began to lift the spirits of the people. One such building was the Andrew Carnegie Library, which was erected at First Avenue and D Street in 1913.

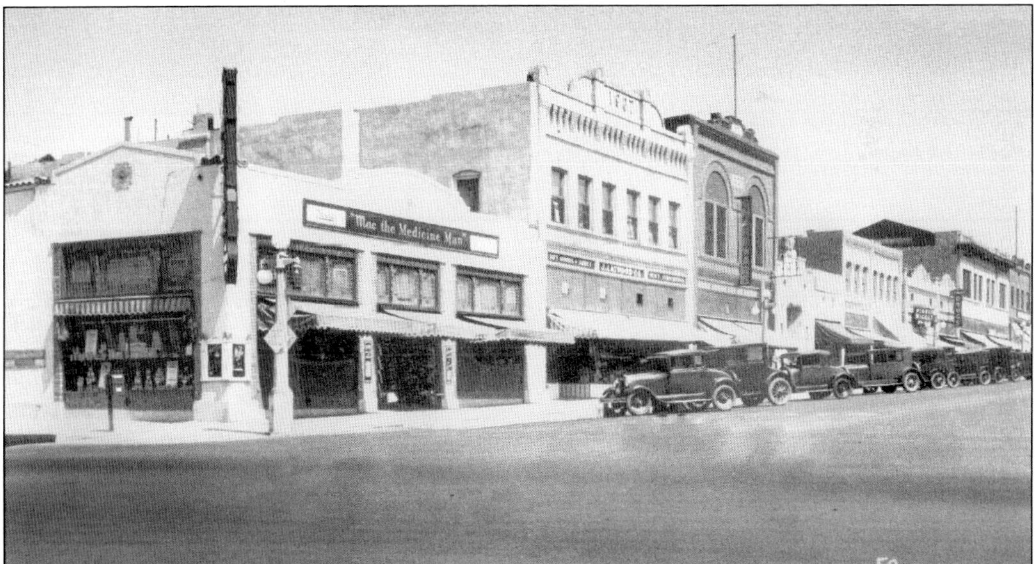


This view of the northwest corner of Second Avenue and Ninth Street was photographed in the 1920s. The building on the corner housed Patrick "Mac the Medicine Man" McQuillen's department store, and the building third from the corner was the Odd Fellows Hall, where a meeting was held and the decision was made to seek incorporation for Upland as a city in 1906.

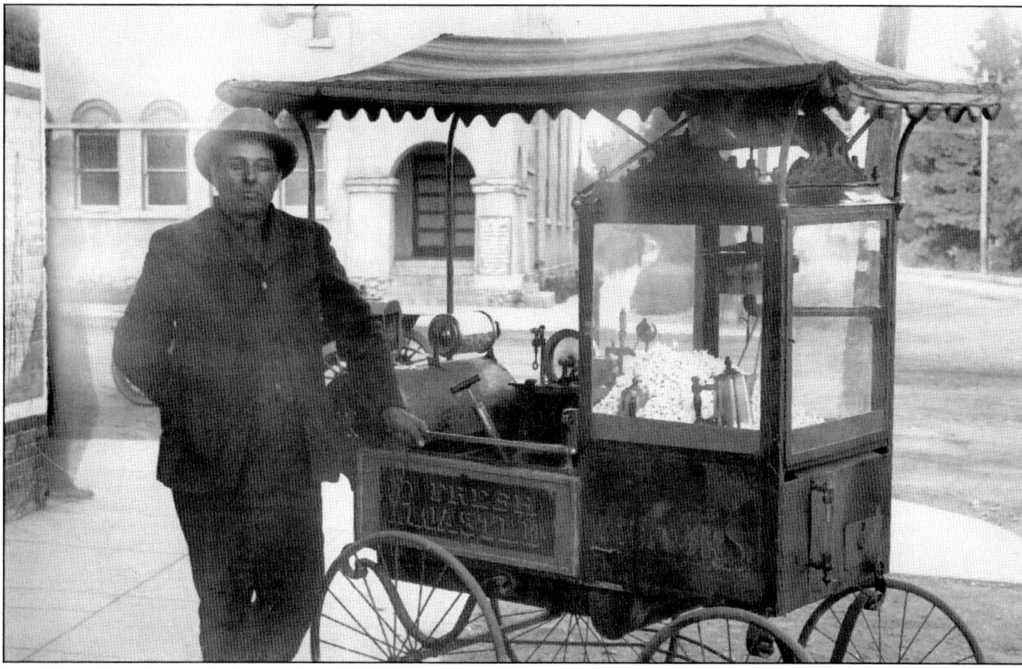

This 1920s popcorn vendor was ready to delight customers with a hot tasty treat at the corner of Third Avenue and Ninth Street. (UPL.)

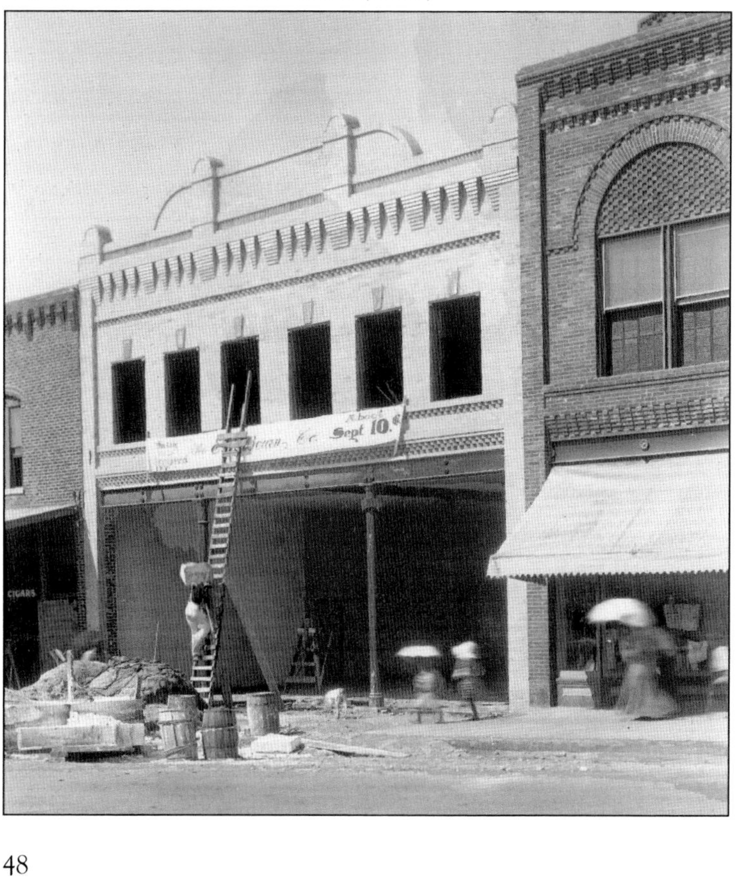


E. A. Bowen operated a butcher shop on Second Avenue in the early 1900s. It is seen here in the construction stages before opening. (UPL.)

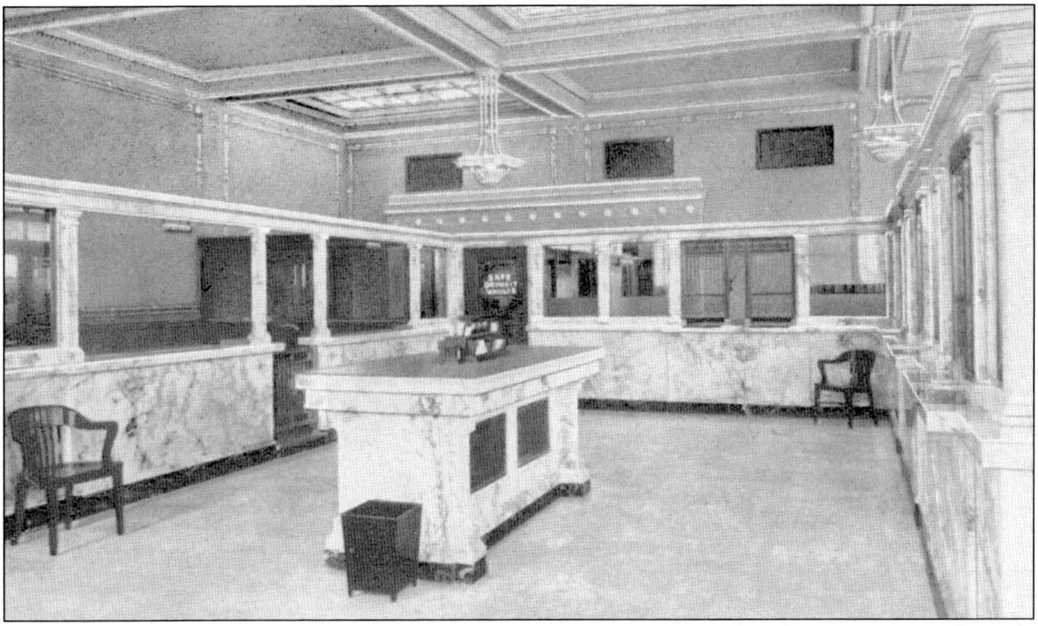

Anyone going downtown to shop would certainly be in need of funds. The First National Bank, seen here in 1920, was one of the financial institutions that was always willing to help out.

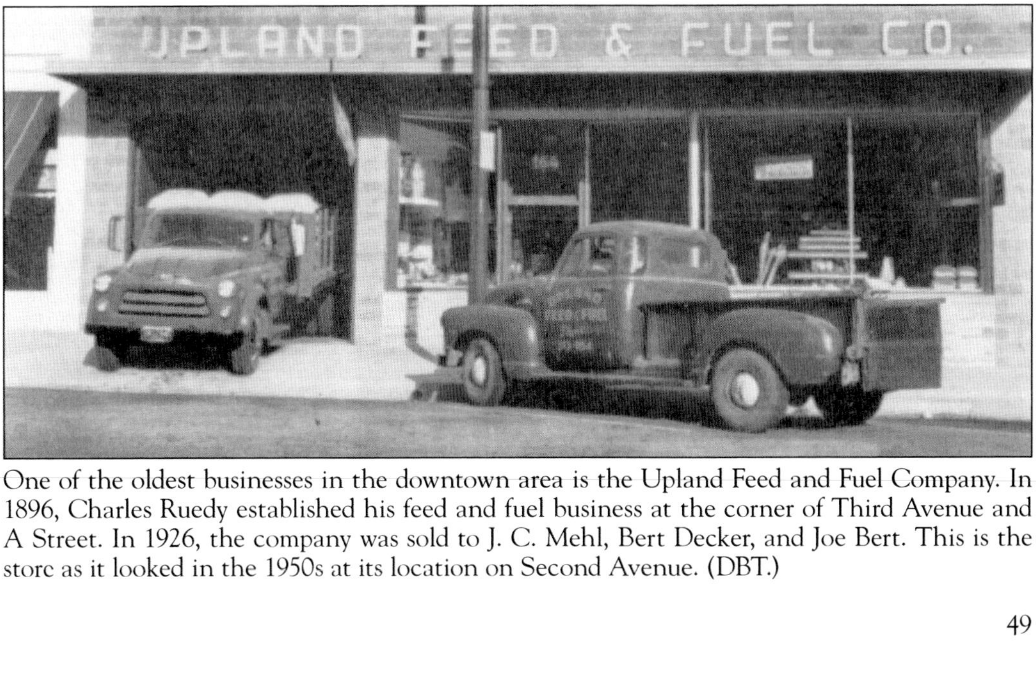


One of the oldest businesses in the downtown area is the Upland Feed and Fuel Company. In 1896, Charles Ruedy established his feed and fuel business at the corner of Third Avenue and A Street. In 1926, the company was sold to J. C. Mehl, Bert Decker, and Joe Bert. This is the store as it looked in the 1950s at its location on Second Avenue. (DBT.)

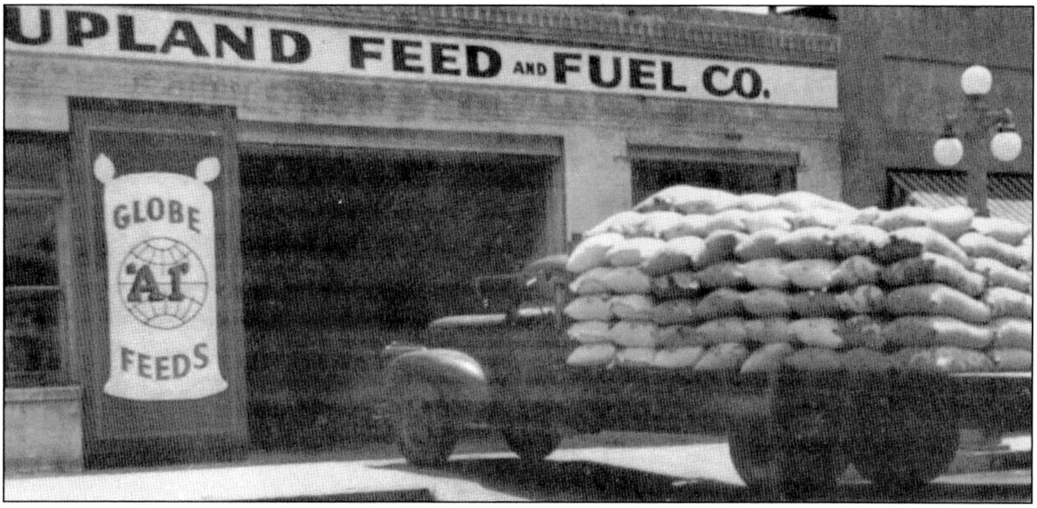


A company truck, loaded with sacks of chicken feed, pulls into the Upland Feed and Fuel Company retail store on Second Avenue. This business moved to this location in 1927. (DBT.)

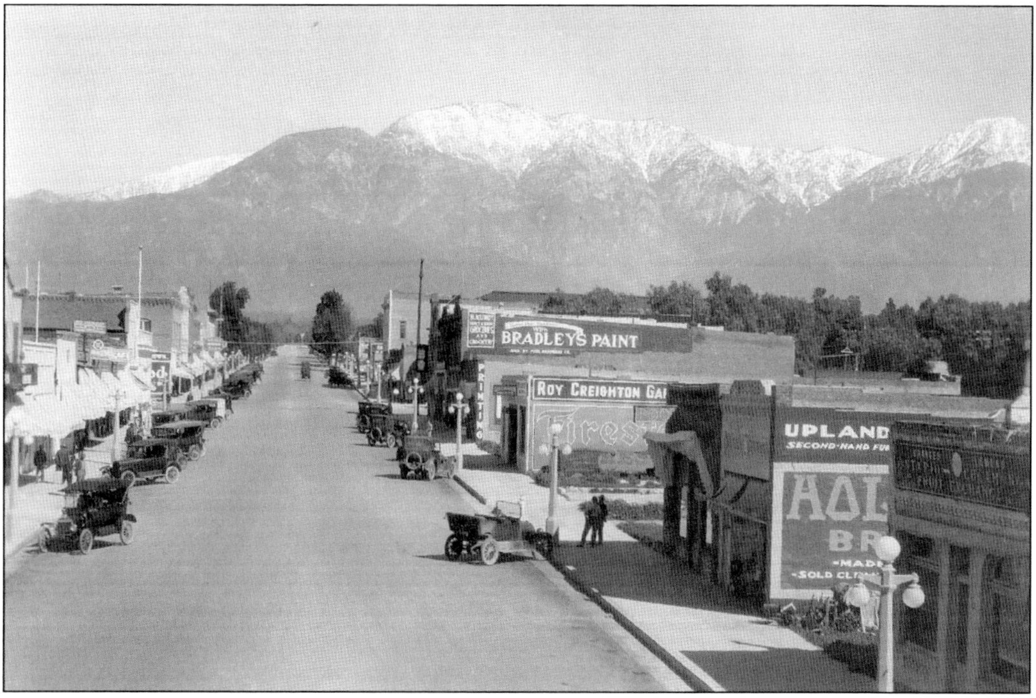


This view looks north on Second Avenue in the 1920s as the downtown area continues to grow with new businesses.

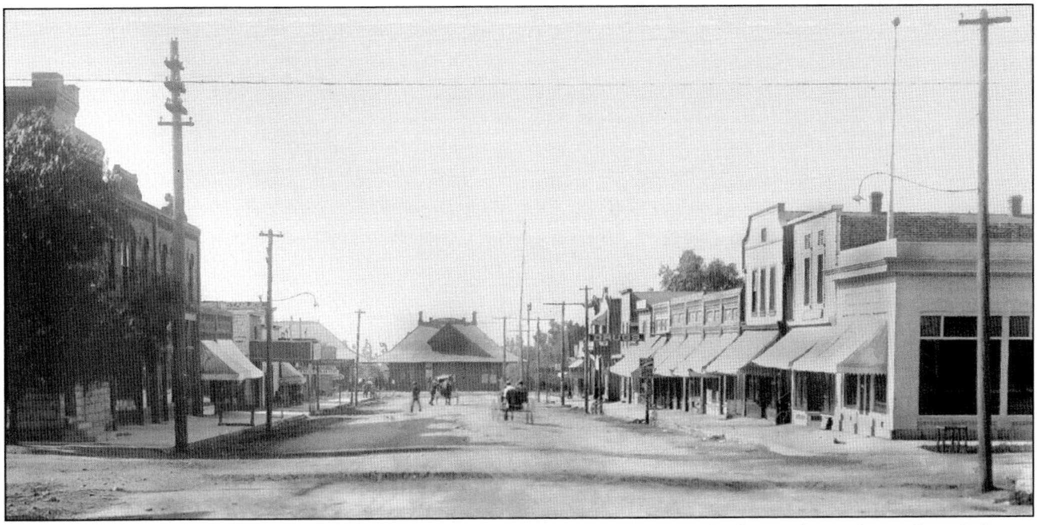

This picture was taken looking south on Second Avenue in the early days when the railroad depot stood at the end of the street, cutting Second Avenue off from what was known as the Stowell district below the tracks. The district was named for Nathan Stowell, who had been a pipe maker for the Chaffey brothers of the Ontario Colony. In 1886, Stowell purchased 60 acres of land on the east side of Euclid Avenue between Seventh and Eighth Streets. This was the beginning of the new colony of North Ontario, which later became Upland. (UPL.)

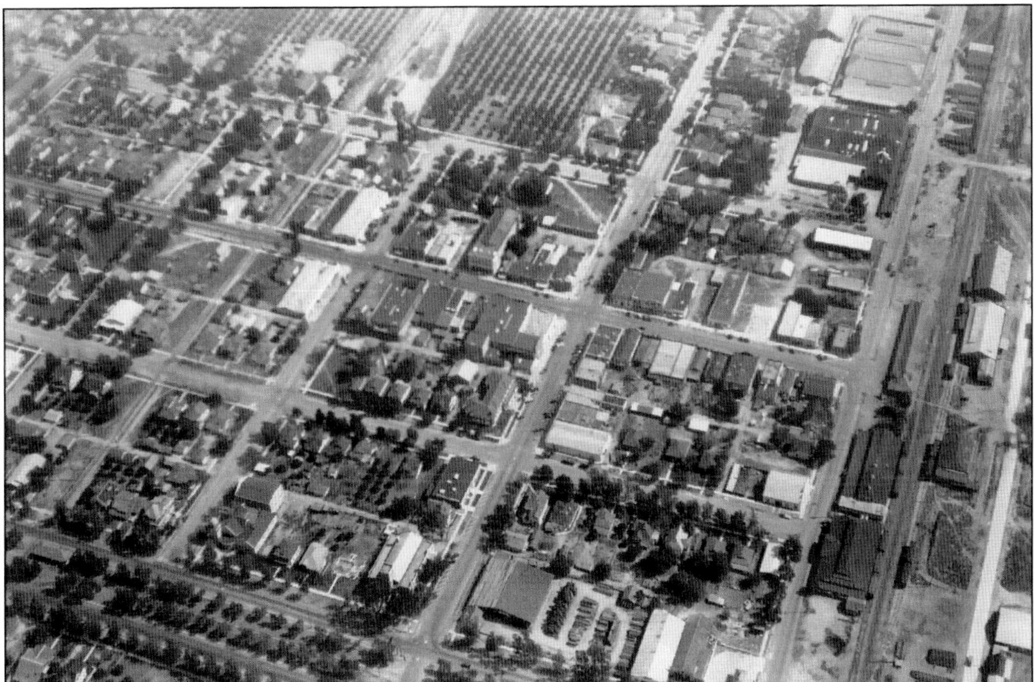

This aerial photograph of Upland, taken sometime in the 1920s, shows how much the city has changed. Old-timers might be able to recognize such places as the Upland (Algonquin) Inn and Mac the Medicine Man's pharmacy and department store near the center of the photograph. The citrus grove near the center top is the present location of the George Gibson Senior Center and Coy D. Estes Senior Housing Complex on Third Avenue.

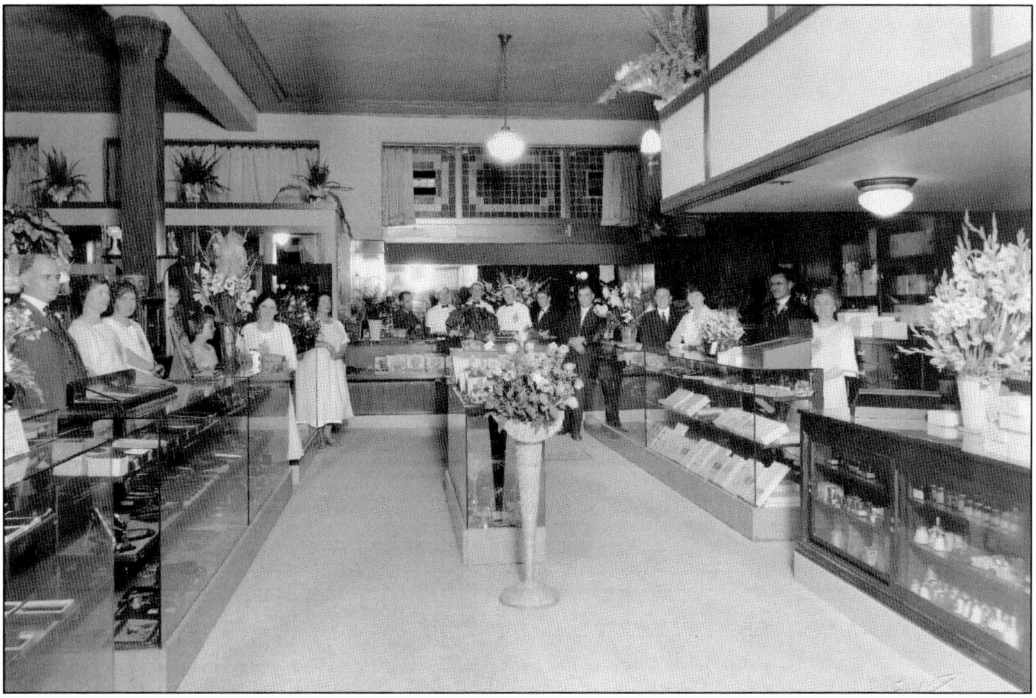

This 1920s photograph was taken inside Patrick "Mac the Medicine Man" McQuillen's pharmacy and department store on Second Avenue. McQuillen is standing behind the counter on the far left.

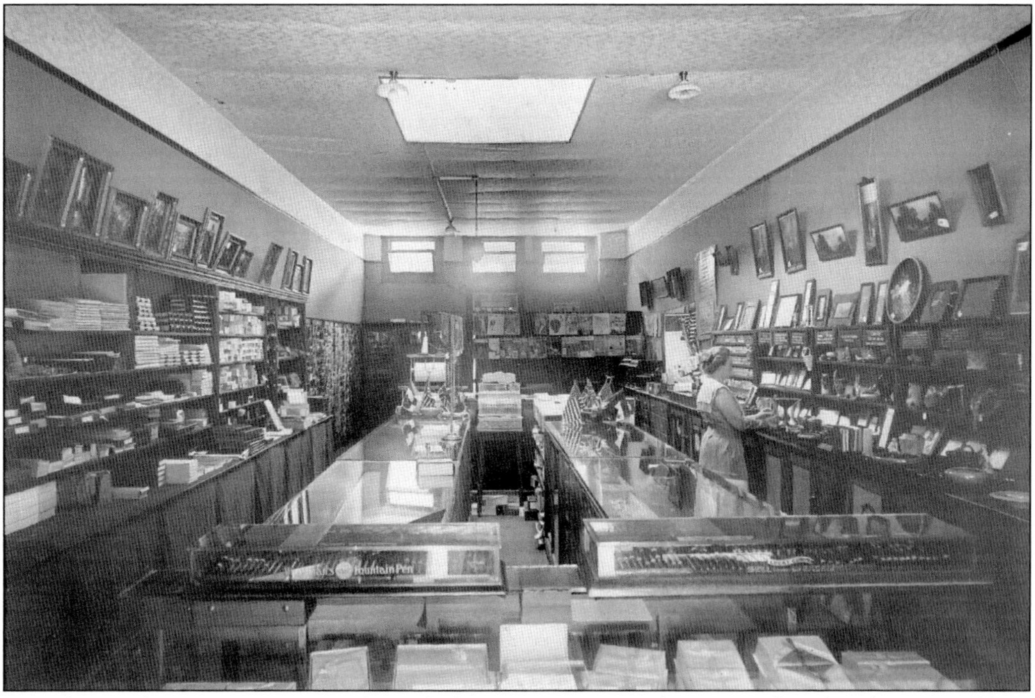

Mac the Medicine Man was not the only businessperson in the McQuillen family. McQuillen's daughters, Teresa and Elizabeth, operated this book and stationery store on Second Avenue.

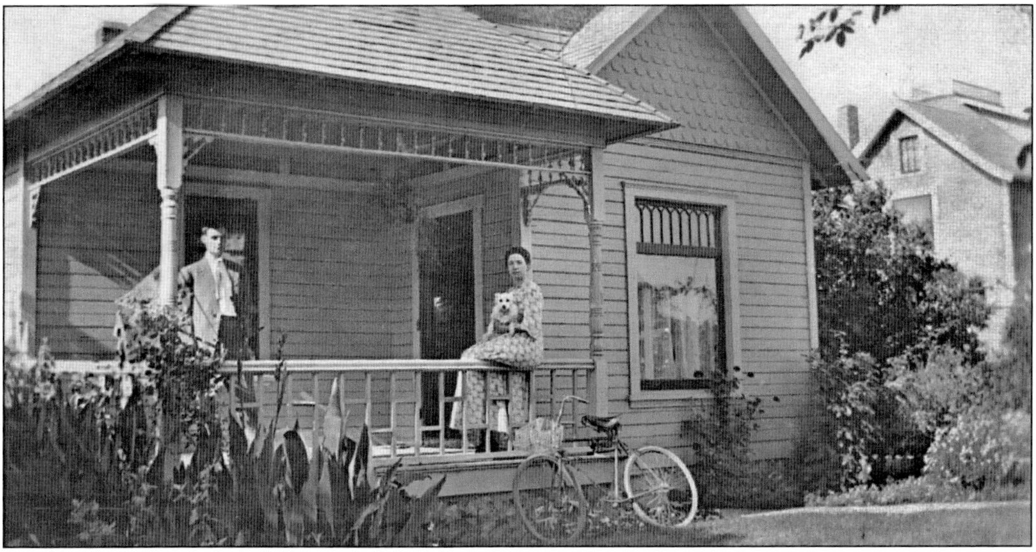

Anyone walking or driving on Ninth Street to the downtown area in the early 1900s might chance to catch Mac the Medicine Man at home with his wife, Jessamine, and their dog, Toodie.

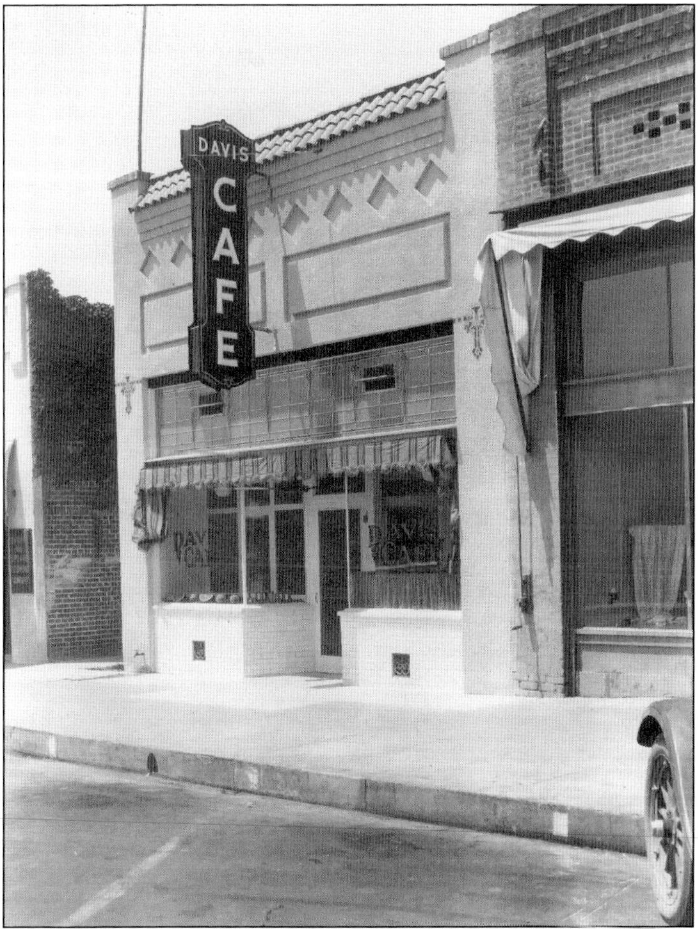


The Davis Café was a popular place to eat downtown. This photograph was taken of the establishment in the 1920s. (UPL.)

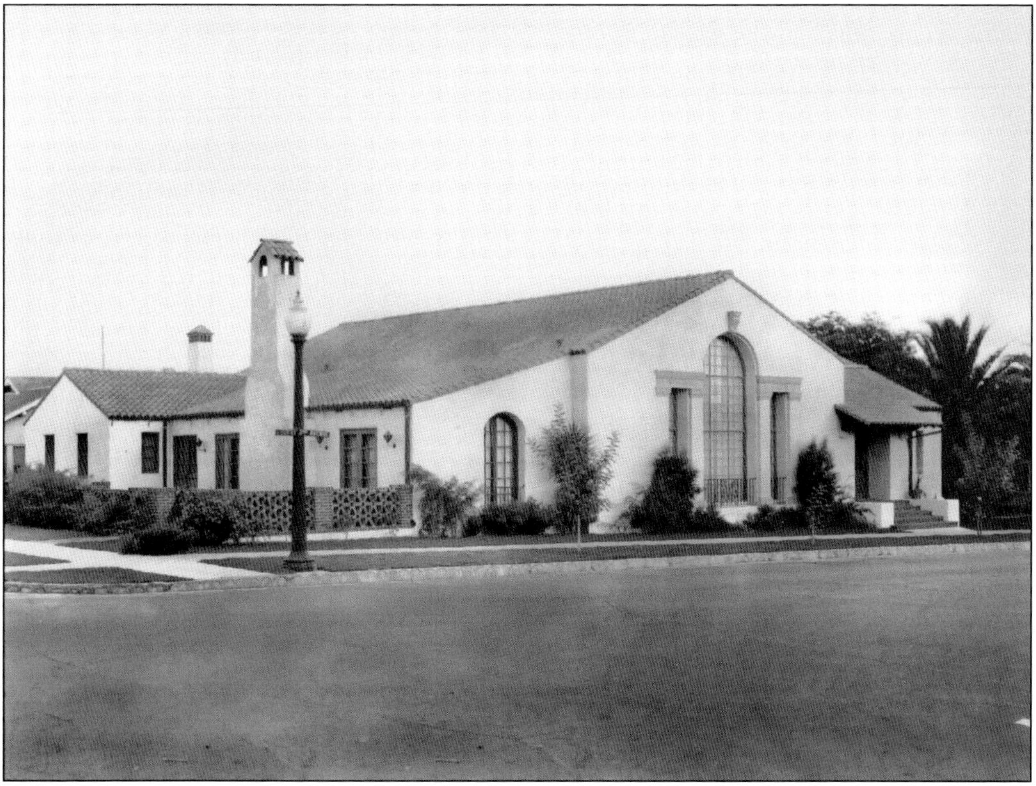

The Upland Woman's Club Building was erected in 1926. It has been the center of numerous civic events not only for the community's women, but also for countless men and youngsters alike.

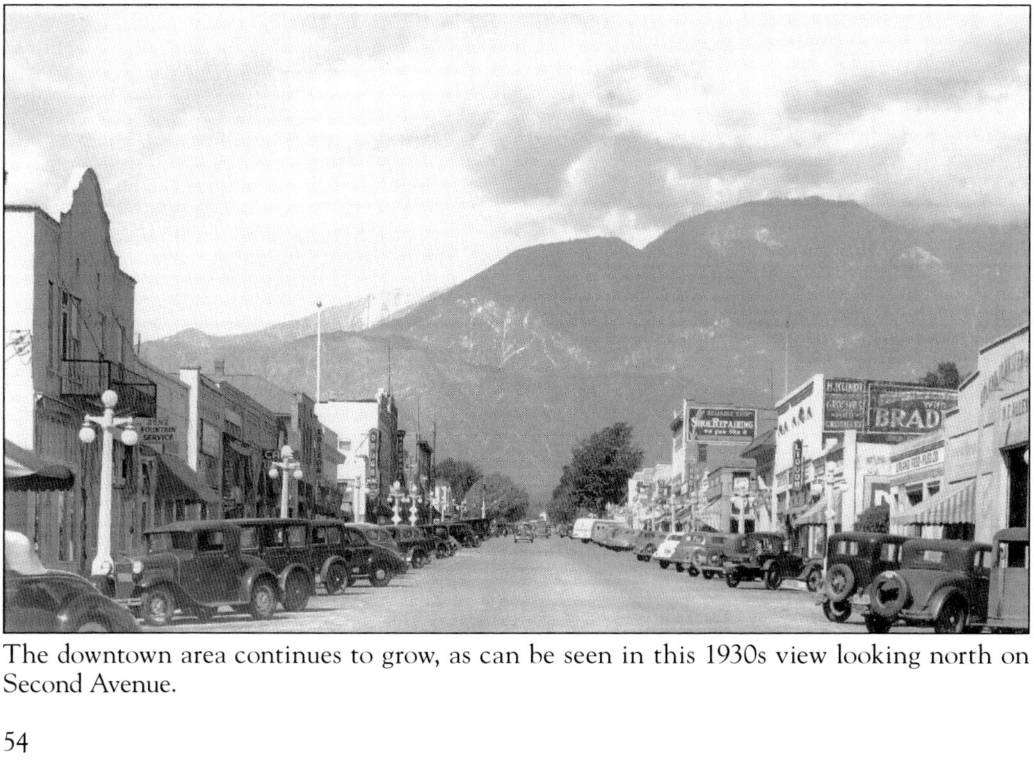


The downtown area continues to grow, as can be seen in this 1930s view looking north on Second Avenue.

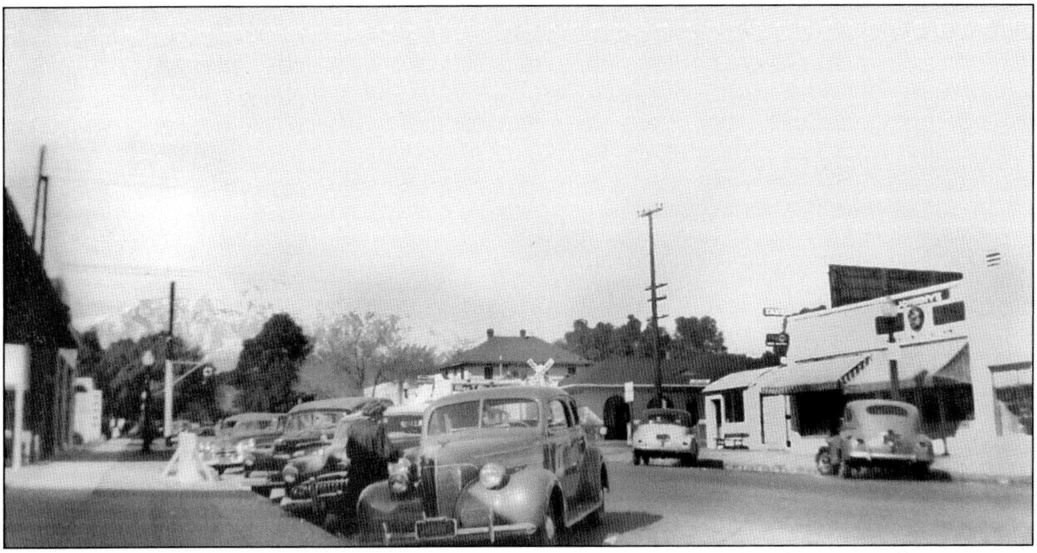

Another view shows downtown Upland about 1930. Note the Pacific Electric Railway Station just beyond the last automobile on the right side of the street.

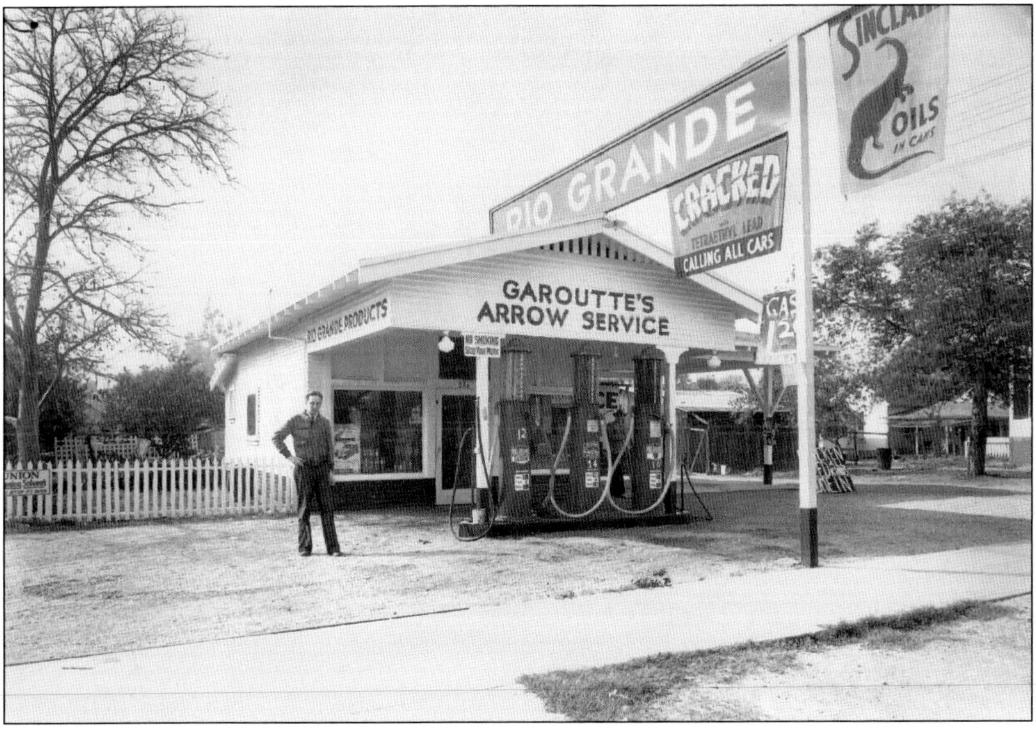


John Herman Moore was ready and able to give full service to customers at Garoutte's Arrow Service on the corner of Third Avenue and Arrow Highway in 1932.

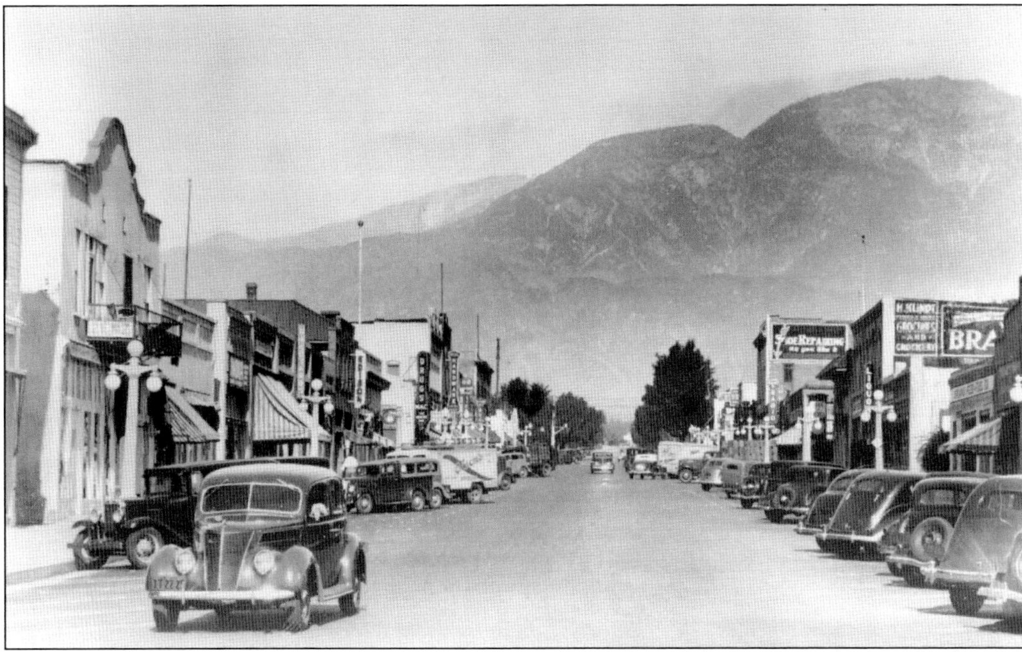

Not much had changed in the downtown area from the early 1930s to the time this photograph was taken in 1938.

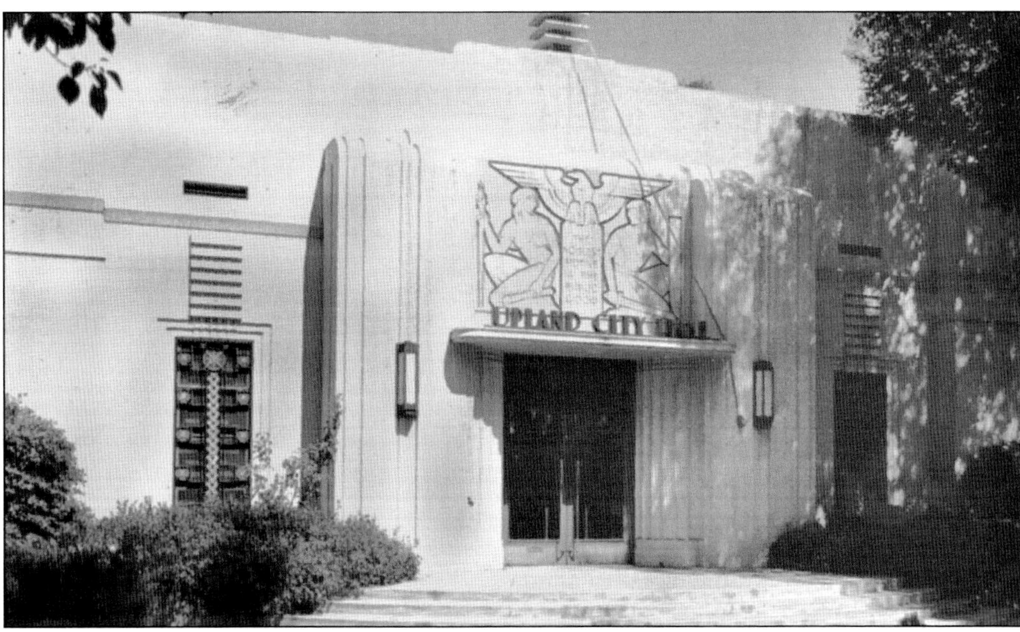


Erected and dedicated in 1939, the Upland City Hall is one of the most beautiful buildings to grace the landscape of the downtown area. (OCL.)

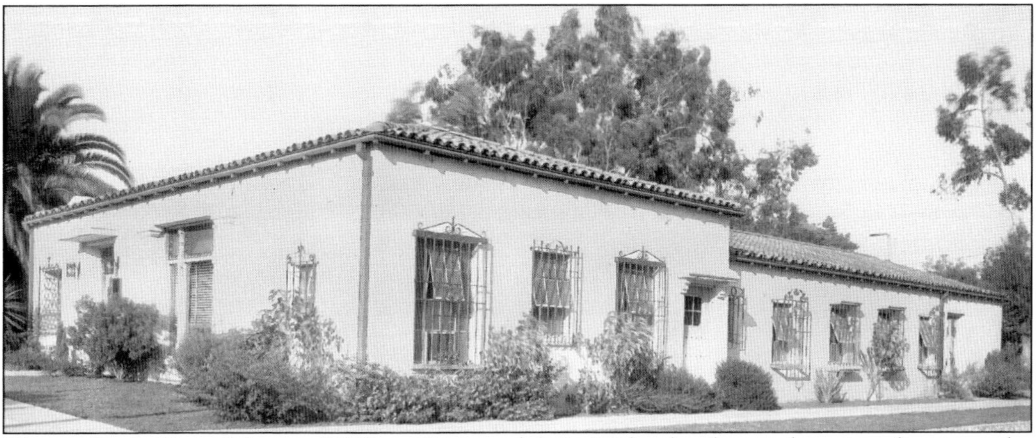

The medical office of doctors William Craig and A. L. Weber has been a longtime fixture at the northeast corner of Second Avenue and D Street in the downtown area. Dr. Craig began his practice in another building in 1896, followed later by Dr. Weber.

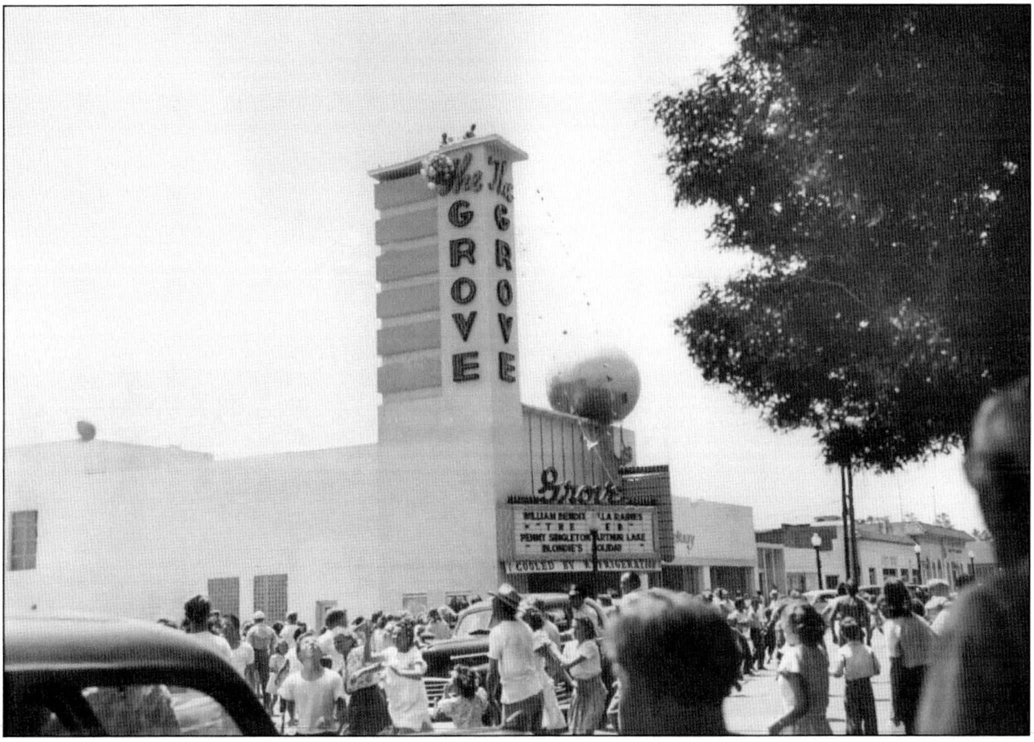


In 1947, a contest was held to name a new theater being built at the southwest corner of Third Avenue and Ninth Street. Mrs. Steve D. Allee was the winning entrant with her suggestion of the Grove Theatre.

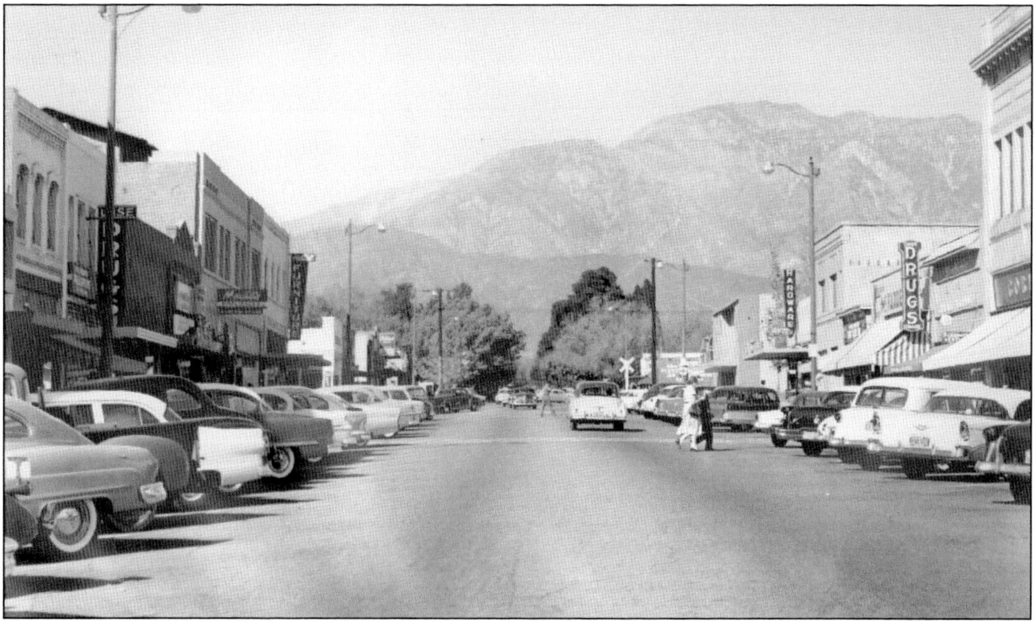


By the 1950s, automobiles were numerous in the downtown area, which caused city officials and downtown merchants to begin thinking about new ways to handle the traffic. In later years, parking would be established in the center of Second Avenue, and parking lots would be opened in the rear of the stores.

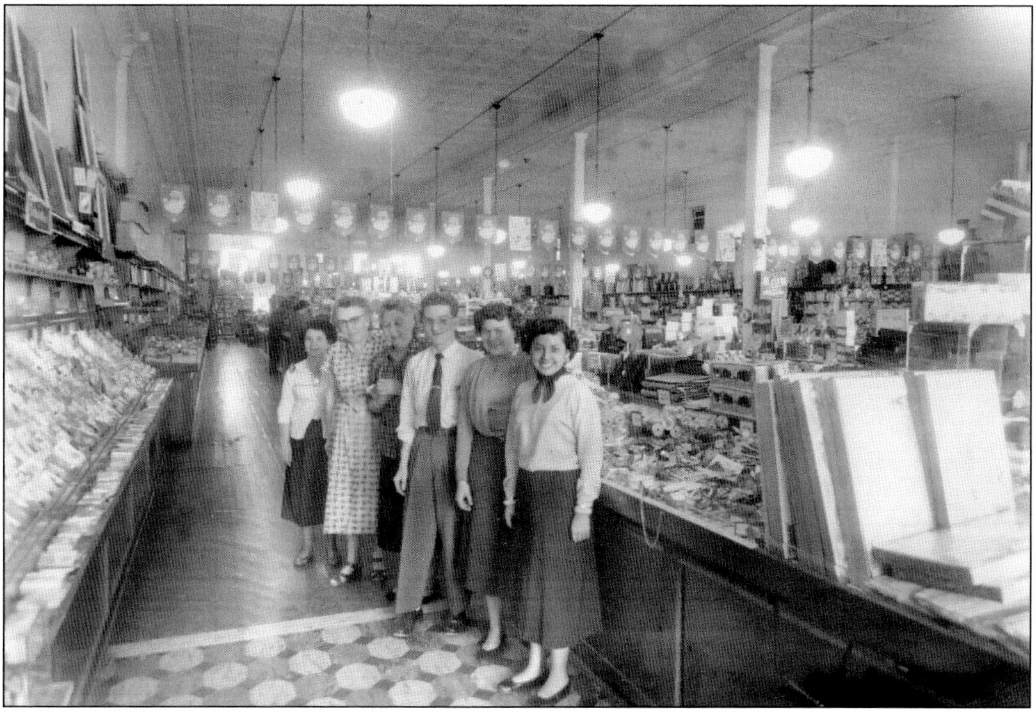

Some of the staff pose in this 1951 photograph at the Cornet Store on Second Avenue. The "five and ten" was a favorite shopping place for young and old alike.

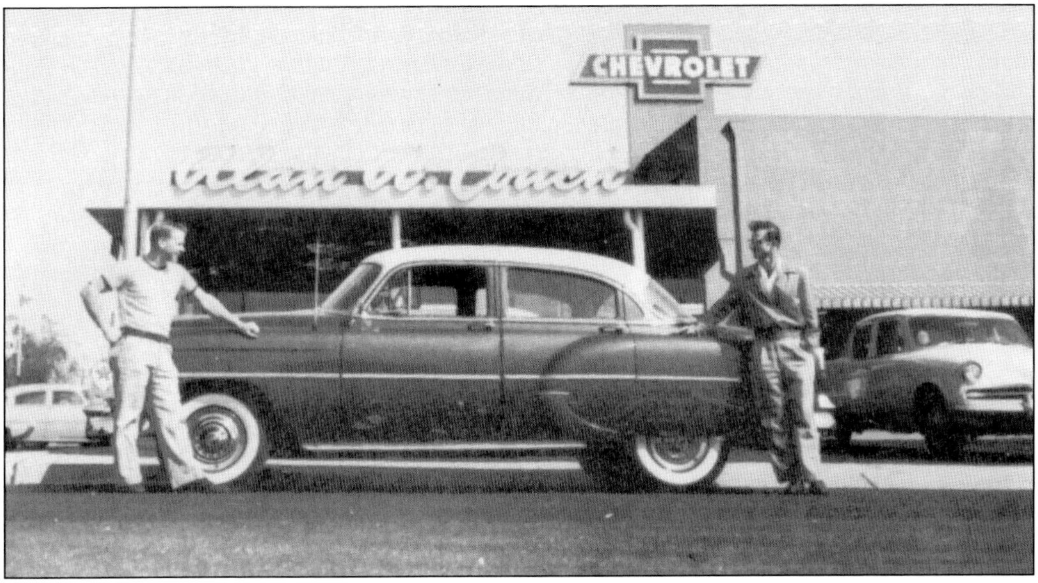

Alan B. Couch Chevrolet on Foothill Boulevard was the place for a young man to go if he had dreams of owning a brand new 1954 Chevy. (RDX.)

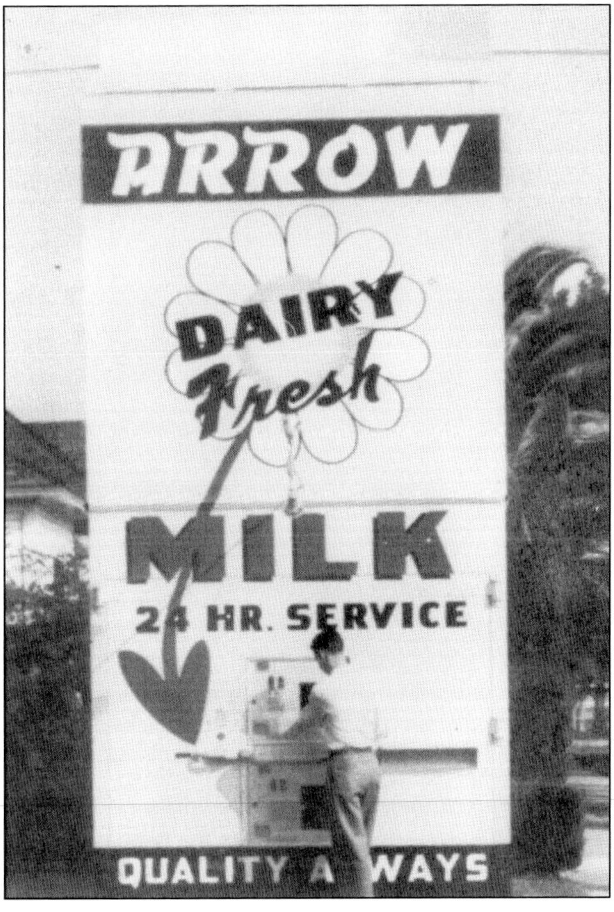

It was always fun to get fresh delicious milk from the Arrow Creamery milk dispenser at the corner of First Avenue and Arrow Highway in the 1950s. (RDX.)

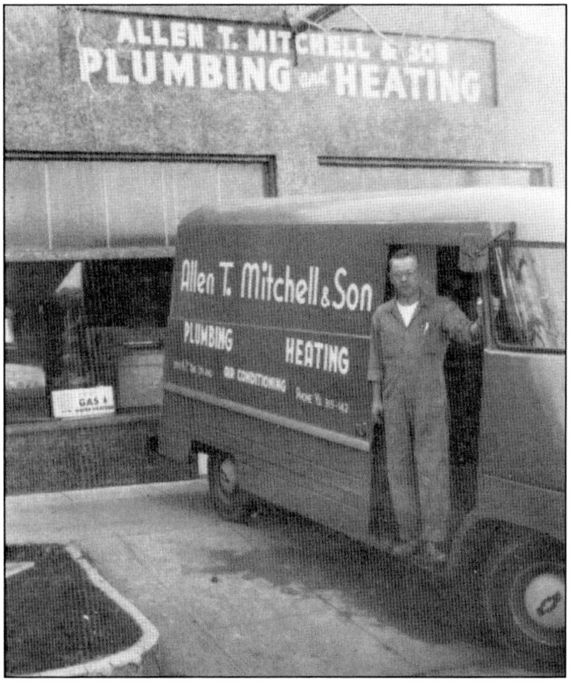


This 1957 photograph shows Allen T. Mitchell and Son, a plumbing and heating business that has been in the downtown area for many years. (RDX.)

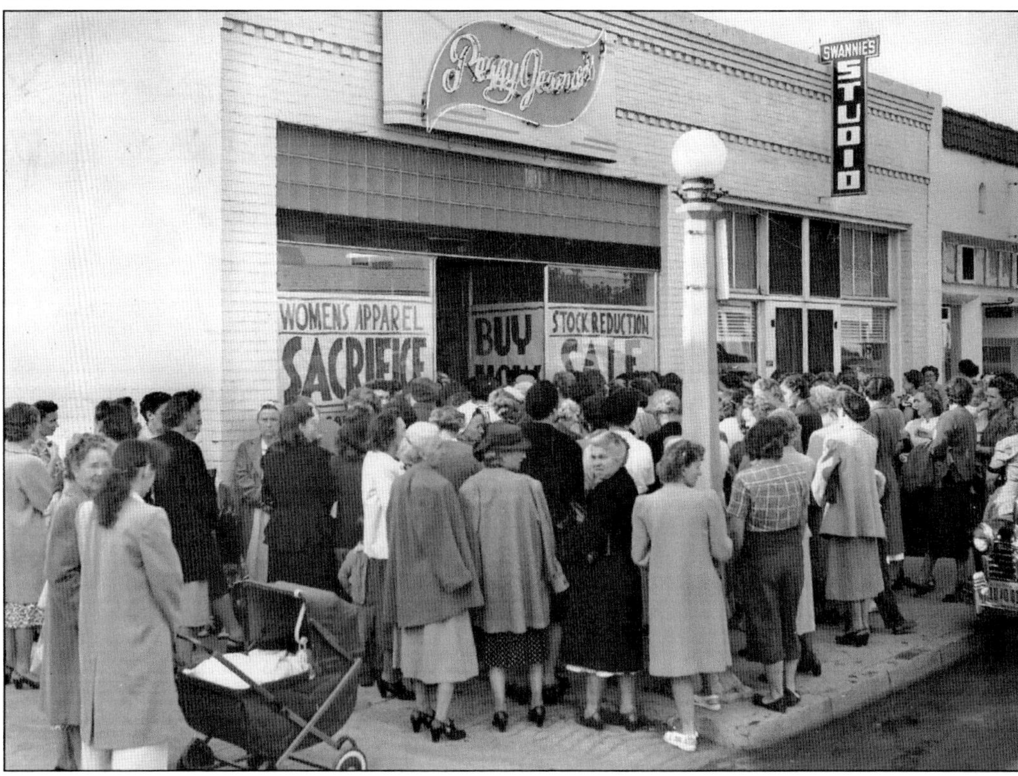


Anxious ladies wait in front of Peggy Jeanne's Dress Shop on West Ninth Street for the doors to open to the 1950 stock reduction sale. Edna Swan's photography studio and the Upland Chamber of Commerce office can also be seen in the photograph.

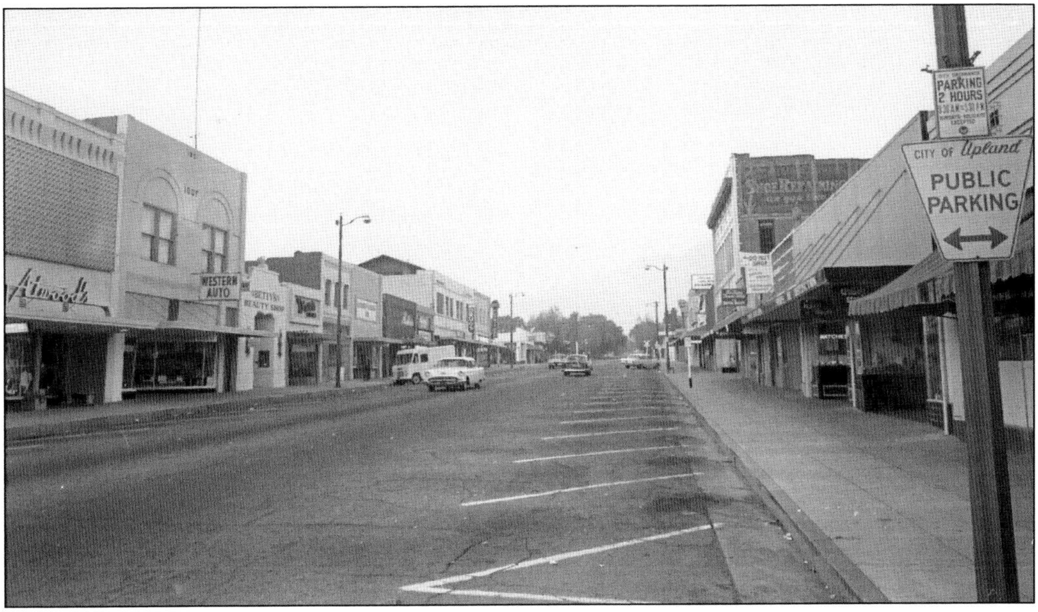


Pictured is Second Avenue in downtown Upland in the 1970s. The Western Auto store on the left is the old International Order of Odd Fellows building.

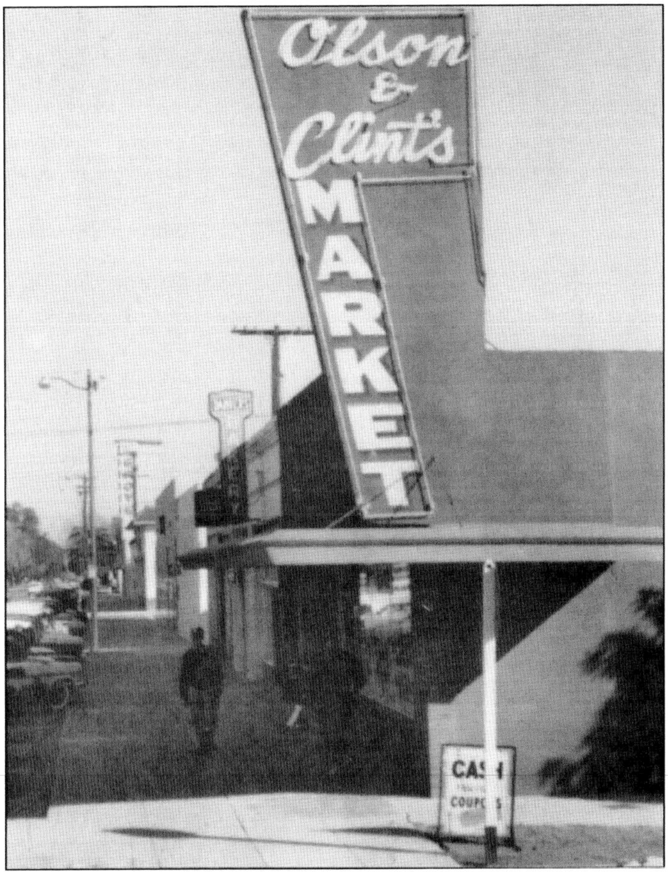


Olson and Clint's Market on Ninth Street had been in business for more than 25 years when this photograph was taken in 1957. (RDX.)

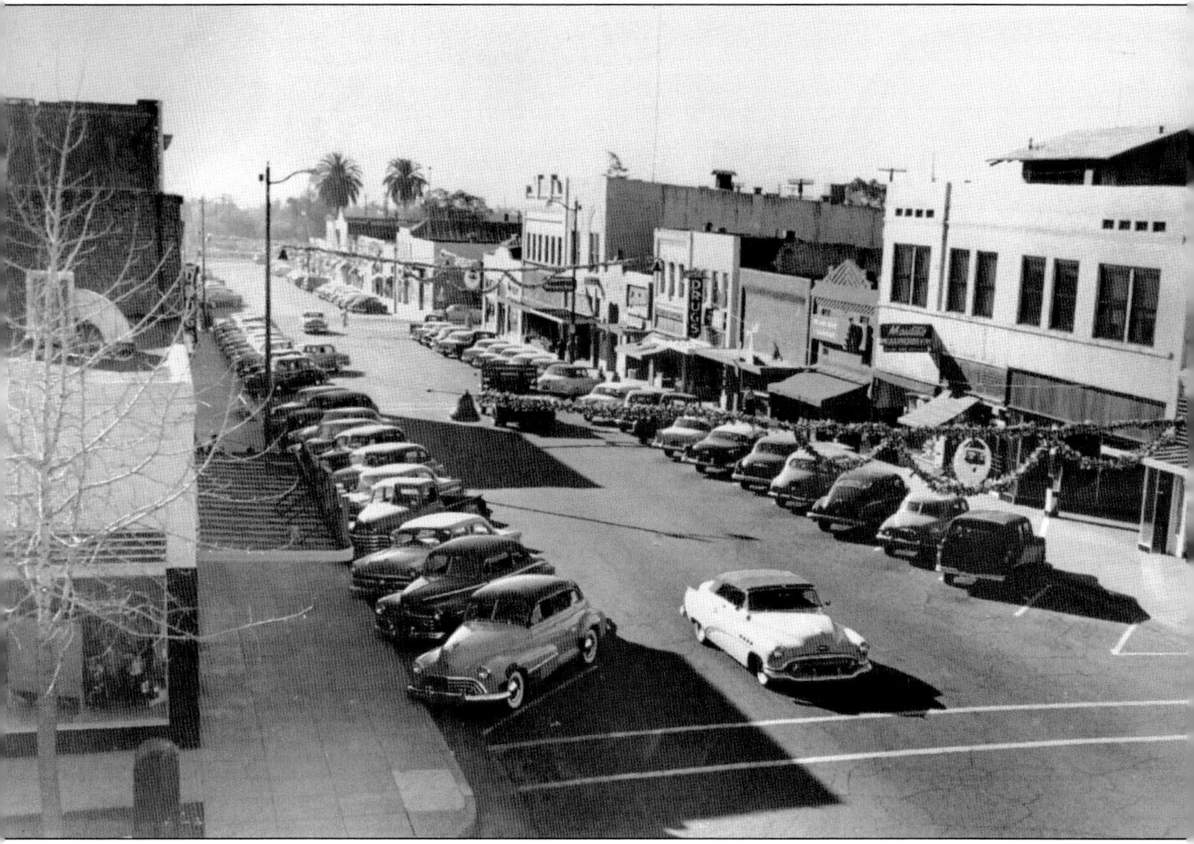

A view of Second Avenue shows a Christmas shopping season in the 1970s. (UPL.)

# *Four*

# TAKING CARE OF THE TOWN

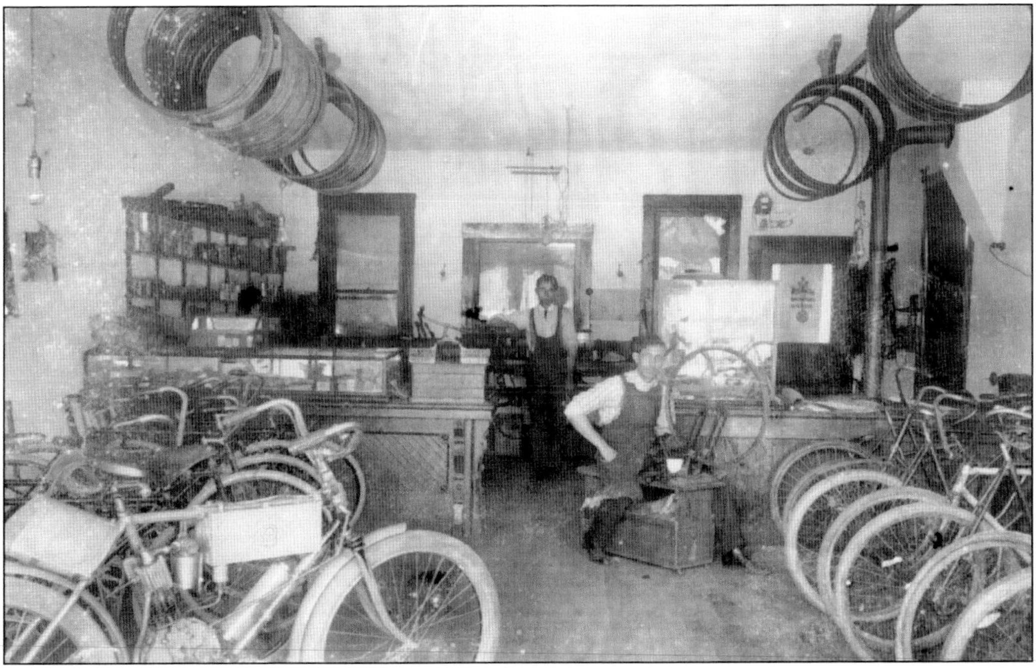

If the distance between home and downtown was too great to walk in the early 1900s, or if someone was looking for a good method of transportation other than a horse, this downtown bicycle shop was the place to go. (UPL.)

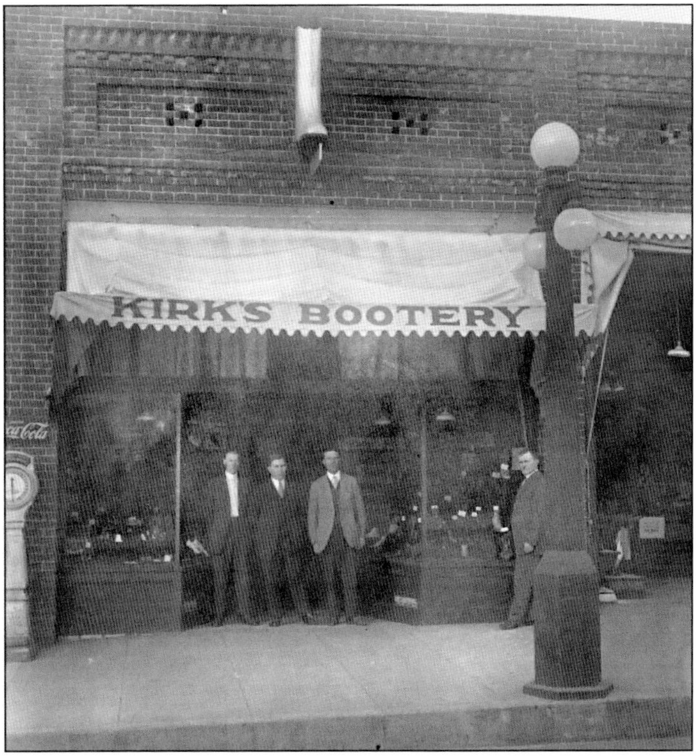


During Upland's early days, Kirk's Bootery on Second Avenue was the place to buy a good pair of shoes or work boots. (UPL.)

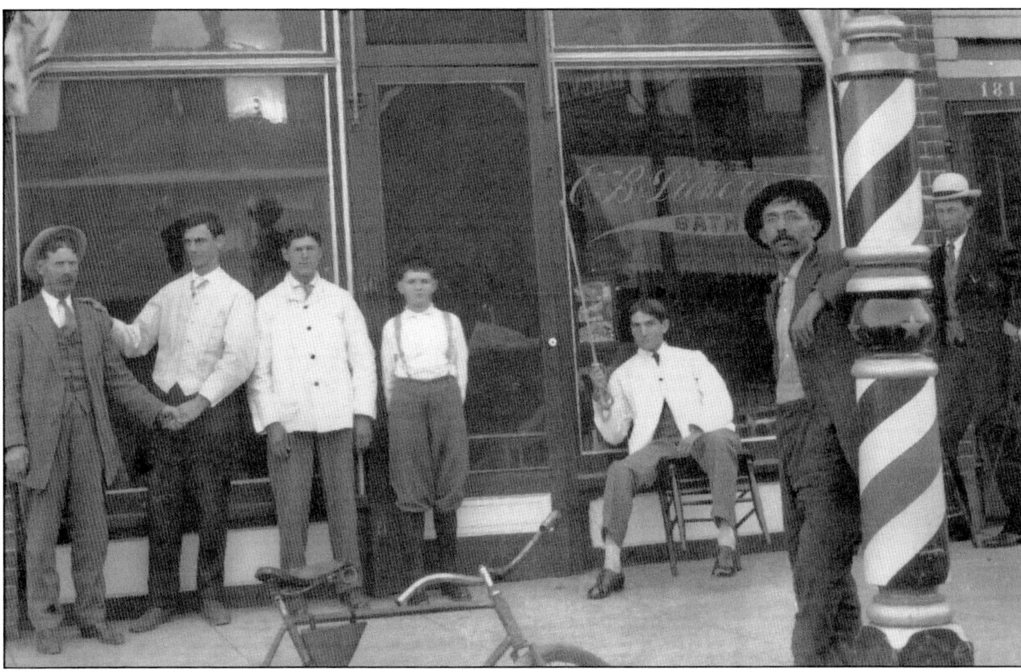


One of the oldest businesses serving Upland is the barbershop now known as Smothers Barbers on Second Avenue. The establishment has been operated by various owners, including Perry Long, who cut Gen. George Patton's hair when he came into the shop during a march of his troops to the Mojave Desert during World War II. This photograph was taken in June 1900. (RHS.)

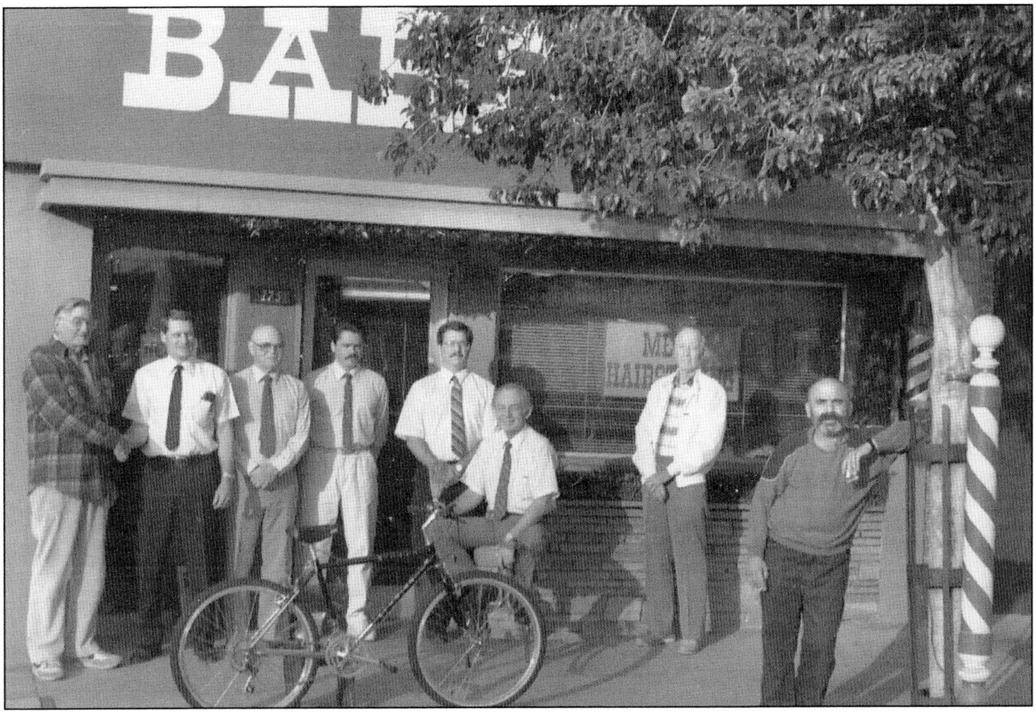

Several years later, in January 1990, the crew of Smothers Barbers reenacts the photograph from 1900. Ed Smothers, owner of the shop at the time, is standing second from the left. Ben Meza, fourth from the left, is still a barber at the establishment, and Rick Hess, fifth from the left, is the current owner. Rick continues to retain the name Smothers Barbers. (RHS.)

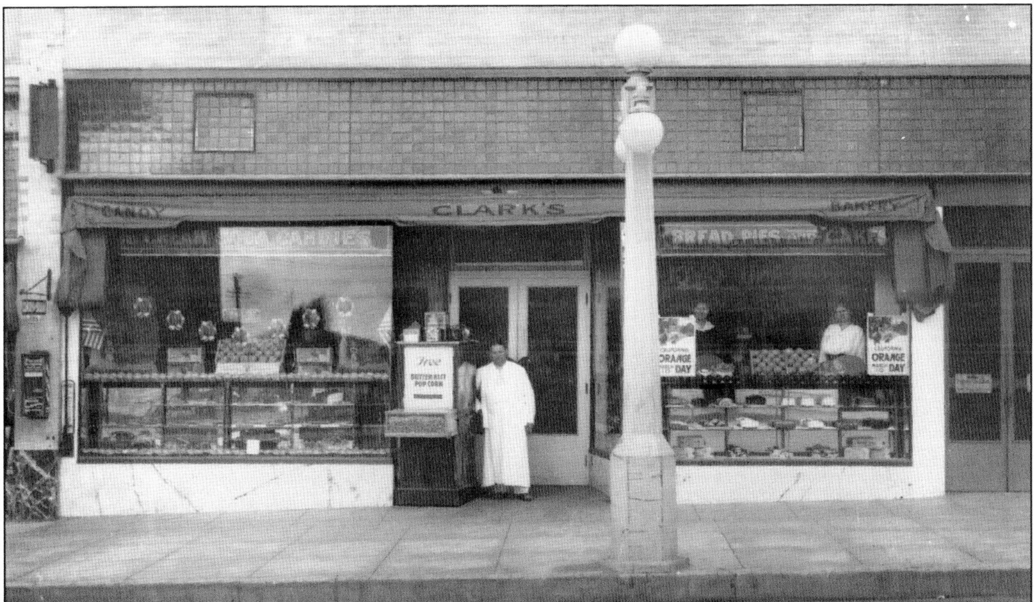


This 1920s photograph is of Clark's Bakery on Second Avenue. The shop was a favorite place to satisfy a sweet tooth with pastries and candy.

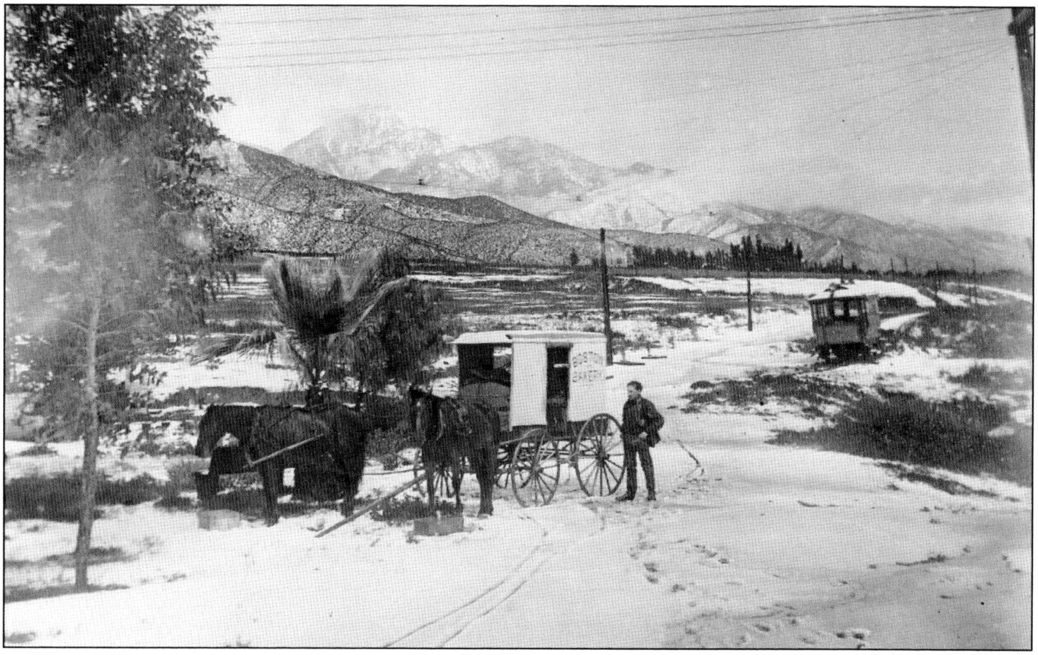

Everyone has heard that the mail goes through even when it is snowing. From the looks of this 1915 photograph, the Boston Bakery deliveryman was just as determined to make certain his Upland and San Antonio Heights customers received their baked goods.

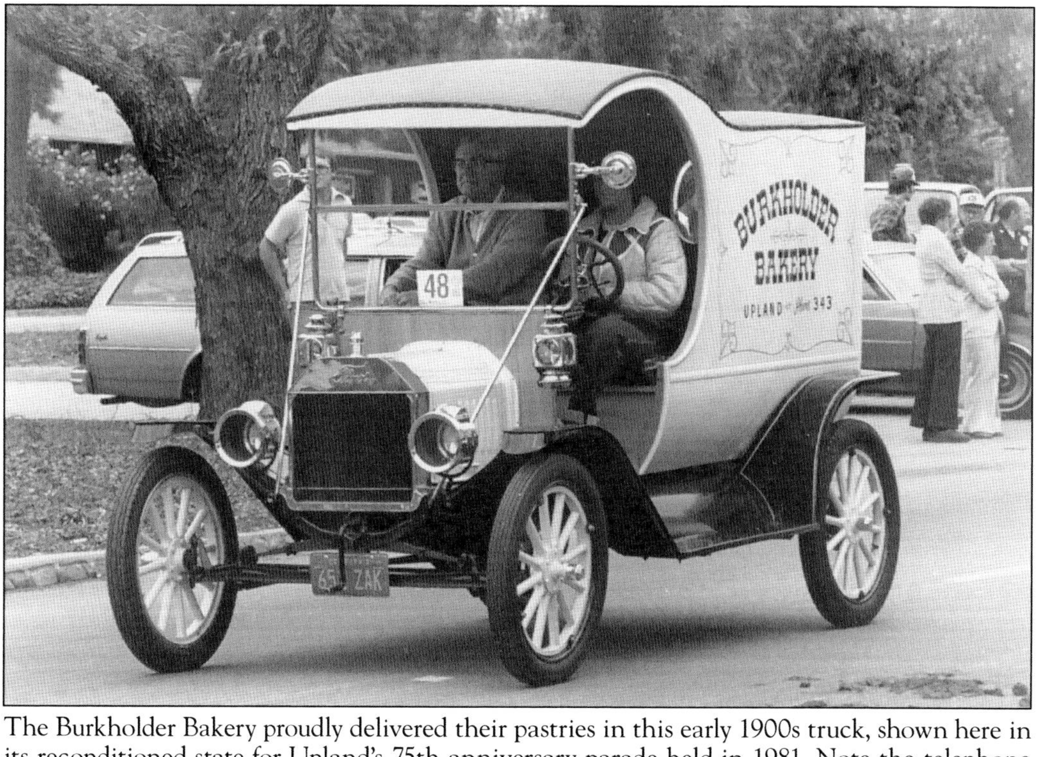


The Burkholder Bakery proudly delivered their pastries in this early 1900s truck, shown here in its reconditioned state for Upland's 75th anniversary parade held in 1981. Note the telephone number of "343" on the side of the vehicle.

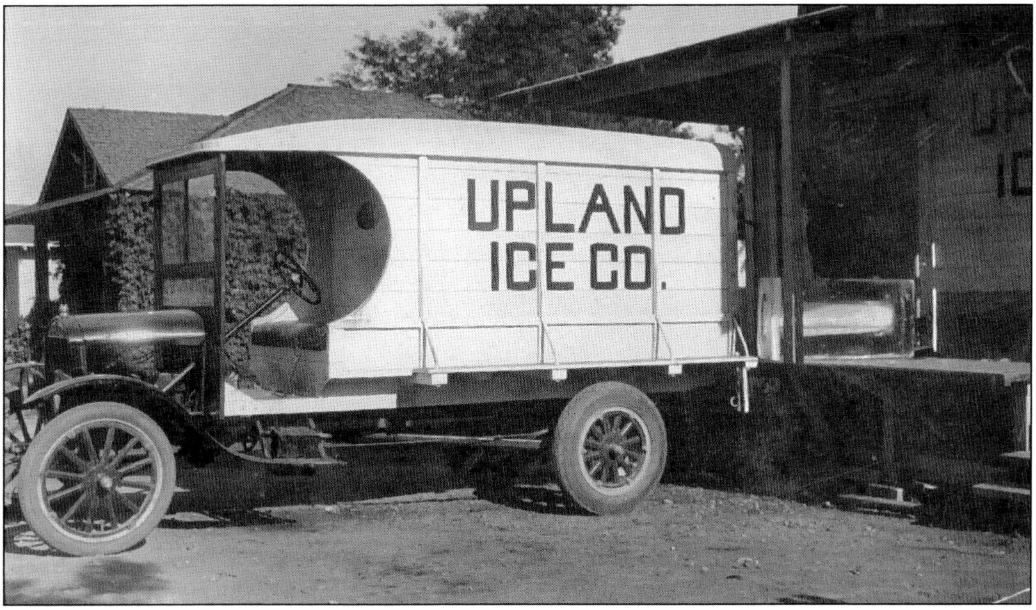


During the days before electric refrigeration was common, a necessary service to the community was the delivery of ice. This 1920 photograph shows the Upland Ice Company truck at the plant located at Arrow Highway near Second Avenue.

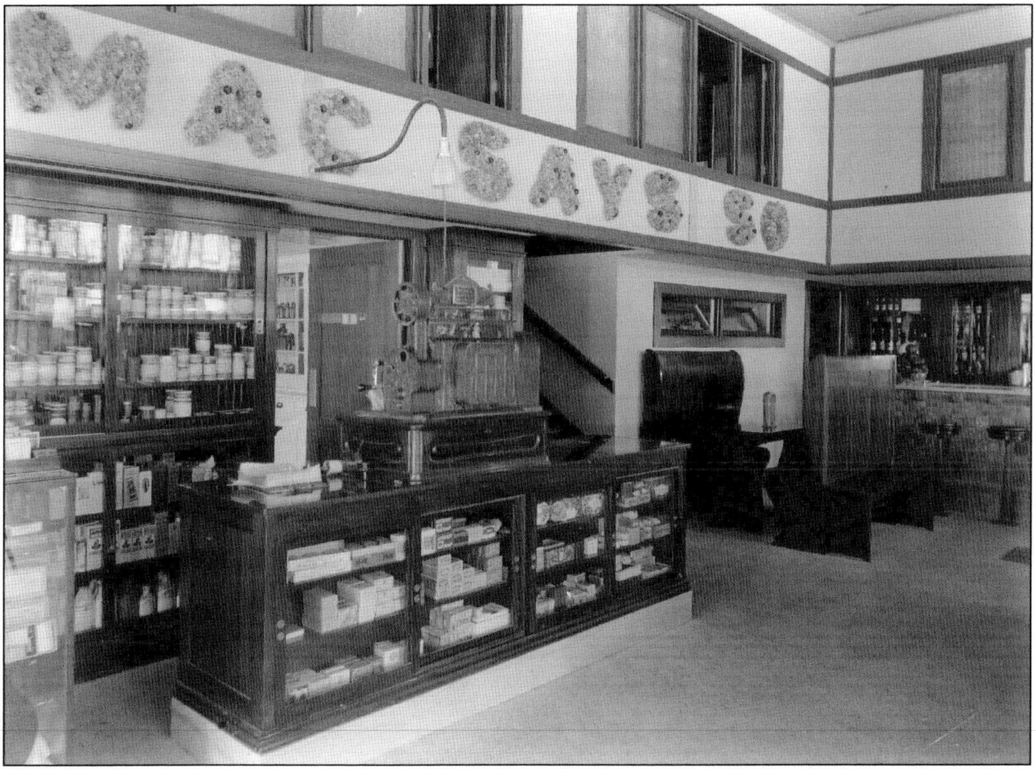


Proof of the fact that Mac was, indeed, a pharmacist was his stock of medicines at the department store. Apparently, the customer was to heed Mac's advice, as the sign states, "Mac Says So."

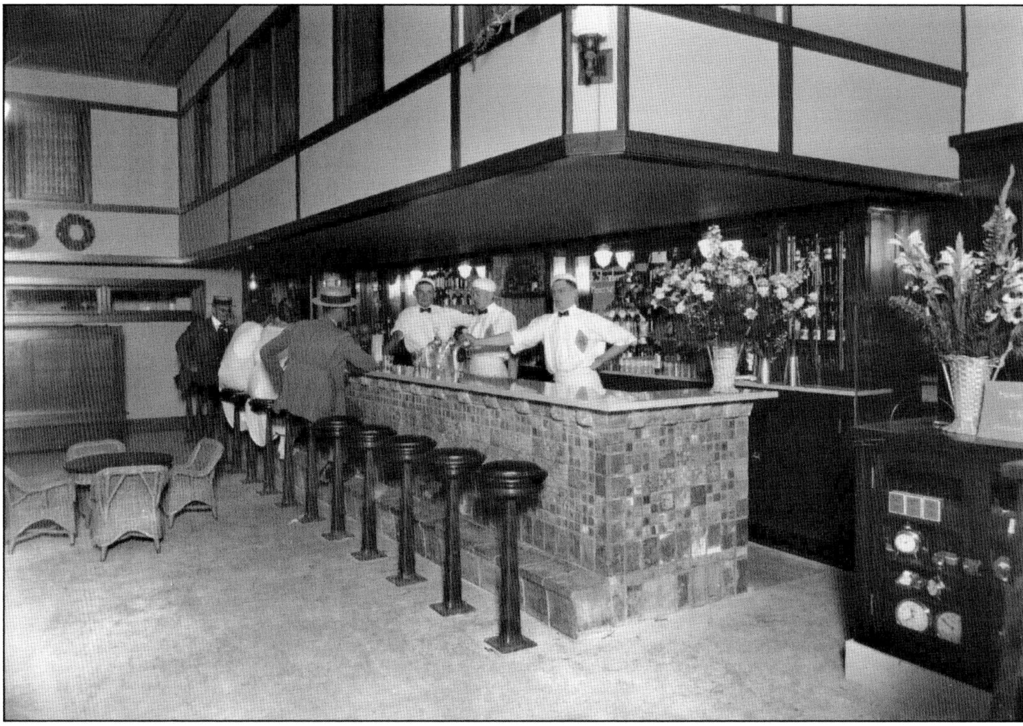

Sweet treats were also served up at the soda fountain inside Mac the Medicine Man's store.

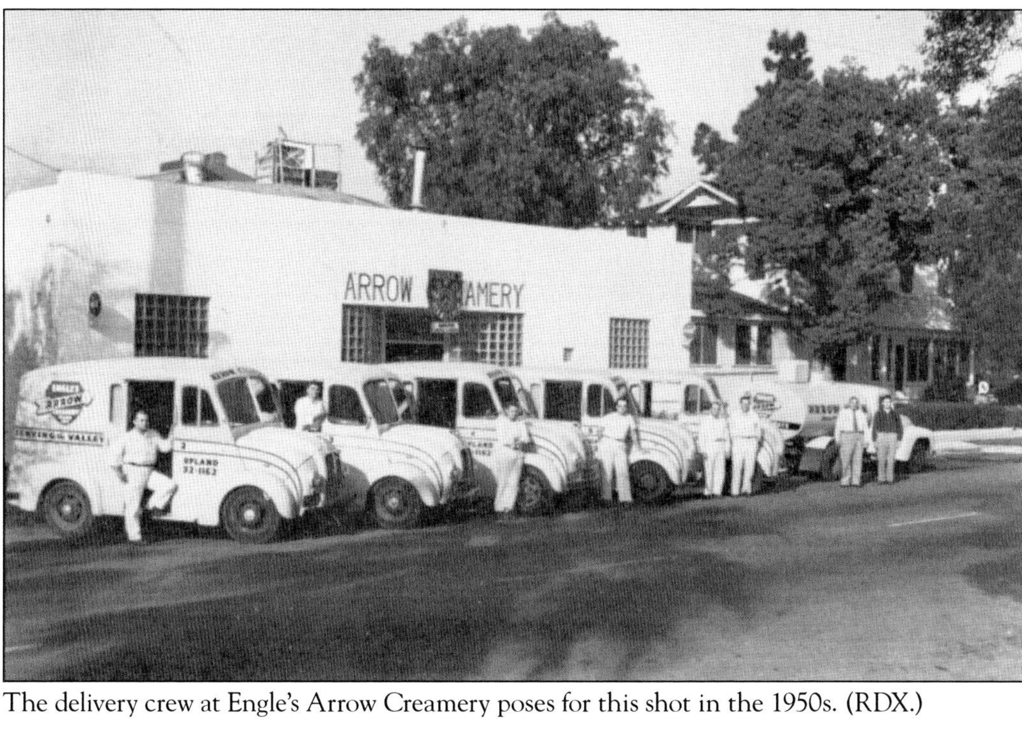


The delivery crew at Engle's Arrow Creamery poses for this shot in the 1950s. (RDX.)

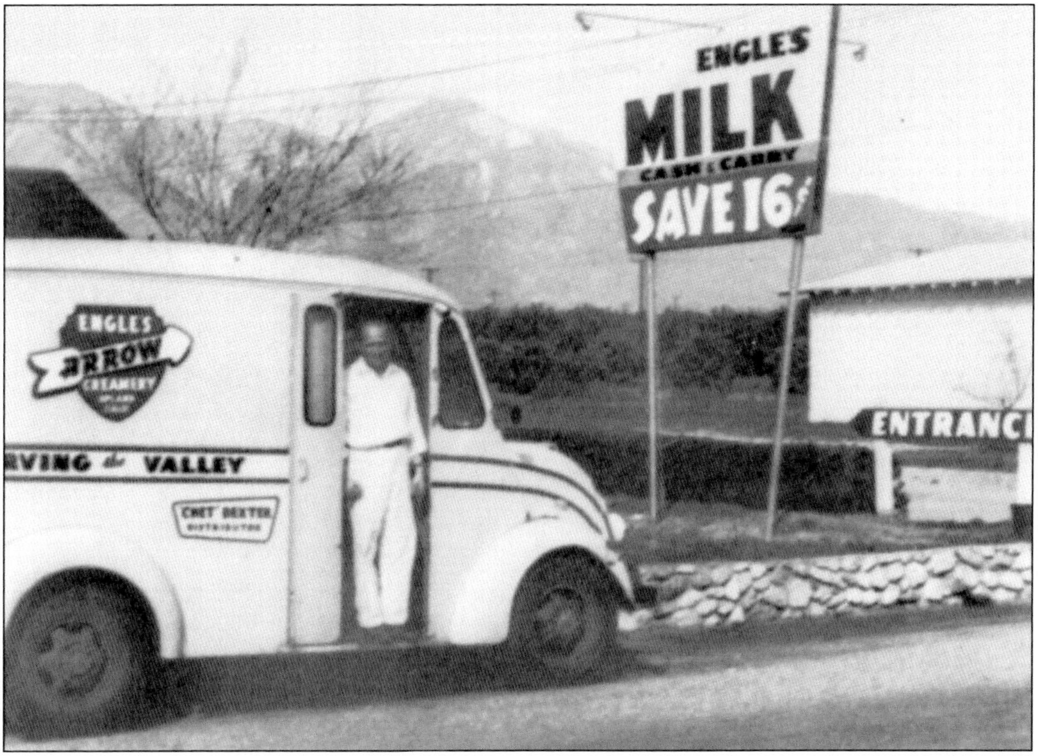


Distributor Chet Dexter stands at the door of his Engle's Arrow Creamery delivery truck in 1957. (RDX.)

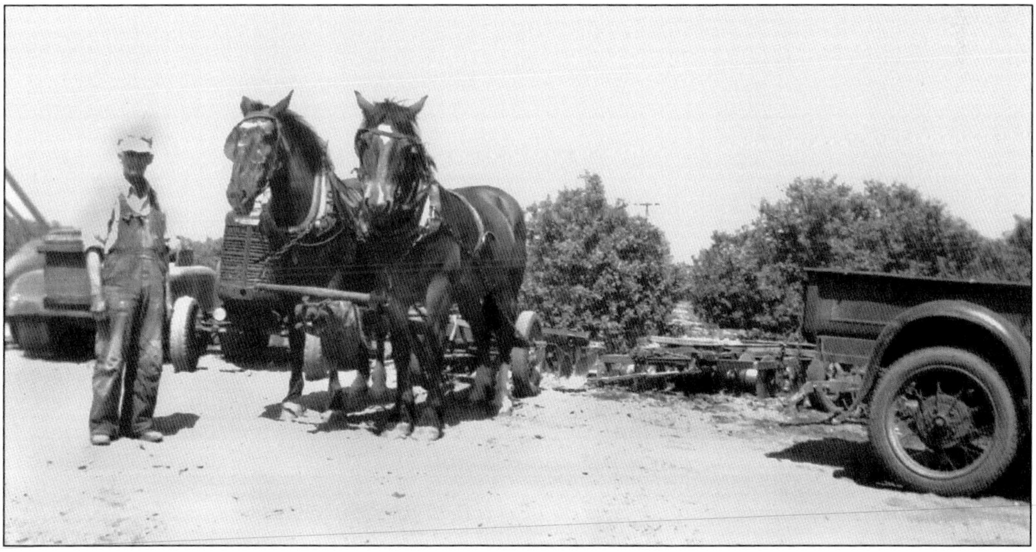

This worker, along with his team, was part of the vast number of people who served the community by helping take care of Upland's numerous citrus groves. (UPL.)

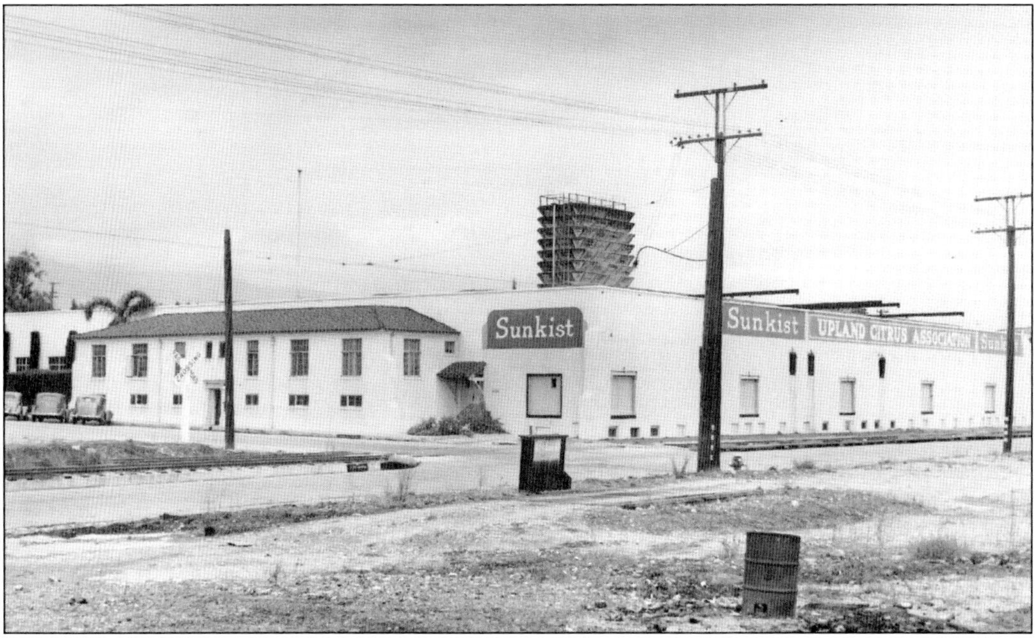


By the 1940s, the Upland Citrus Association had erected a new packinghouse at the northeast corner of Third Avenue and A Street to replace the old wooden structure that had served part of the need for fresh delicious fruit within the local community and the United States.

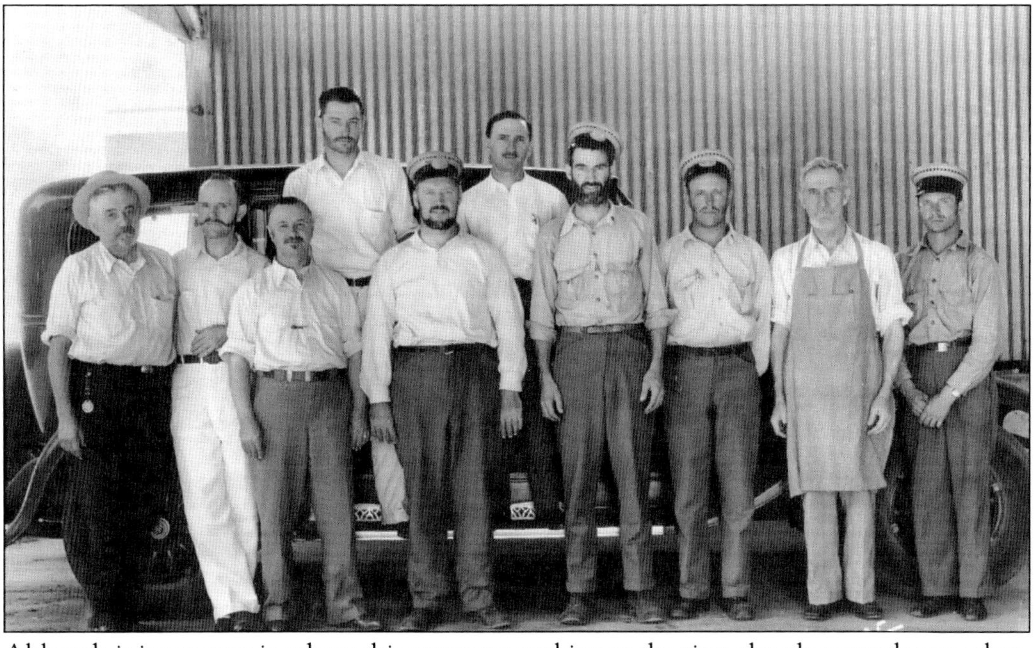

Although it is not certain where this crew was working at the time the photograph was taken, these men do appear to be ready and able to handle whatever task they needed to perform to help the citizens of Upland.

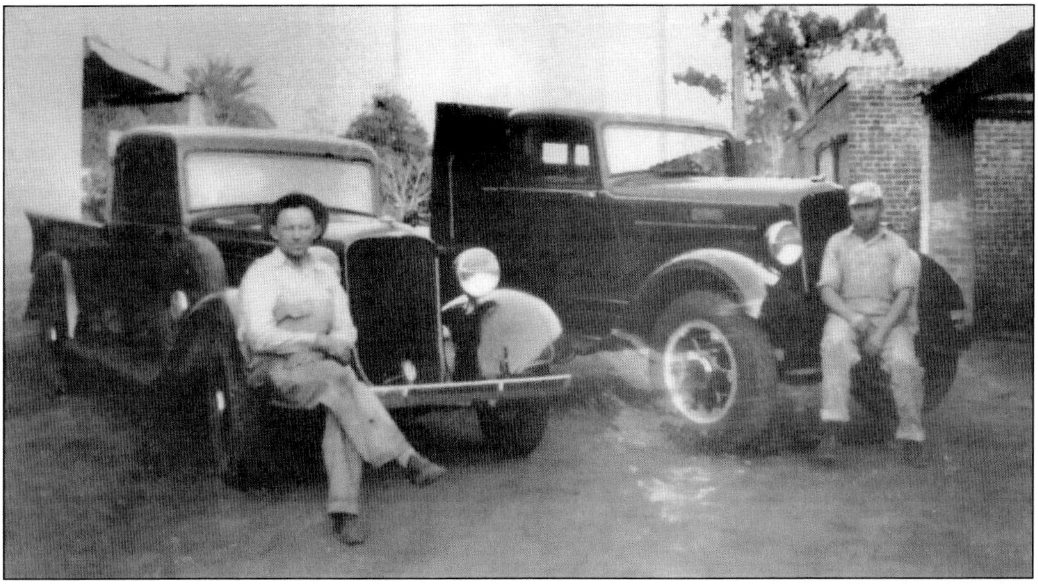

Joe Bert (left) and Oren Decker take a break from serving customers at Upland Feed and Fuel in downtown Upland. (UPL.)

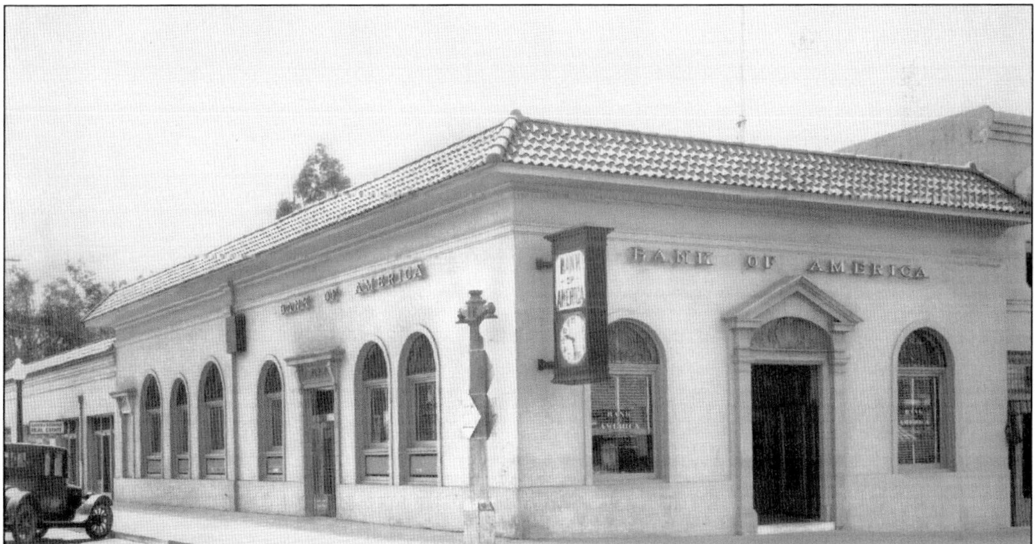


The Bank of America was at the southeast corner of Second Avenue and Ninth Street. This was one of the financial institutions that served the community during the 1930s. The building had previously been occupied by the Commercial National Bank.

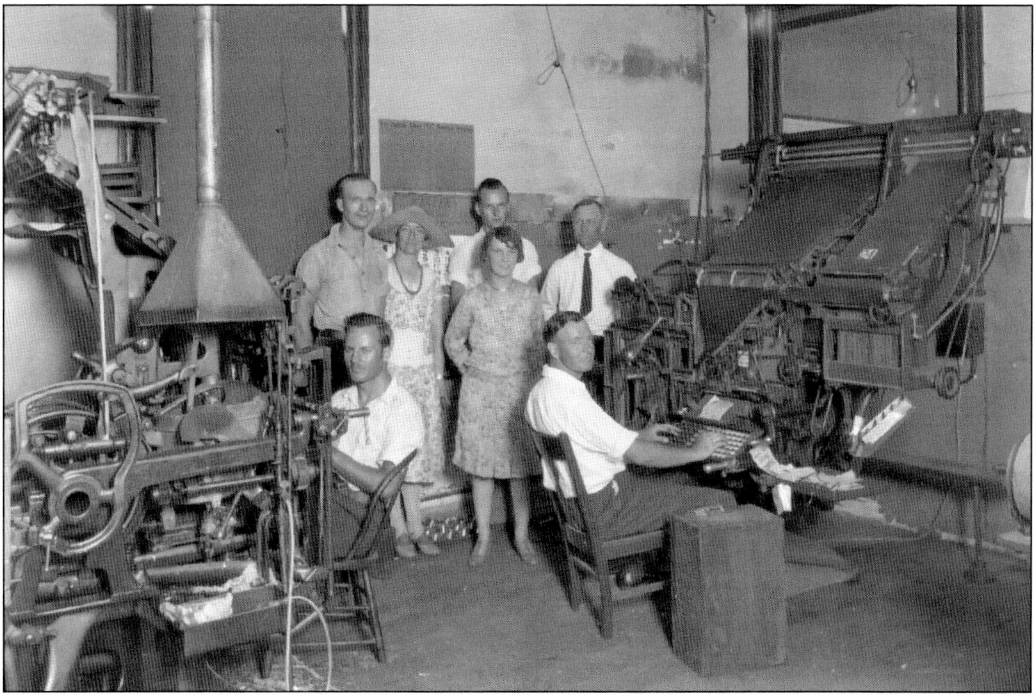

The staff of the *Upland News*, seen here in the 1930s, was always ready to inform the city of what was going on around town. The newspaper had its beginnings in 1897 as the *North Ontario Surprise*. In 1902, four years before the city officially became incorporated and began using the name, the journal became the *Upland News*.

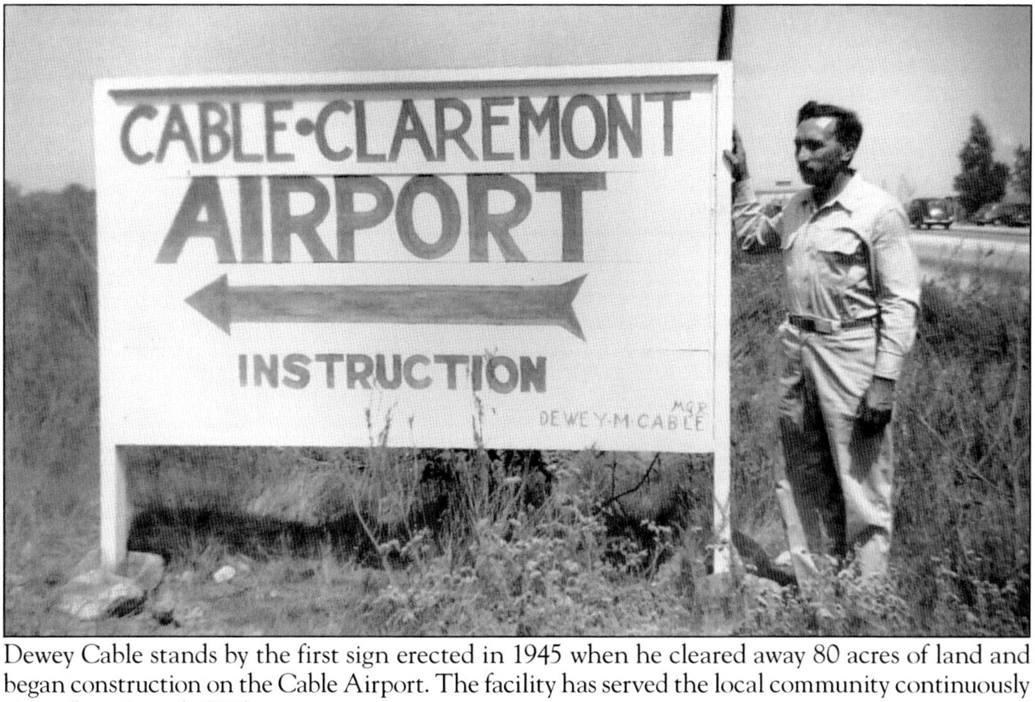


Dewey Cable stands by the first sign erected in 1945 when he cleared away 80 acres of land and began construction on the Cable Airport. The facility has served the local community continuously since that time. (MST.)

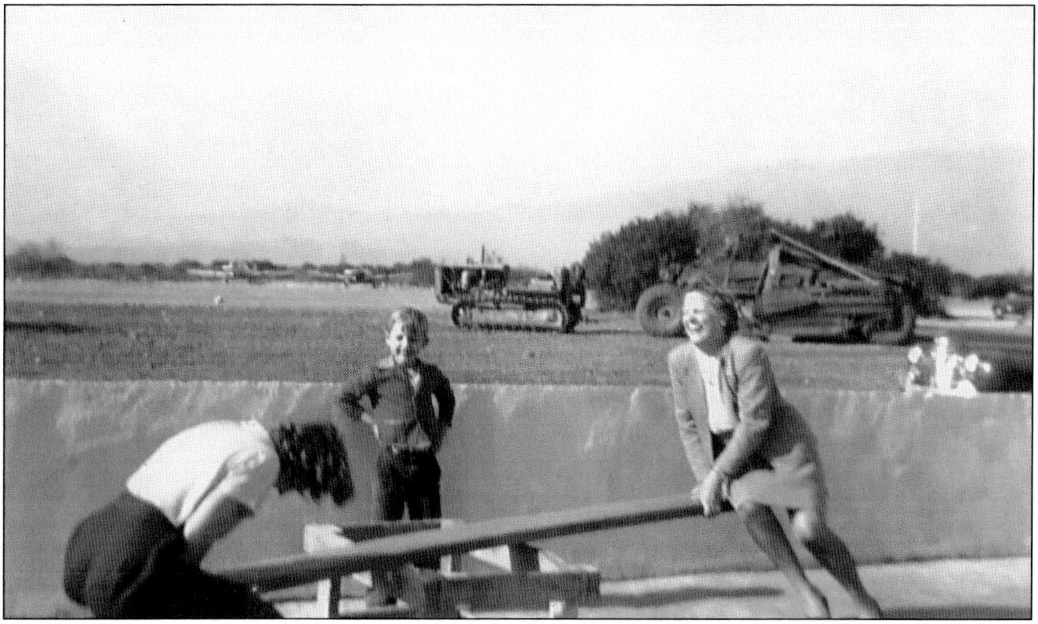

Millie (left) and Maxine Cable are having fun at a party to celebrate the eighth birthday of Millie's brother Roger (center). The makeshift teeter-totter they are sitting on was made from some lumber used in the construction of the airport. The low wall in the photograph is the same foundation wall still standing today in "Maniac-Mike" Stewart's Restaurant at the airport. (MST.)

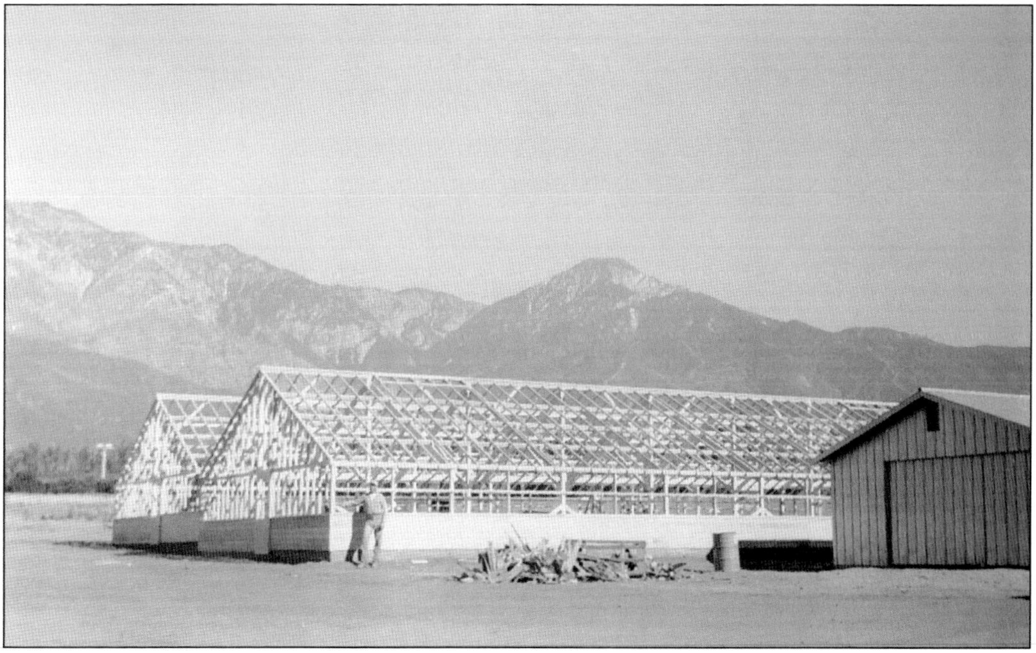

Ray Rietkerk inspects the construction of the original greenhouses for the new business he and his wife, Cora, established on Twenty-first Street in 1958. Bella Vista Orchids first developed and marketed the tropical plants from which the business derived its name. (RKT.)

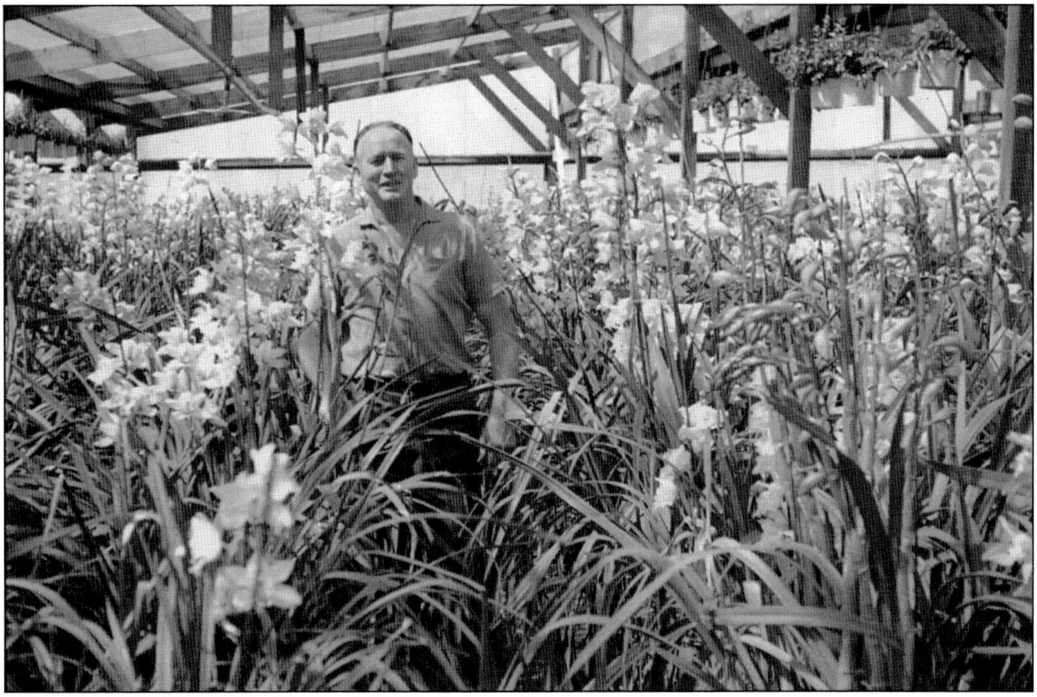

In 1974, with a new demand for indoor plants, the name was changed to Bella Vista Nursery, Inc., and the emphasis of the nursery was changed to green plants and cymbidiums. Here Ray Rietkerk stands among a greenhouse full of cymbidiums. (RKT.)

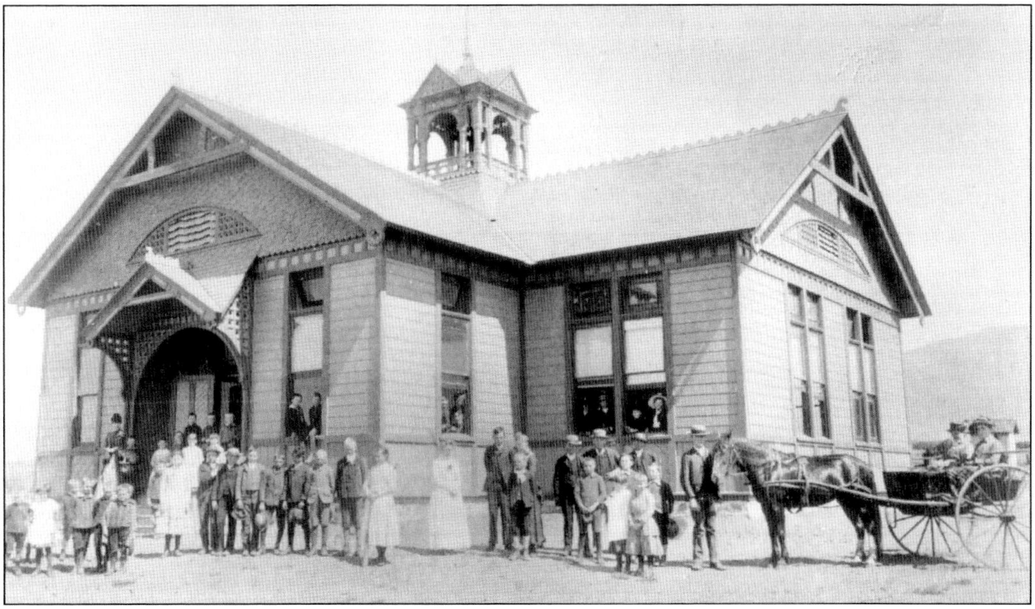

Upland parents and teachers have always made certain they took care of the educational needs of the children of the community. The public school system in Upland began as the San Antonio School District in 1886. This building, shown in the 1890s, once stood on Eighteenth Street where Pioneer Junior High School is now located.

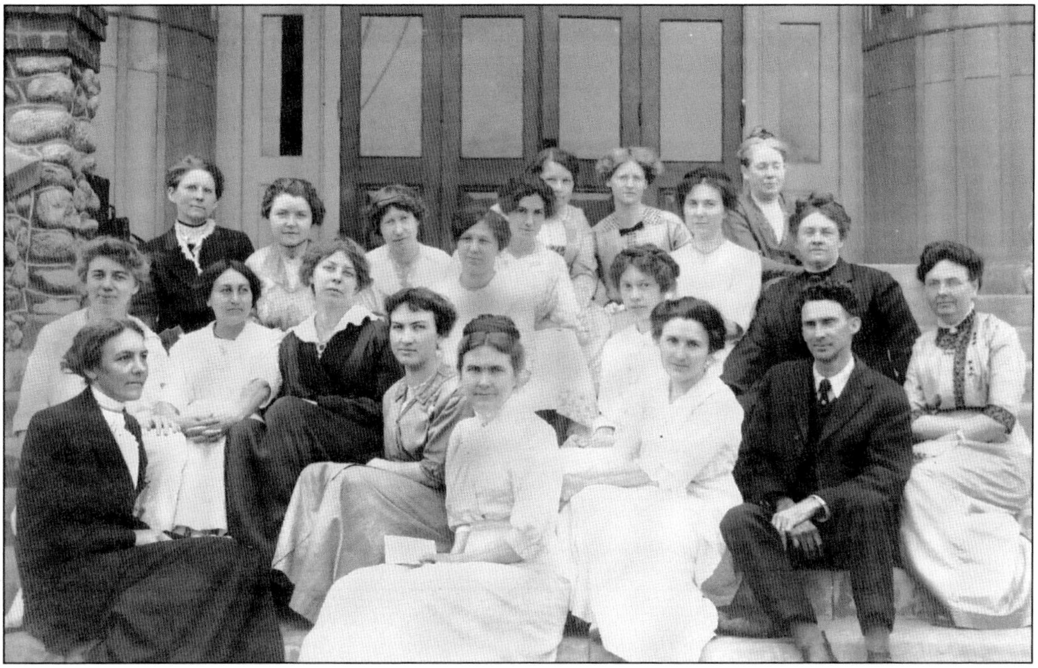

If this photograph of teachers is any indication, male instructors were few and far between during the early years of Upland Grammar School.

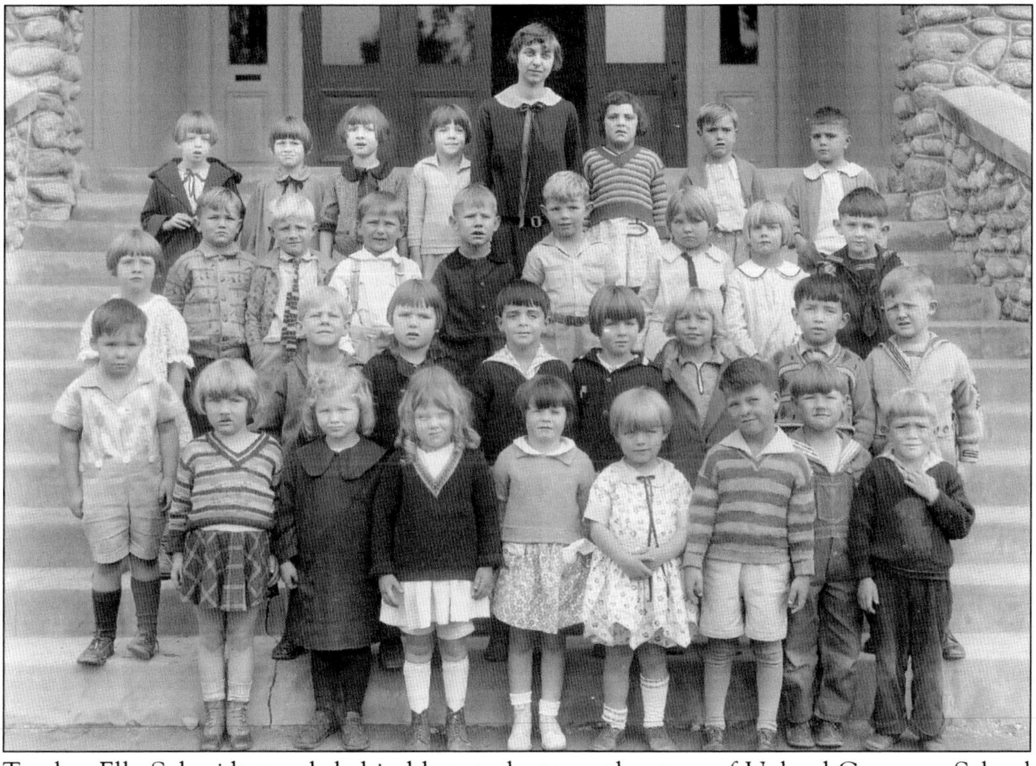

Teacher Ella Schmidt stands behind her students on the steps of Upland Grammar School in 1928.

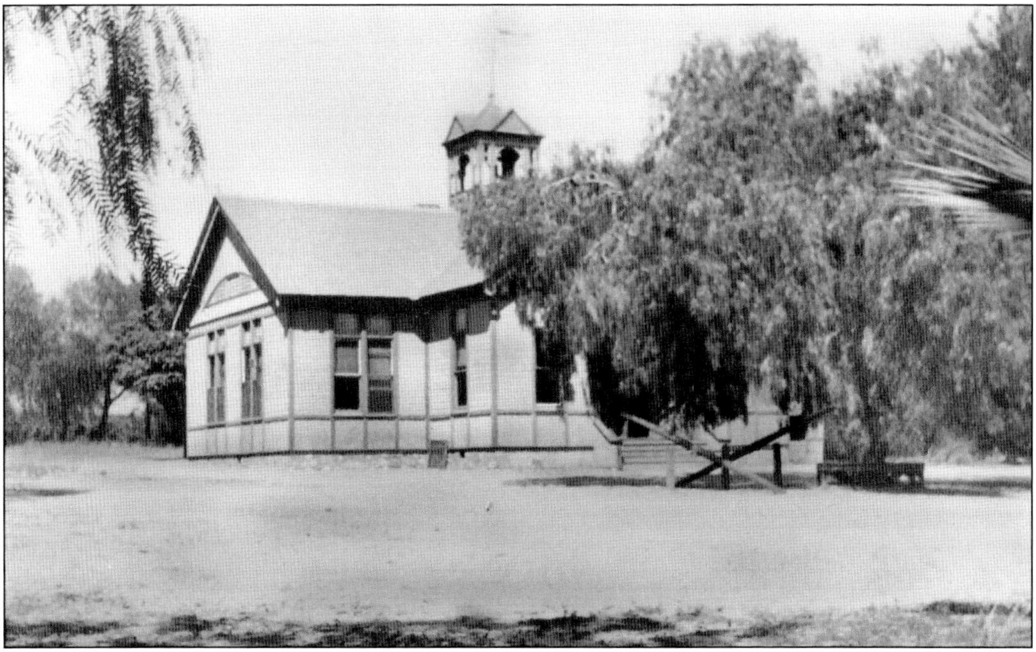

The original school building on Eighteenth Street was moved in 1919 to the corner of Campus Avenue and Thirteenth Street. It was renamed the Sierra Vista School and served the community for several more years.

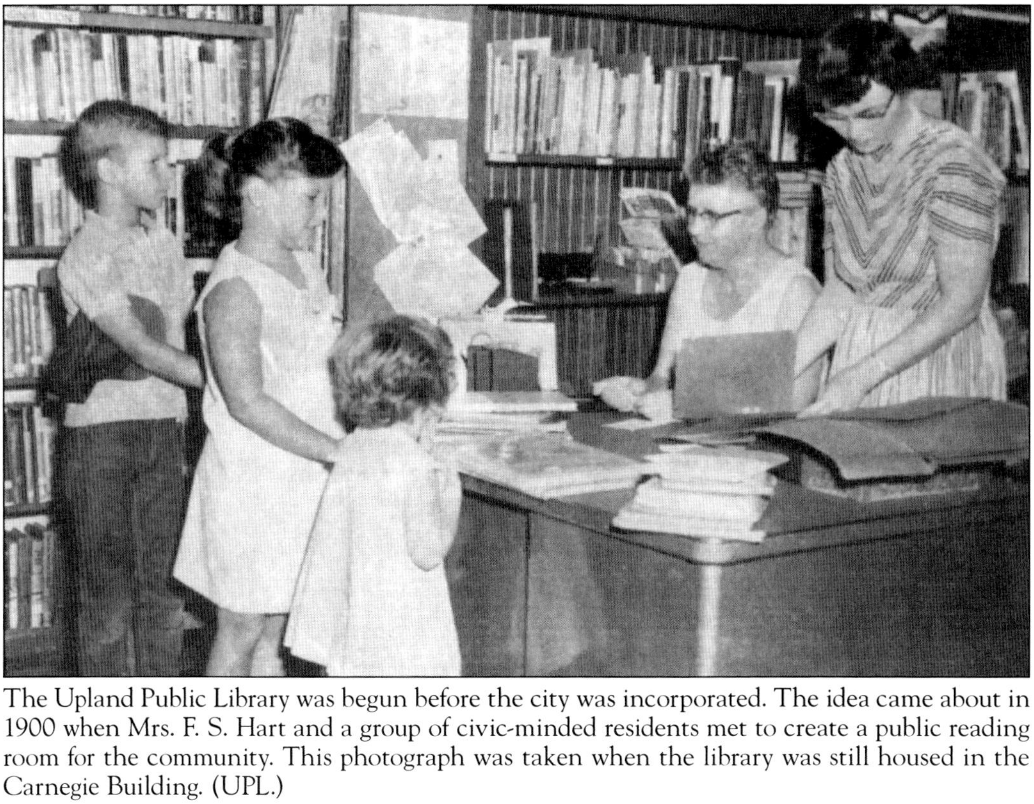

The Upland Public Library was begun before the city was incorporated. The idea came about in 1900 when Mrs. F. S. Hart and a group of civic-minded residents met to create a public reading room for the community. This photograph was taken when the library was still housed in the Carnegie Building. (UPL.)

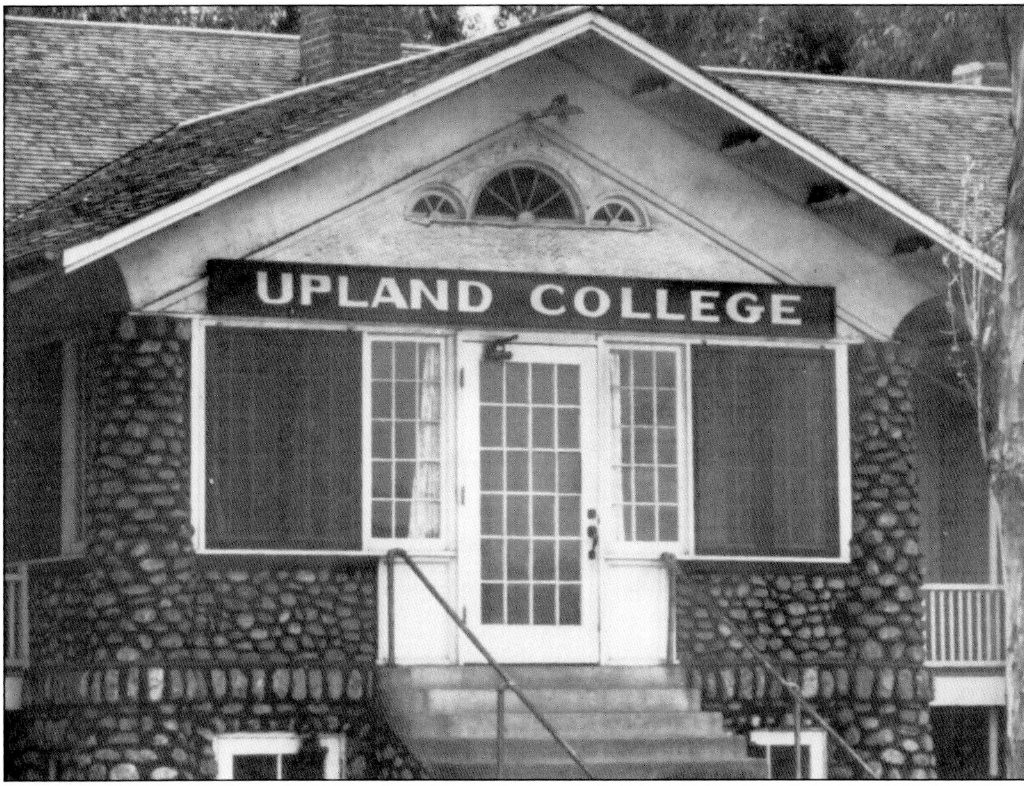


This building served as part of Beulah (later Upland) College beginning in 1935 but had been the original San Antonio Hospital building. It was constructed in 1907 at the southeast corner of San Antonio Avenue and Arrow Highway. It had also served as the Alpine Resort before the college occupied the facility.

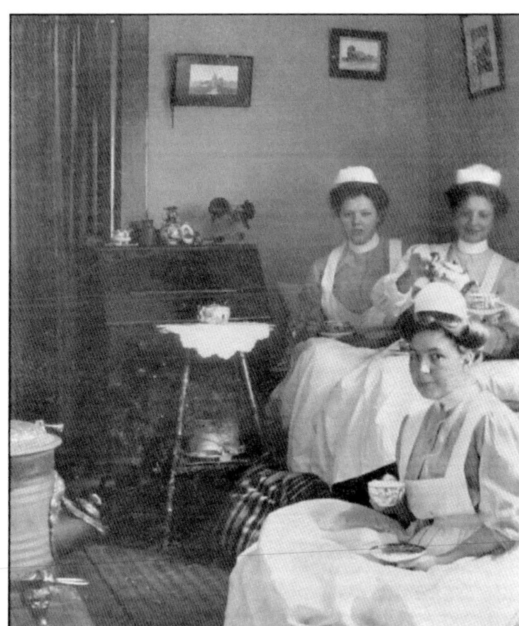

These three nursing students are enjoying an afternoon break from their studies at the original San Antonio School of Nursing boardinghouse at 59 East Ninth Street.

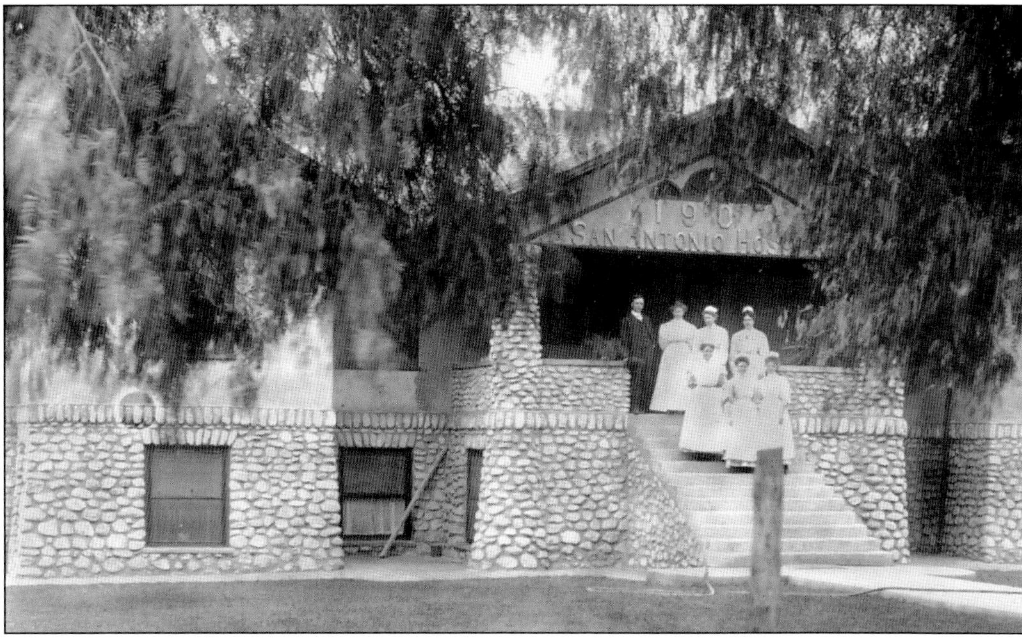


The San Antonio Hospital staff stand in front of the 18-bed facility, which opened in 1907.

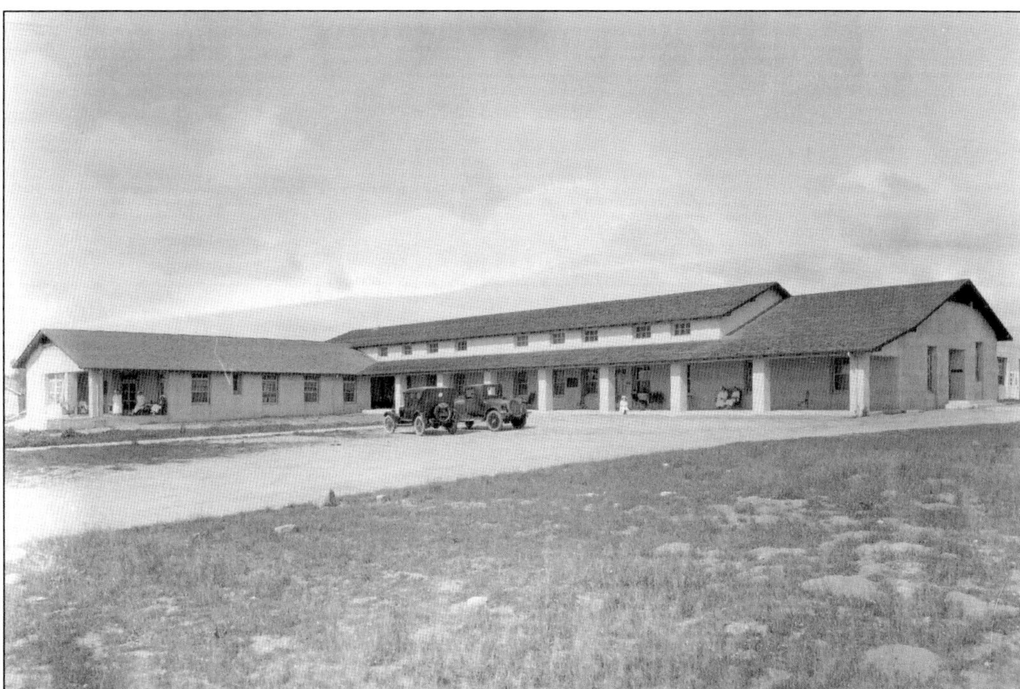

The new San Antonio Community Hospital on San Bernardino Road was a result of the generosity of Frances Mary Paul and her family. The facility opened for service on August 1, 1924.

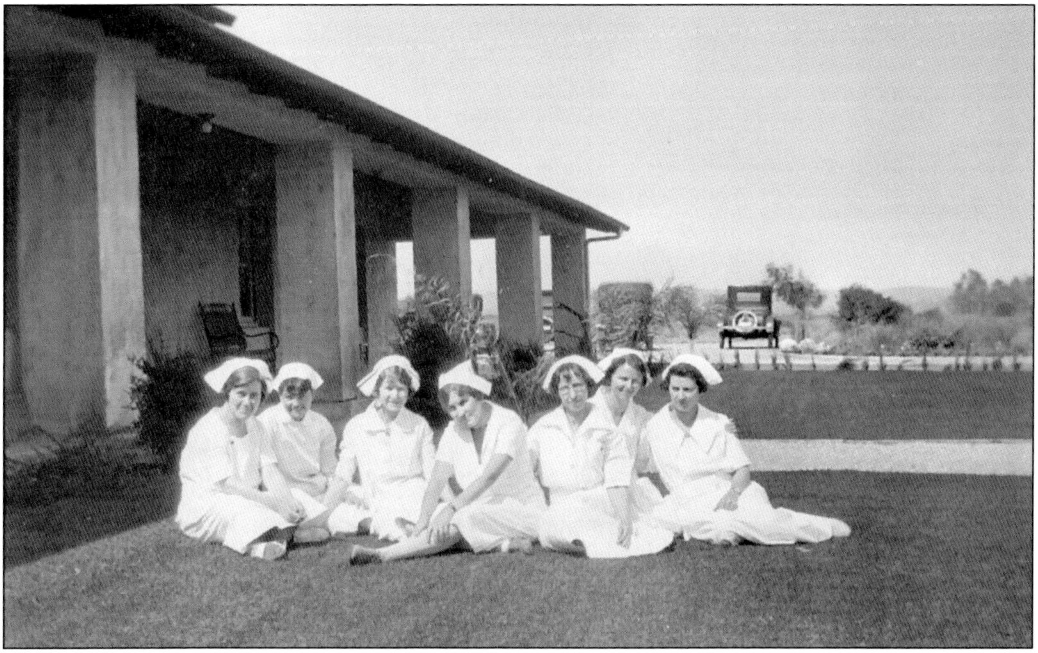

Nurses are enjoying a relaxing moment on the lawn of the new San Antonio Community Hospital facility. Pictured from left to right are Ada Stainsby, unidentified, Genevieve Bickmore, Aletha White, Eva Campbell, Bertha Schwarzwaelder, and Elizabeth Lehman.

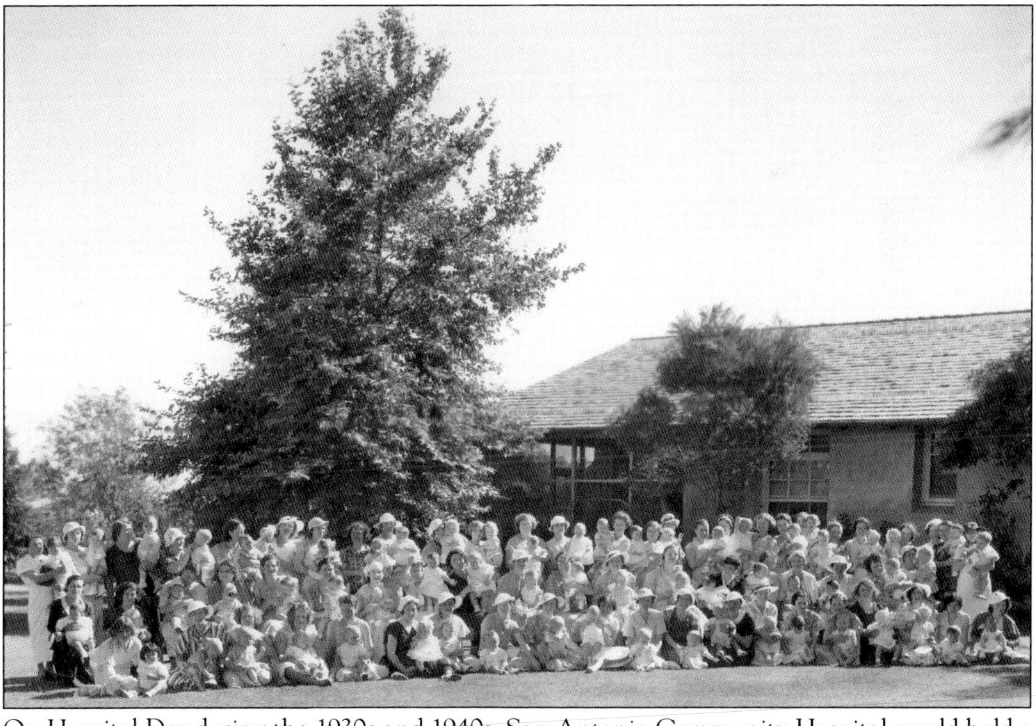

On Hospital Day during the 1930s and 1940s, San Antonio Community Hospital would hold a reunion for mothers and babies born during the previous year. This photograph was most likely taken at either the 1939 or 1940 reunion. (SACH.)

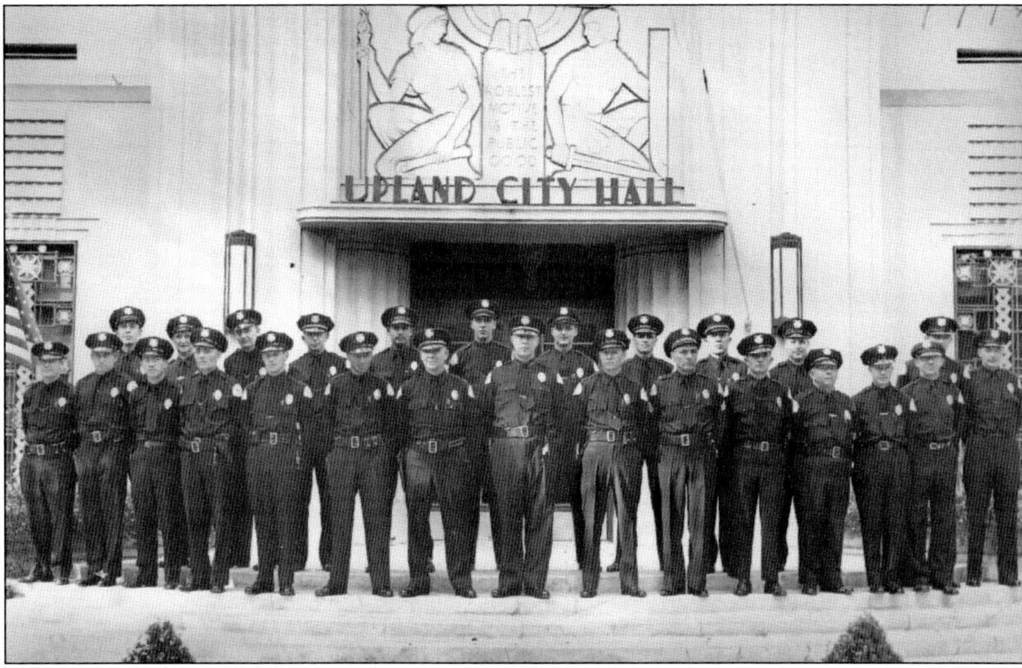


"Proud to Serve" is today's motto of the Upland Police Department. Although the motto was not being officially used in 1940, it is certain the officers at that time lived by the same ideal. (UPL.)

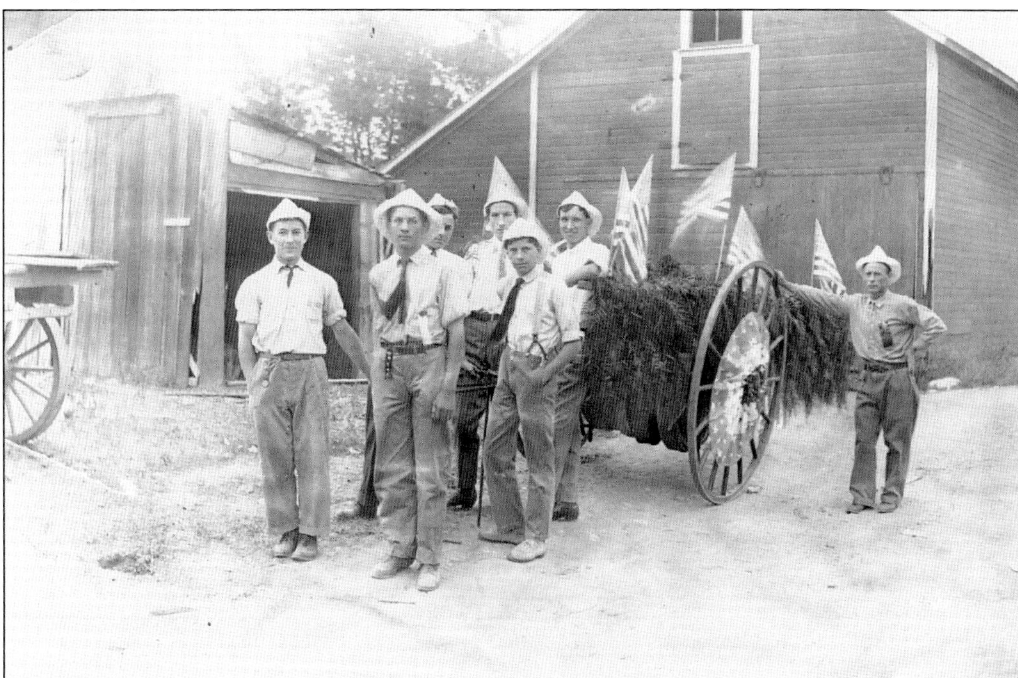

During the years 1909 to 1913, Upland's volunteer fire department had only one piece of equipment. It was a handcart carrying 500 feet of hose. Here the firefighters are shown with that cart all decked out for what is probably a Fourth of July parade.

Fletcher H. Manker served as one of the city's original volunteer firemen. He also served as chief of the Upland Fire Department from 1925 to 1927. (UPL.)

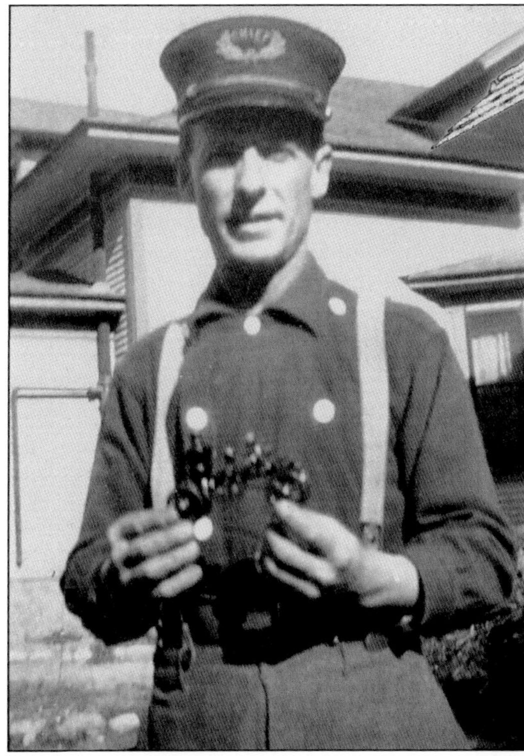

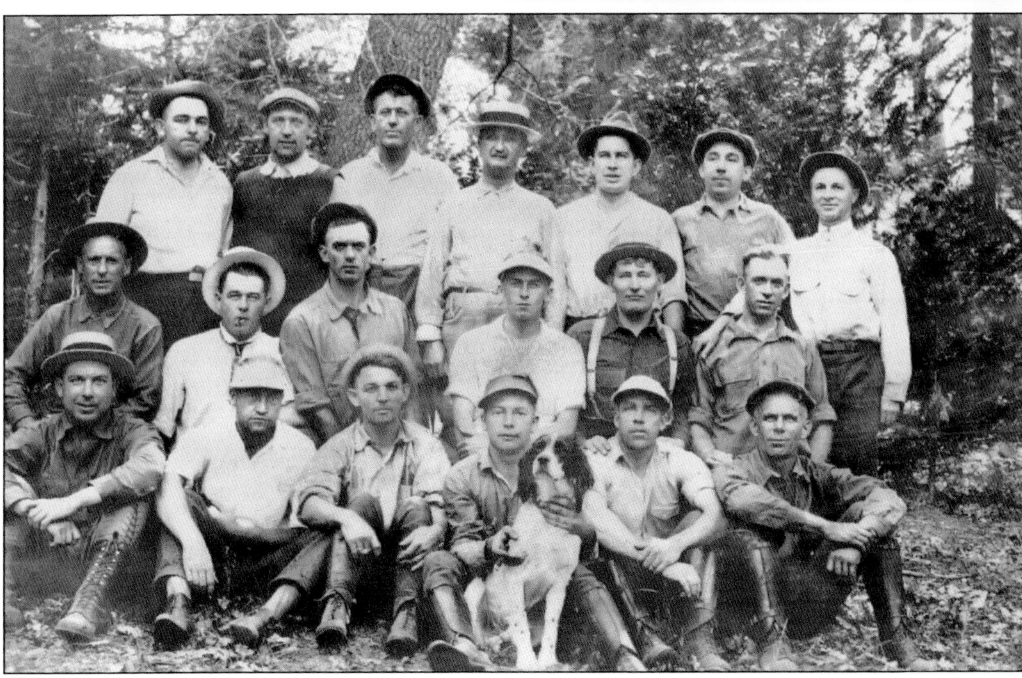

Upland's volunteer fire department was sent from time to time to help fight fires in the mountains around Camp Baldy. This photograph was taken about 1915 in that area. From their looks and the fact they have a dog with them, they may have been on a casual outing rather than getting ready to battle a blaze.

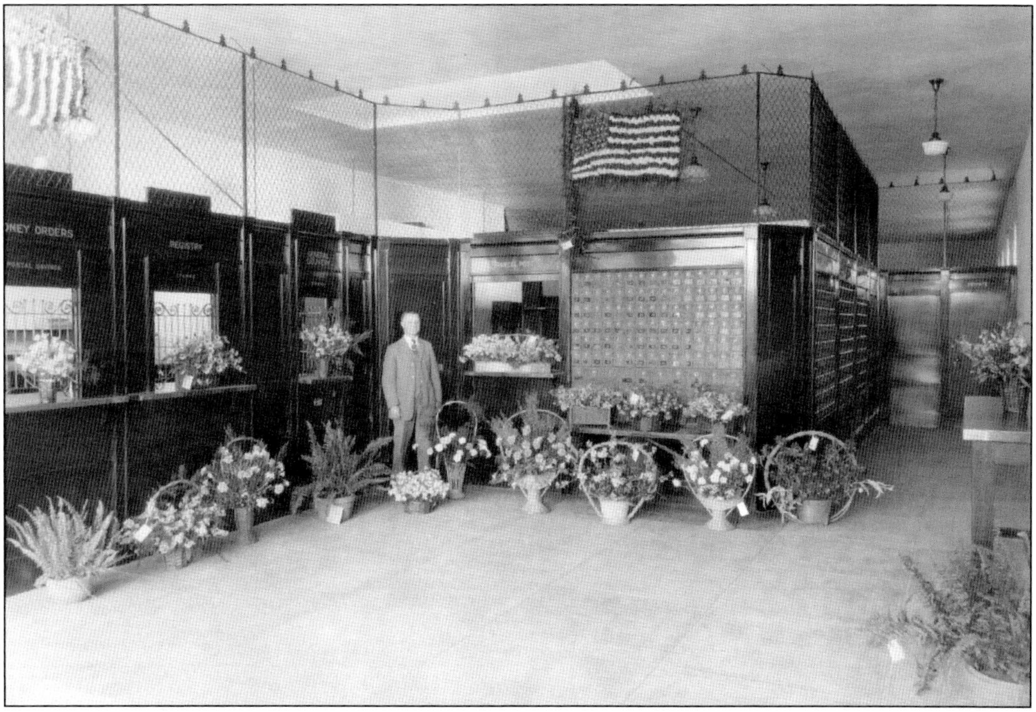

The opening day for the new U.S. Post Office on Ninth Street between Second and Third Avenues was a grand affair. At one time, mail was delivered by a Ford Model T. In 1922, city carrier service was begun. (UPL.)

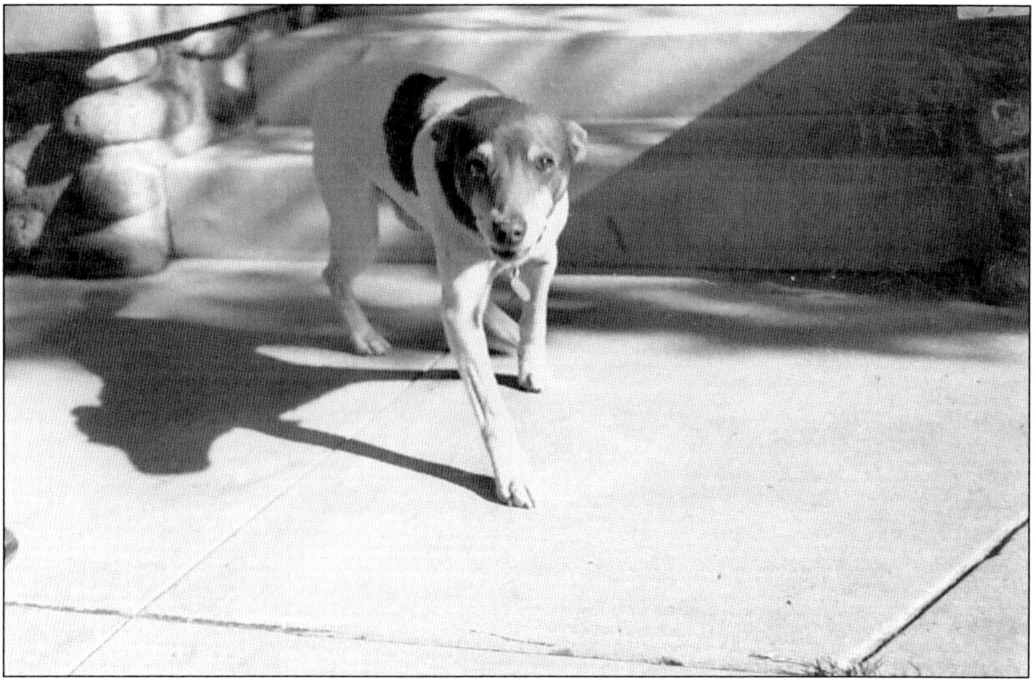

Many Uplanders might remember Pancho, the unofficial mascot of the Upland Post Office during the 1950s.

Mailman Charles Deverts is delivering the mail with Pancho in 1950.

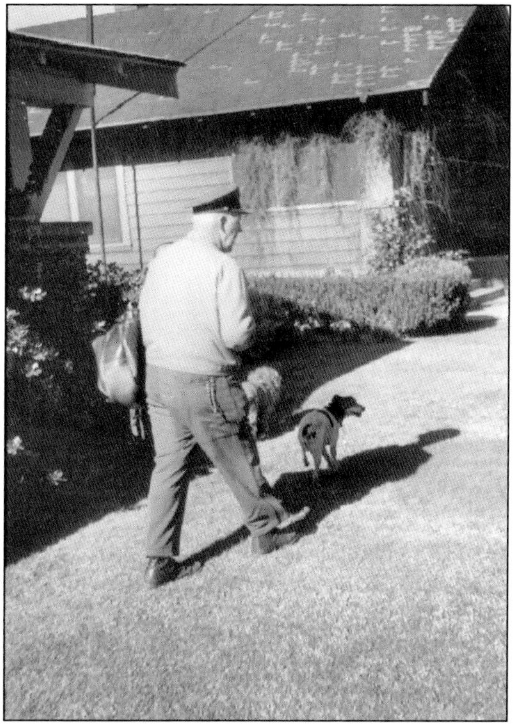

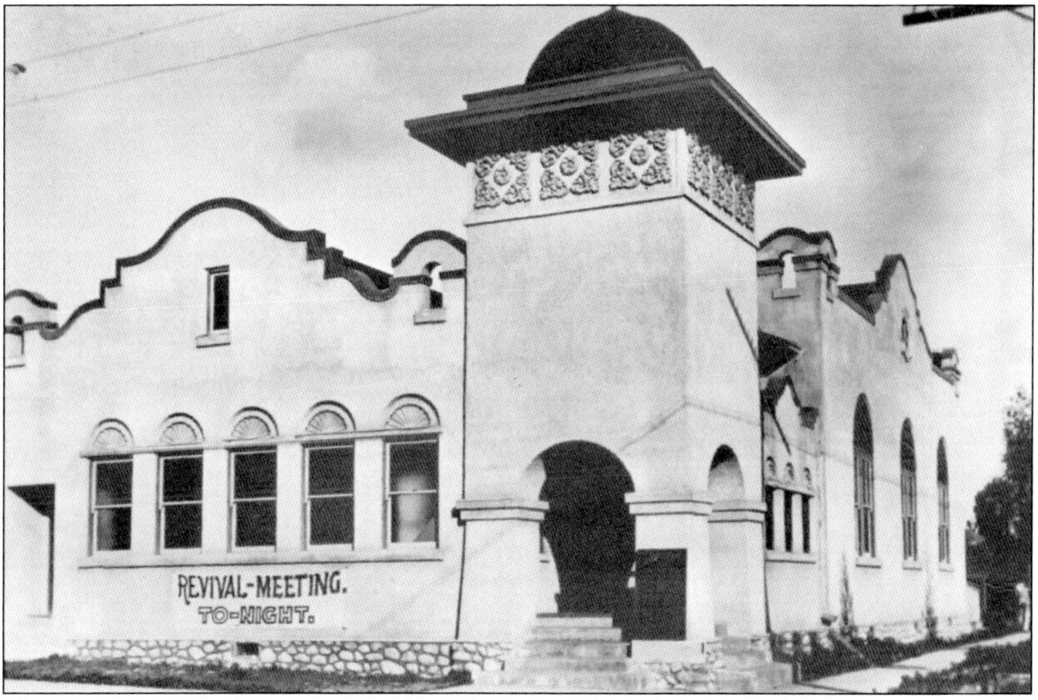


The Nazarene Church began its work in Upland in 1906, the year of the city's incorporation. This building was erected that same year at the northeast corner of Second Avenue and Ninth Street. It was later moved one block east to its present location at Third Avenue and Ninth Street. (UPL.)

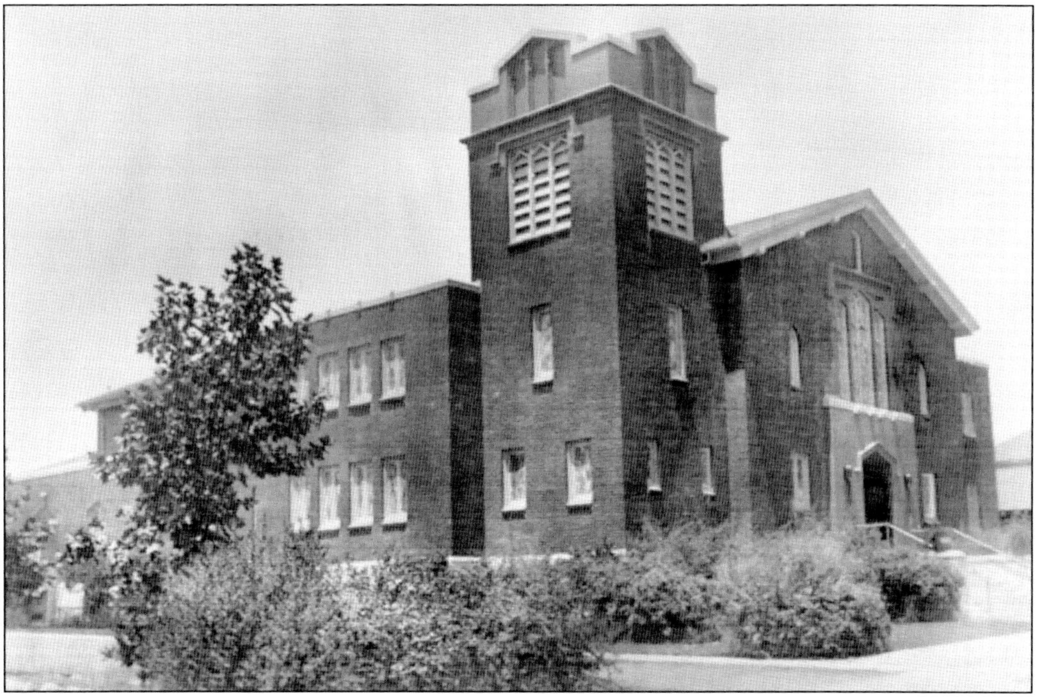

The Mennonite church building was erected on Campus Avenue in 1898. Because the majority of the church members were of German origin, most of the church records were written in German. (UPL.)

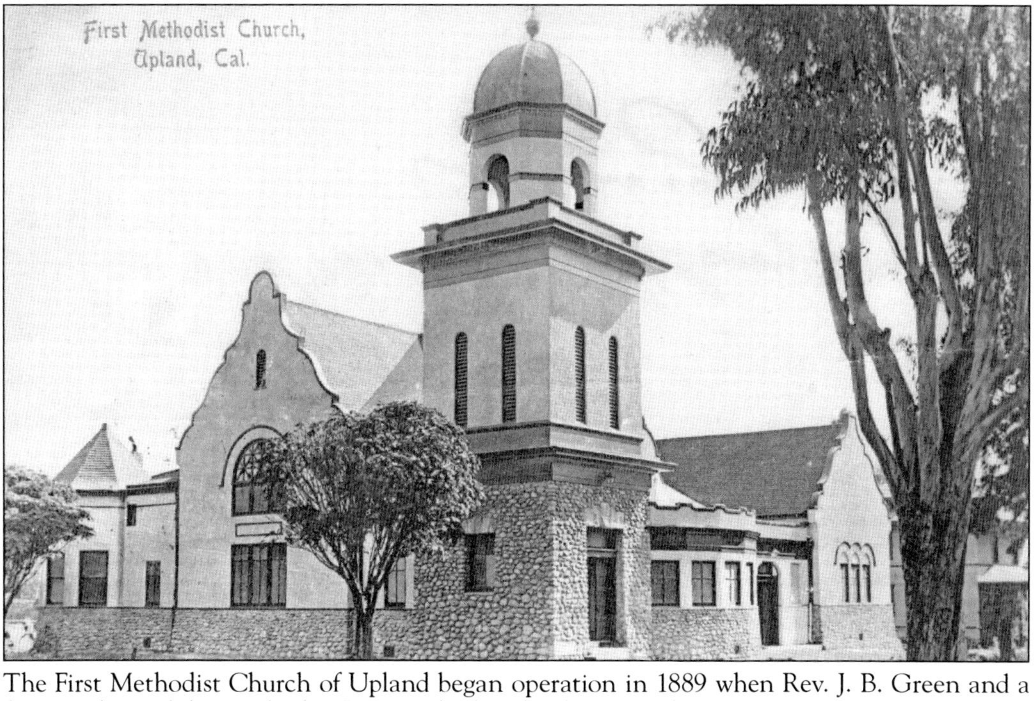


The First Methodist Church of Upland began operation in 1889 when Rev. J. B. Green and a few members of the Methodist Episcopal Church of Ontario began mission work among local Chinese field workers in the vineyards.

*Five*

# Getting around Town

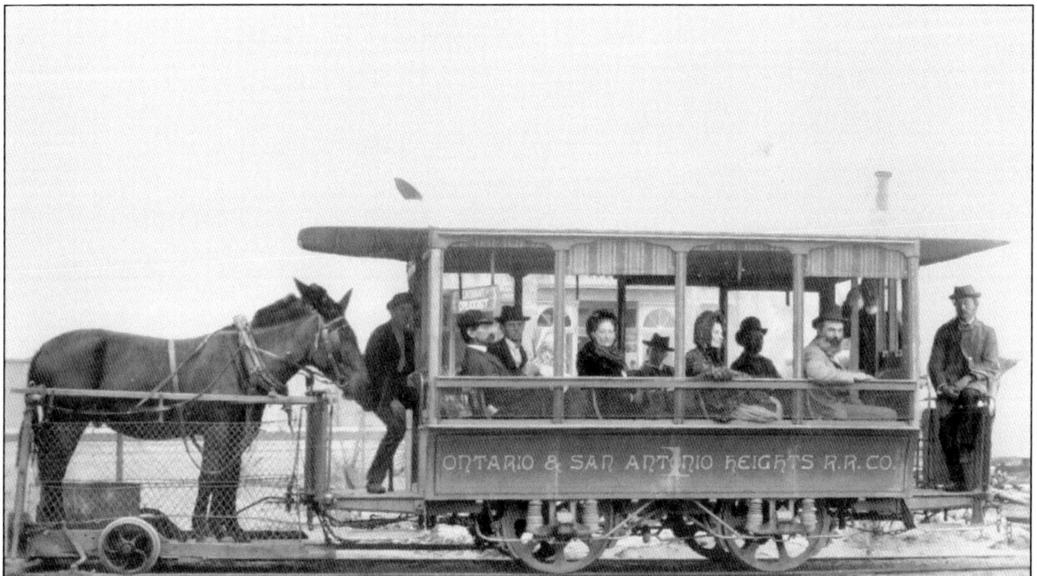


Along with the Madonna of the Trail, the old mule car that ran the length of Euclid Avenue carrying passengers from Ontario, through Upland, and to San Antonio Heights is synonymous with area history. Charles Frankish originally dreamed of an electric railway but settled for a horse-powered system, and later used mules in 1887. A team of two equines pulled the little train on the one-hour trip up the 1,000-foot rise from the center of Ontario to San Antonio Heights, then rode on a platform at the back of the car for the trip back down the hill. (UPL.)

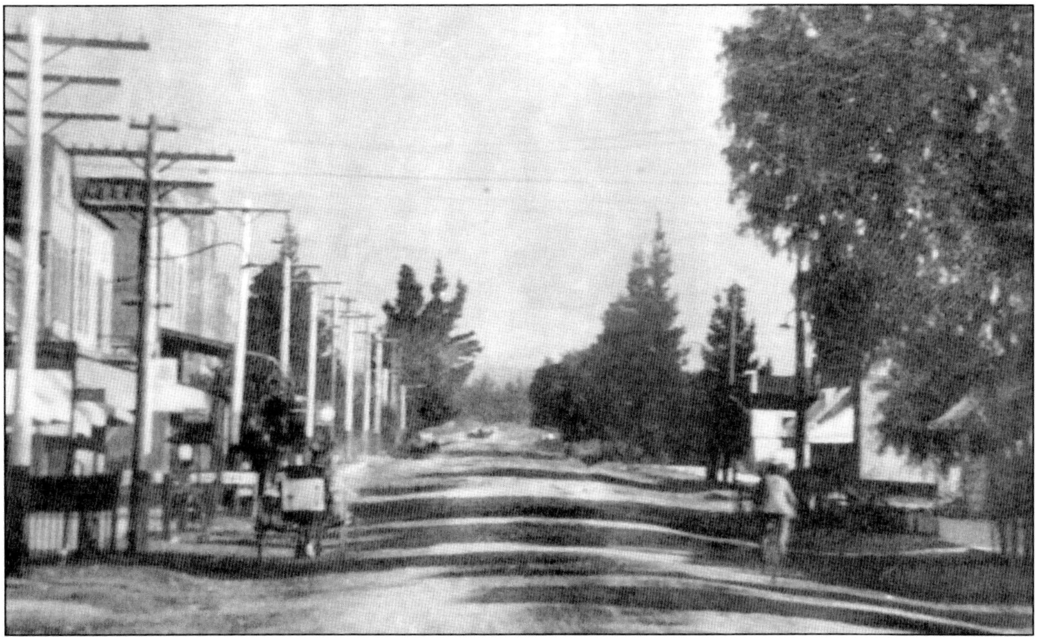

This 1900 view looking north on Second Avenue shows two forms of transportation at the time. At the left side of the unpaved street is a horse and buggy, while a bicycle rider is making his way up the opposite side of the road. (UPL.)

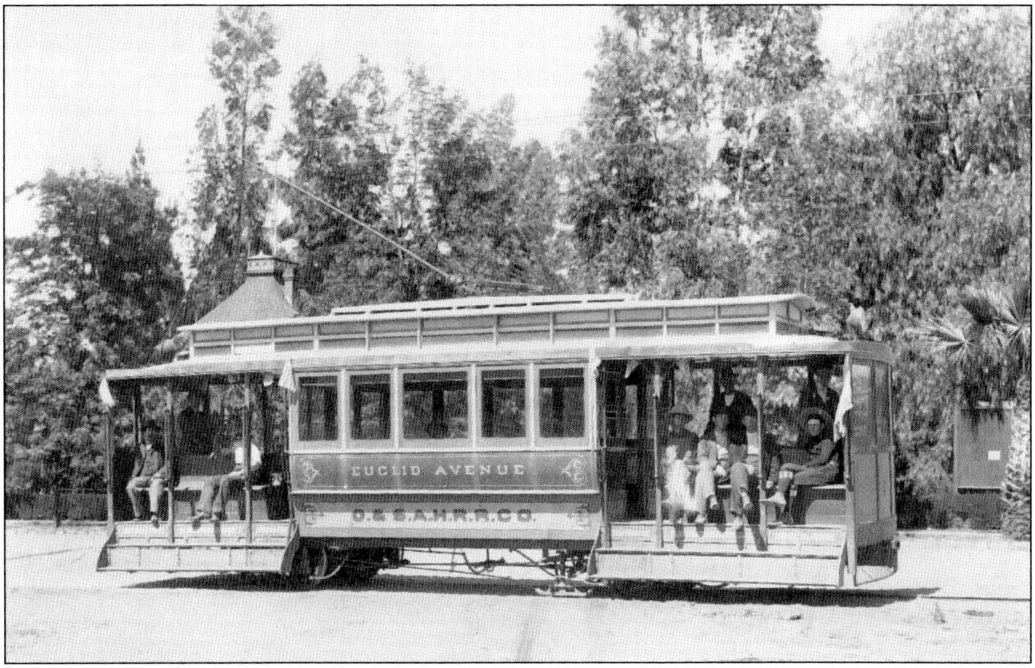


In 1888, the *Ontario Record* newspaper stated, "The tourist . . . will step aboard a handsome electric car." Charles Frankish's vision of an electric rail system did not actually come about until 1895, when he began operation of the Ontario and San Antonio Heights Railway Company. Although "railway" was part of the company's name, the cars were inscribed "O.&S.A.H.R.R. [Railroad] Co." (UPL.)

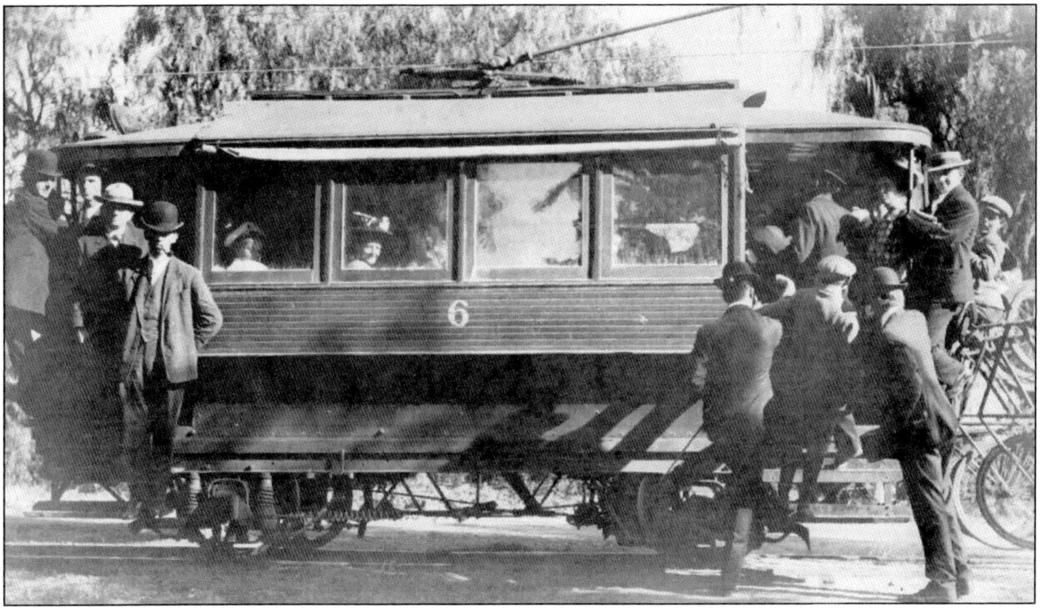

Passengers are climbing aboard one of the electric cars of the O&SAHRR Company. Note the bicycles being carried at the back of the car. (UPL.)

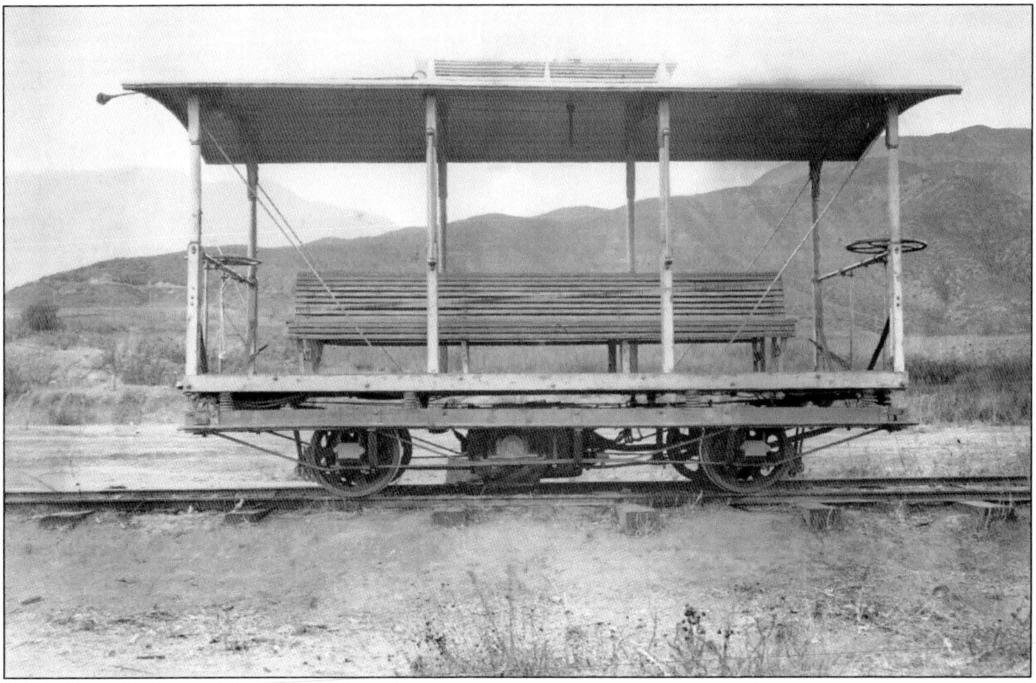

This is one of the original "dummy" (non-powered) passenger cars that would have been attached to the electric rail system on Euclid Avenue.

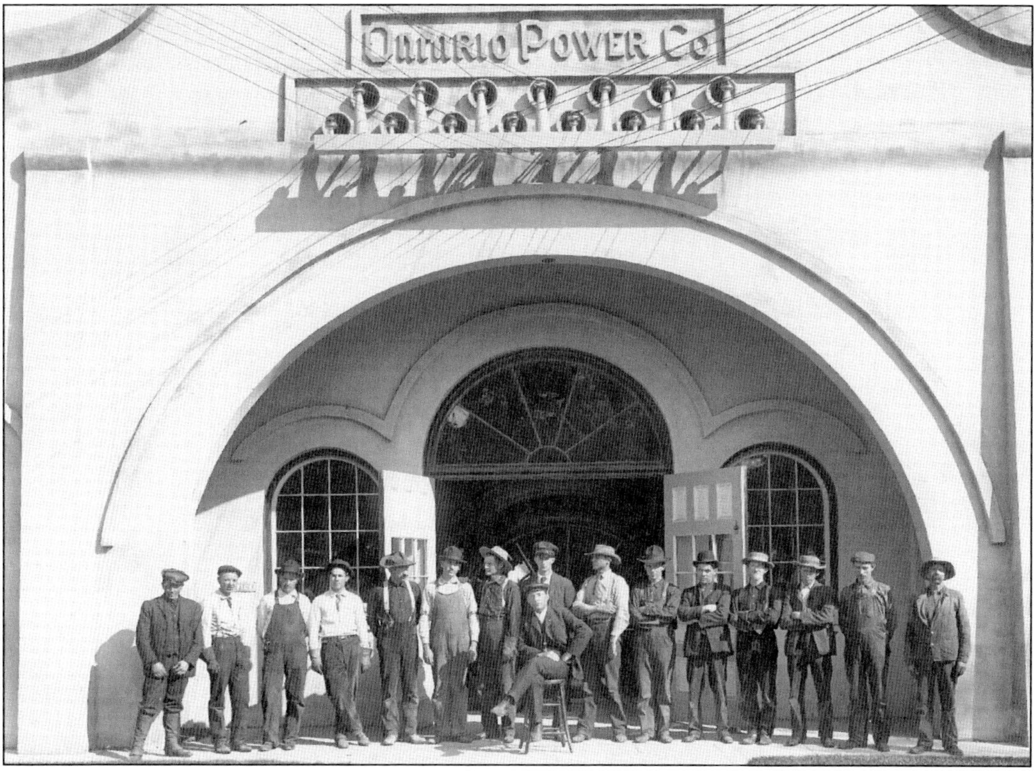


It took a great amount of power to keep the O&SAHRR Company and the Pacific Electric Railway operating for Upland residents. The crew at the Ontario Power Company on Euclid Avenue was able to keep up with the task in every way.

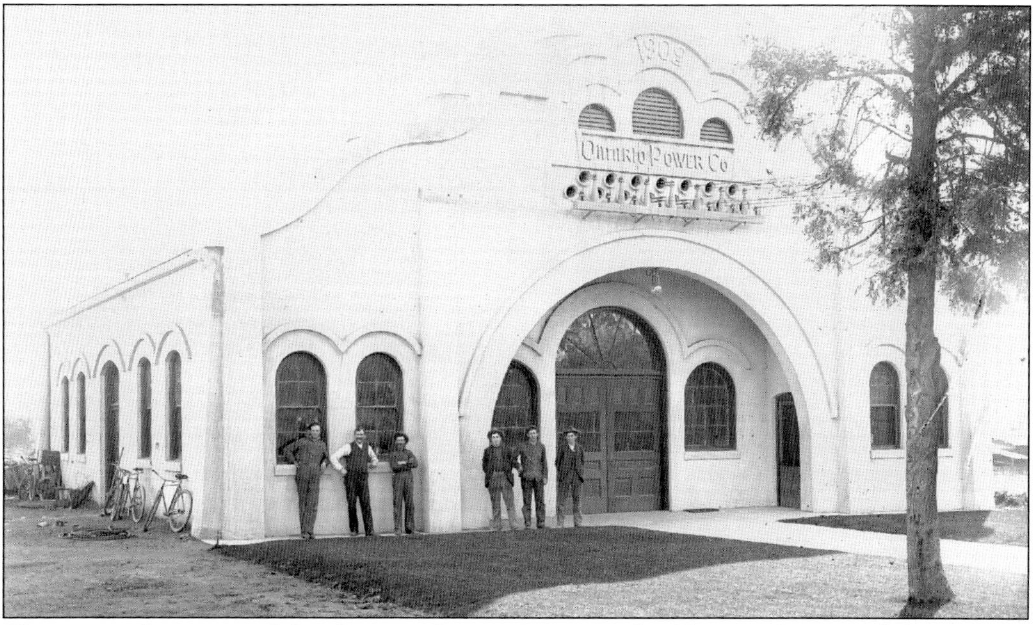


This is another view of the Ontario Power Company building and some of the crew in the early 1900s.

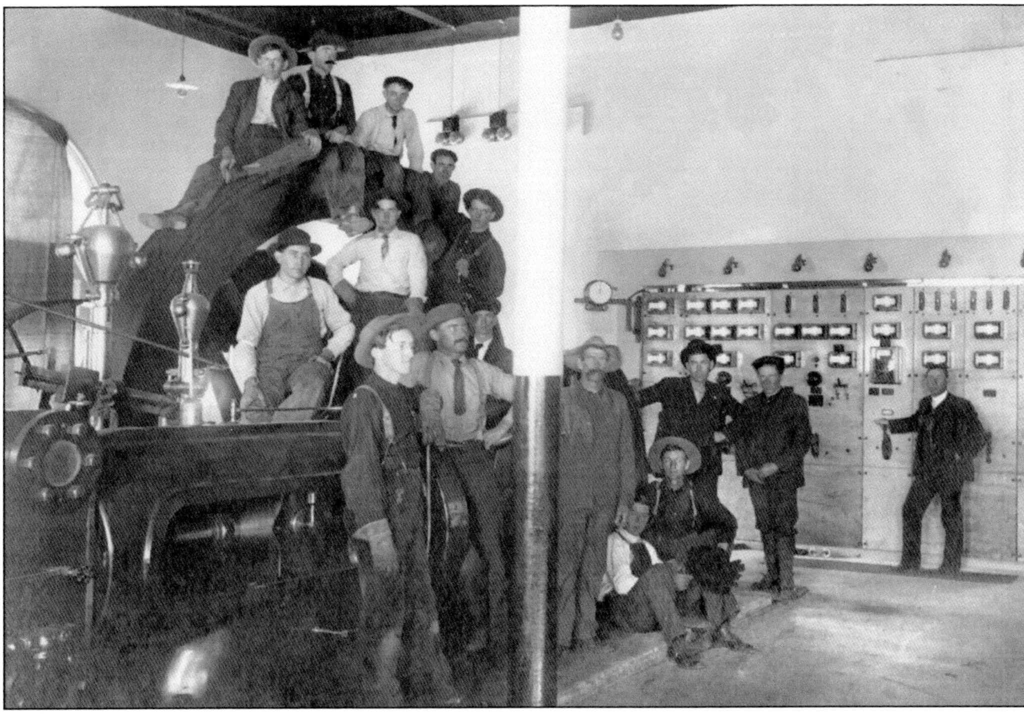

It required an able Ontario Power Company crew to handle the task of providing electricity for homes, businesses, schools, and the railway system in Upland during the early 1900s.

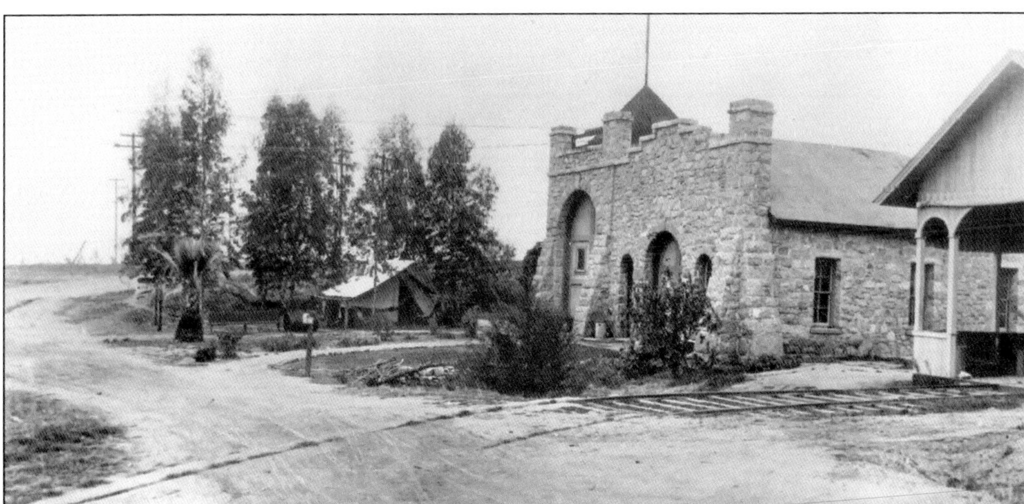

The stone castle electric power station located on the north side of Mountain Avenue in San Antonio Heights was used to help produce electricity for the O&SAHRR Company. (UPL.)

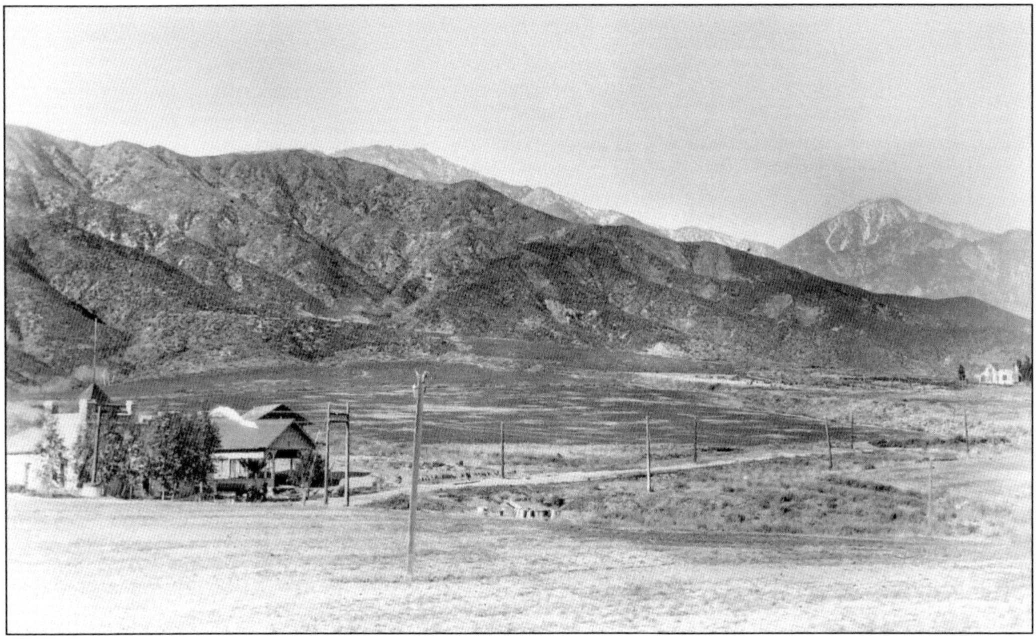

During the late 1890s and early 1900s, the area near the northern end of the O&SAHRR Company tracks was desolate except for the stone castle and the original little waiting station next to it. (UPL.)

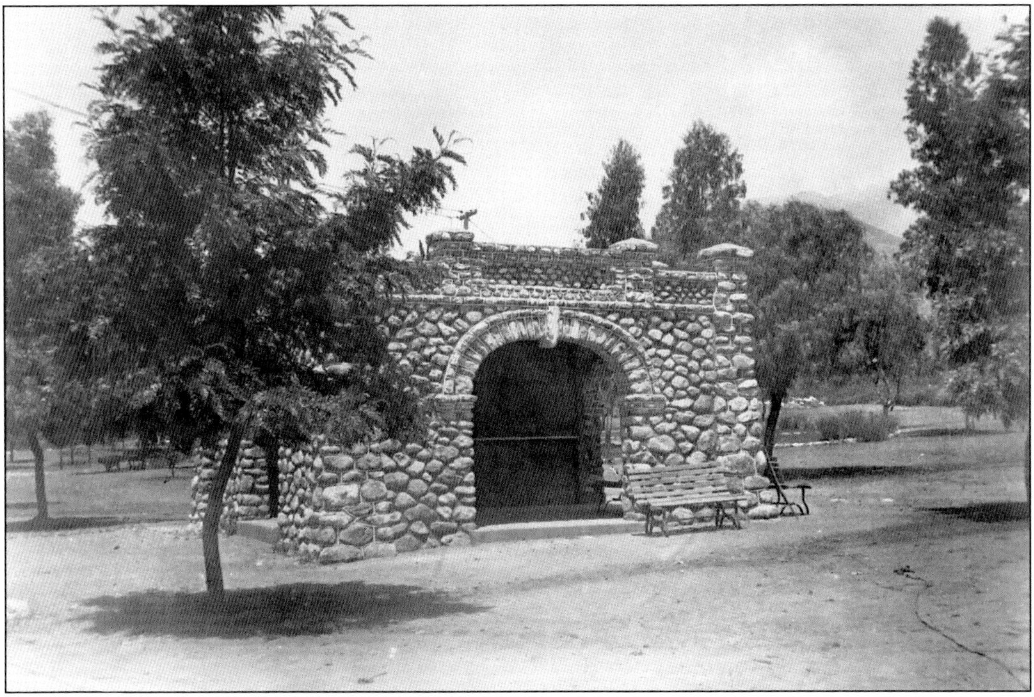

This stone waiting station was erected in 1903 at the terminus of the electric rail line at Mountain Avenue and Twenty-fourth Street. This was also a boarding place for a motorized stage to transport passengers to Camp Baldy at one time. It has been beautifully restored by the Upland Community Foundation with support from individuals and organizations within the area. (UPL.)

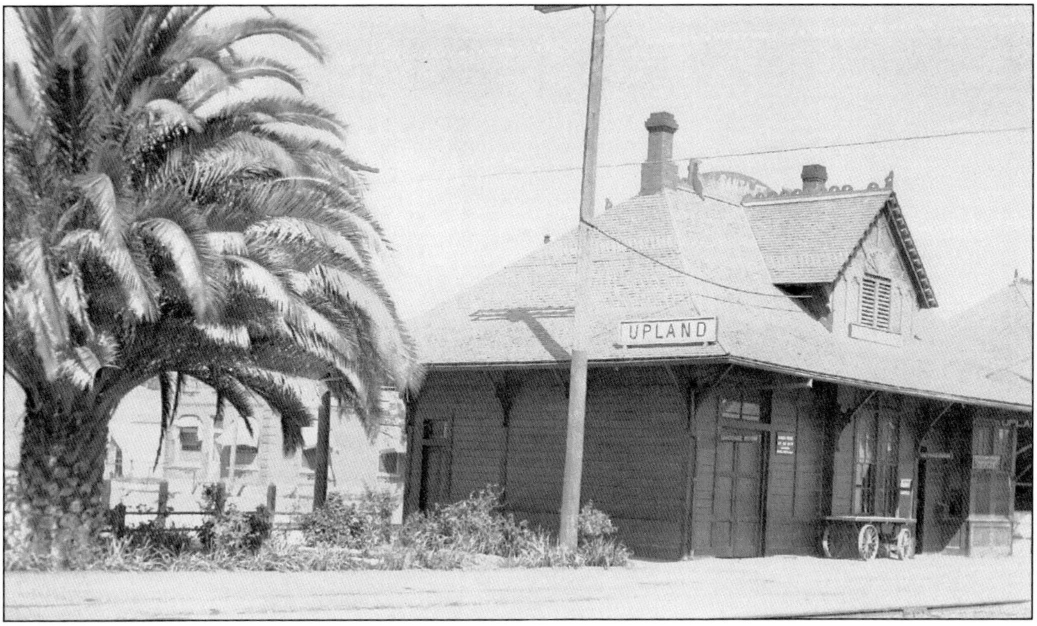


This photograph had to be taken after 1906, as the sign on the depot has been changed from "North Ontario" to "Upland."

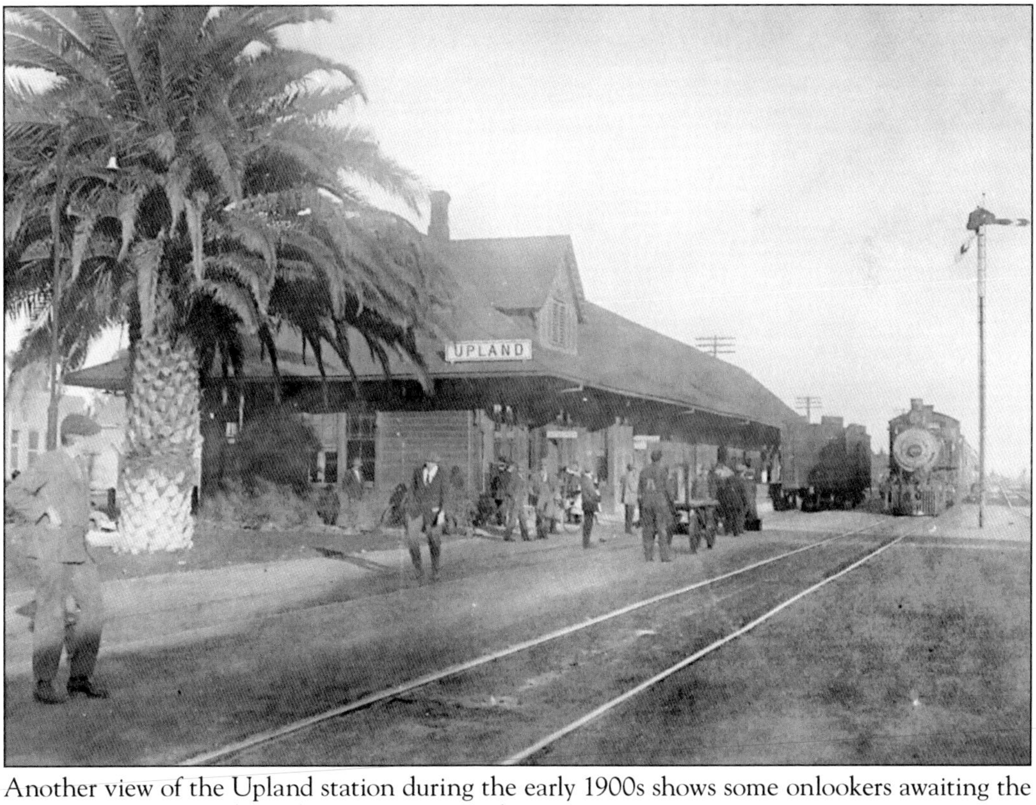


Another view of the Upland station during the early 1900s shows some onlookers awaiting the arrival of a train westbound from San Bernardino.

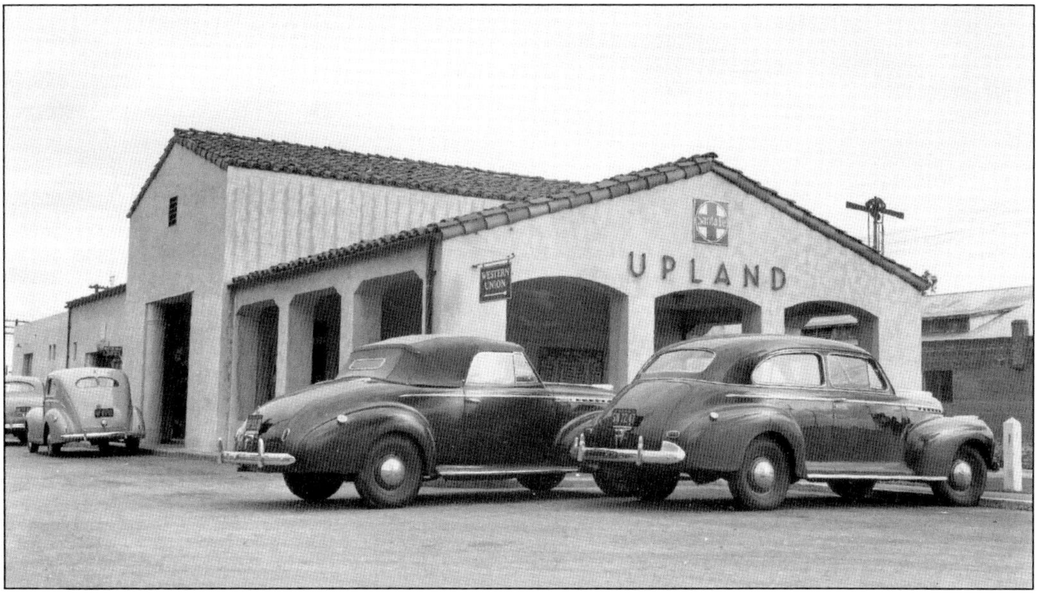


The Santa Fe Station in Upland is pictured during the 1940s. The depot is still in use today as a place for private businesses. An outside station has been built to accommodate passengers traveling on the Metrolink line.

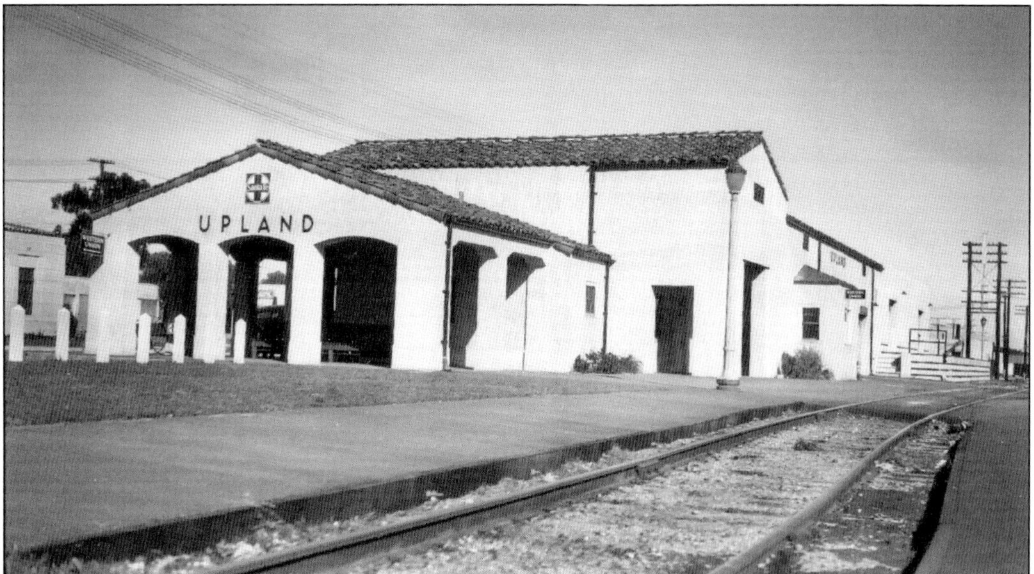


This is another view of the station during the 1950s. Note the small white posts, which created a dead end on Second Avenue and kept motorists from driving across the tracks.

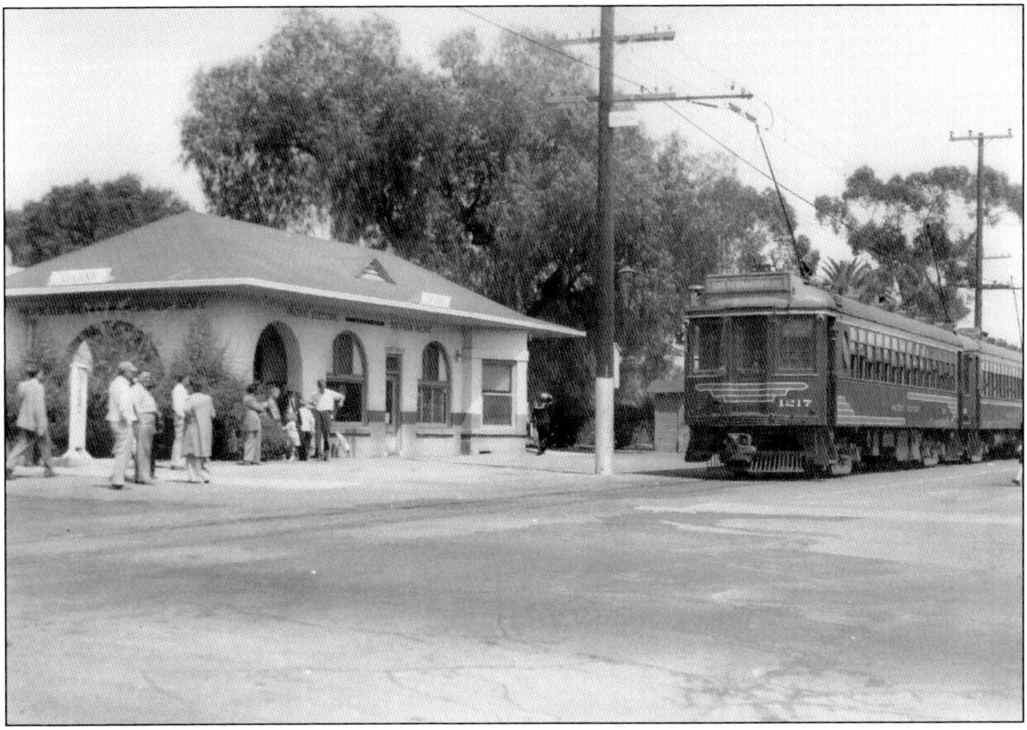


A Pacific Electric Railway "Red Car" rolls into the station at Second Avenue between C and D Streets in the 1950s. (UPL.)

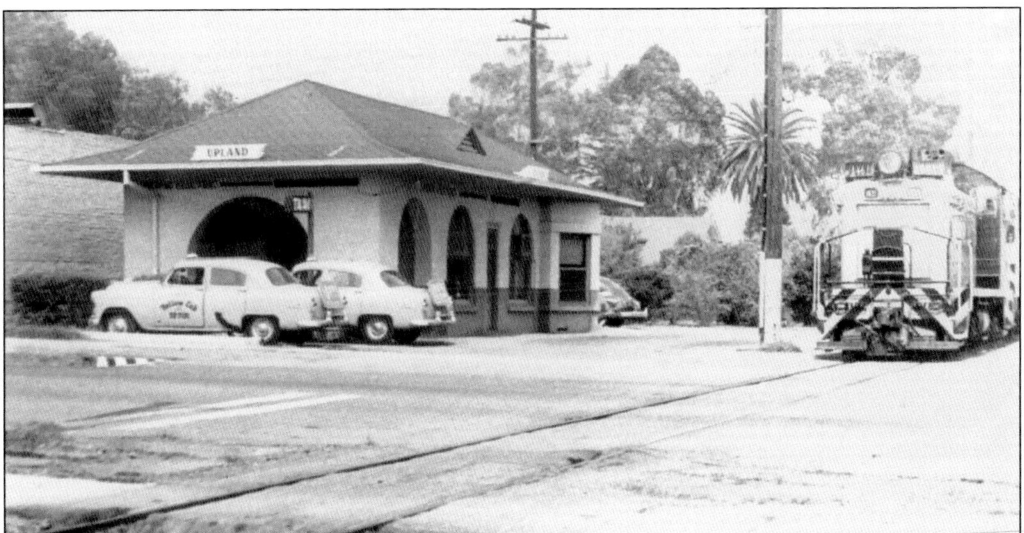


A Pacific Electric Railway freight locomotive also passes by the Second Avenue station in the 1950s. (UPL.)

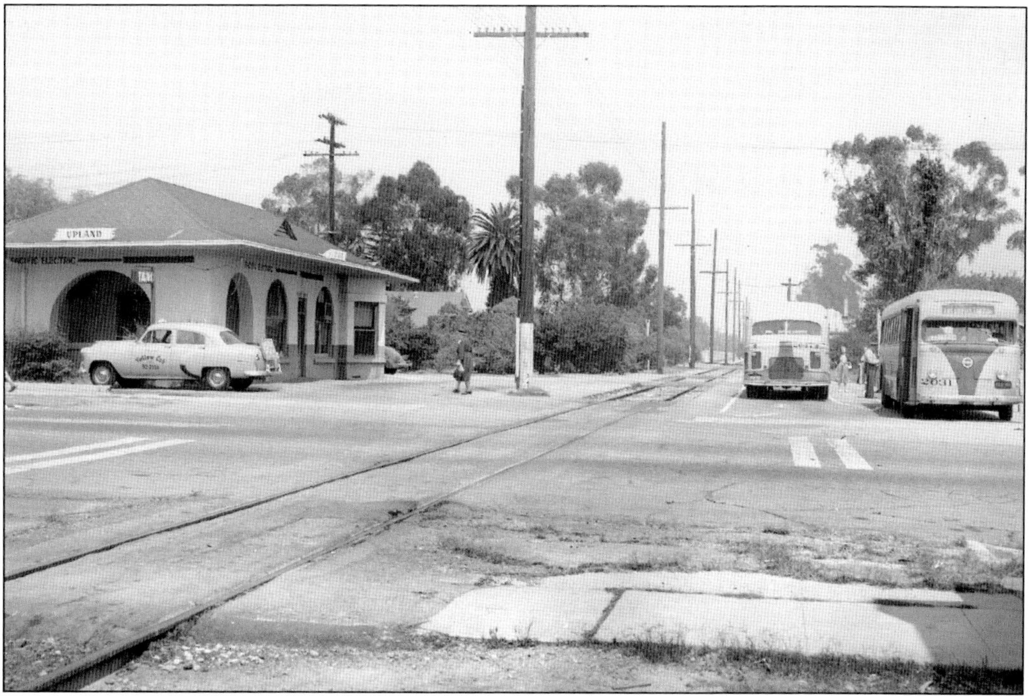


Passengers could be dropped off and picked up by taxi or bus at the Pacific Electric Railway station. At the time, Washington Boulevard ran alongside the tracks.

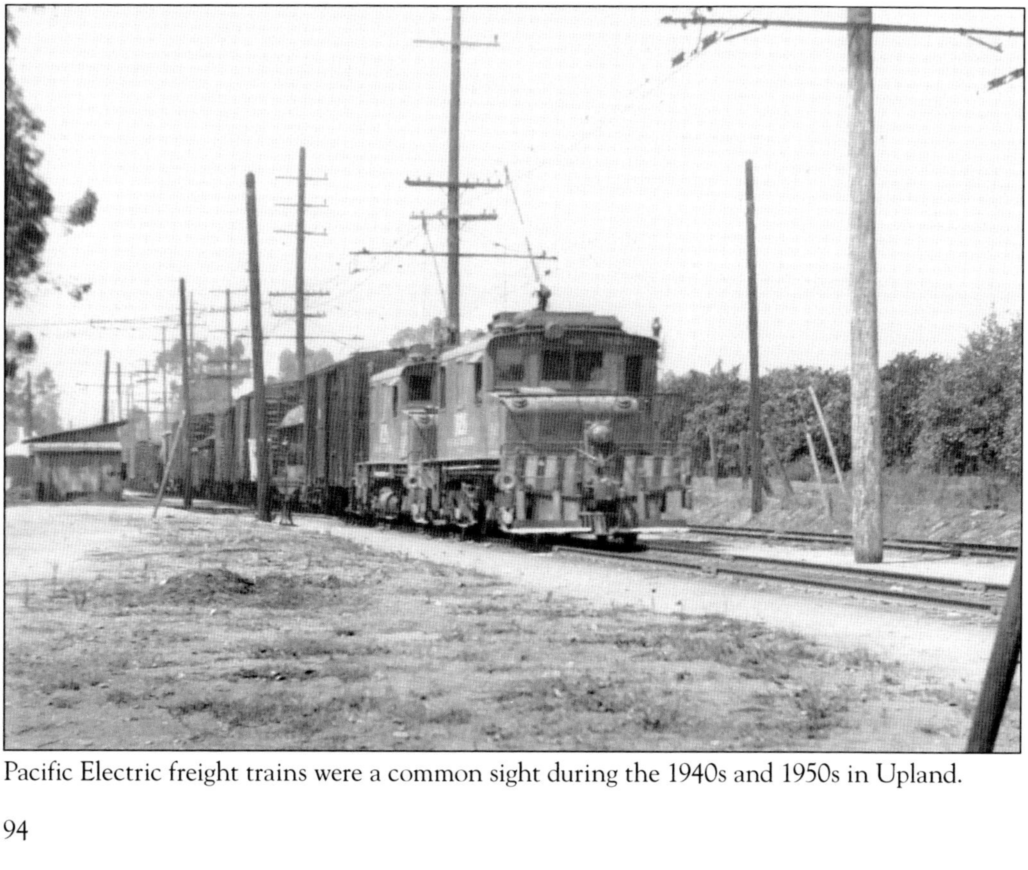

Pacific Electric freight trains were a common sight during the 1940s and 1950s in Upland.

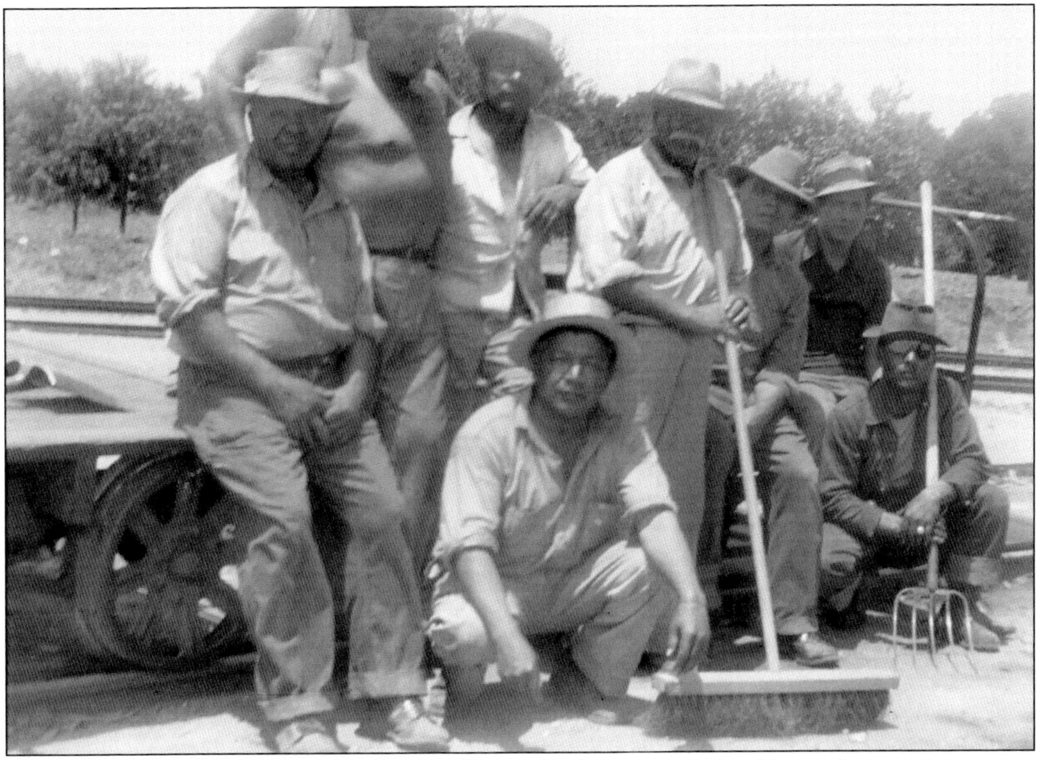

During the 1940s and 1950s, this Pacific Electric Railway crew helped keep the system running through Upland and on to points east and west.

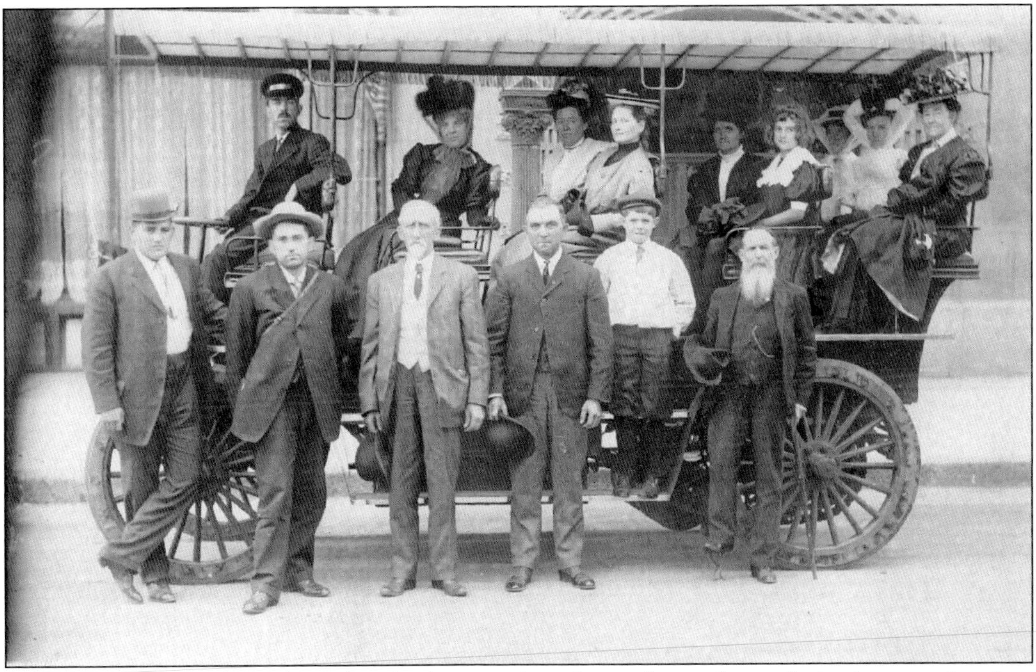

Because of the number of people who have gathered together to have their photograph taken with this automobile, it must have been one of the very first on the roads in Upland.

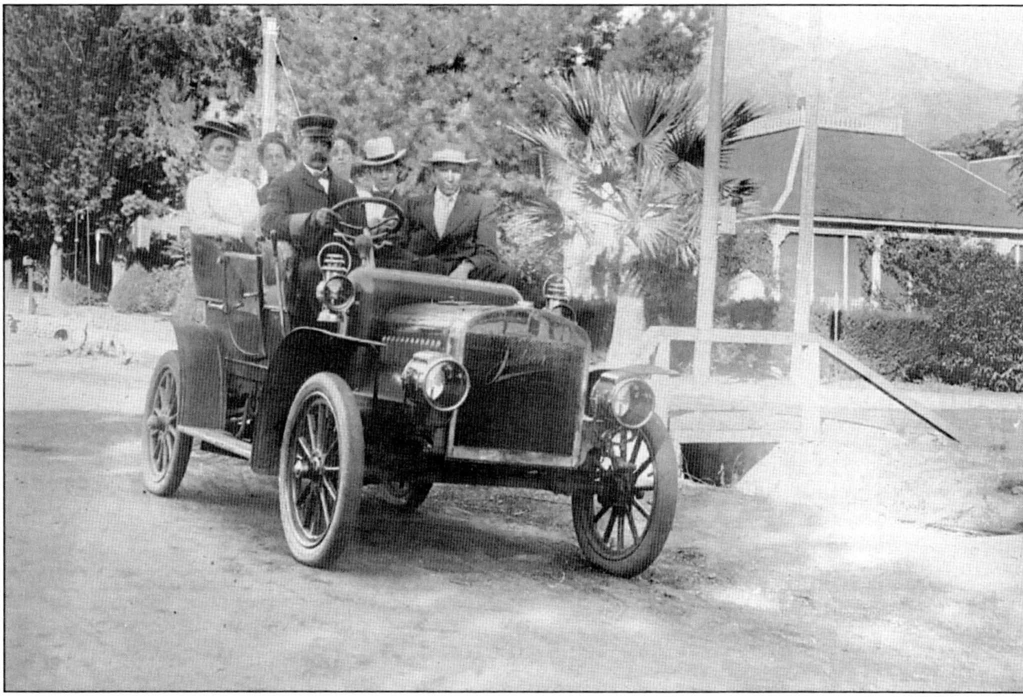

In 1910, the transportation of choice for the Fuller family of San Antonio Heights was their brand new Jackson automobile.

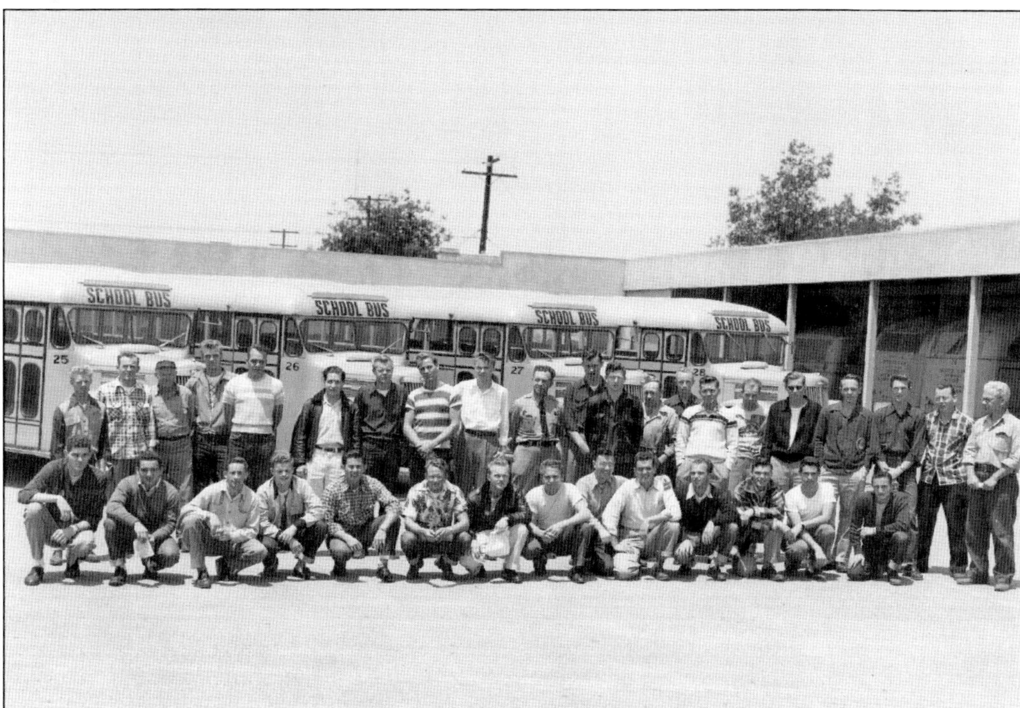


This 1950 group of bus drivers and shop employees helped guarantee the safe transport of Upland students to and from Chaffey Union High School.

*Six*

# Having Fun around Town

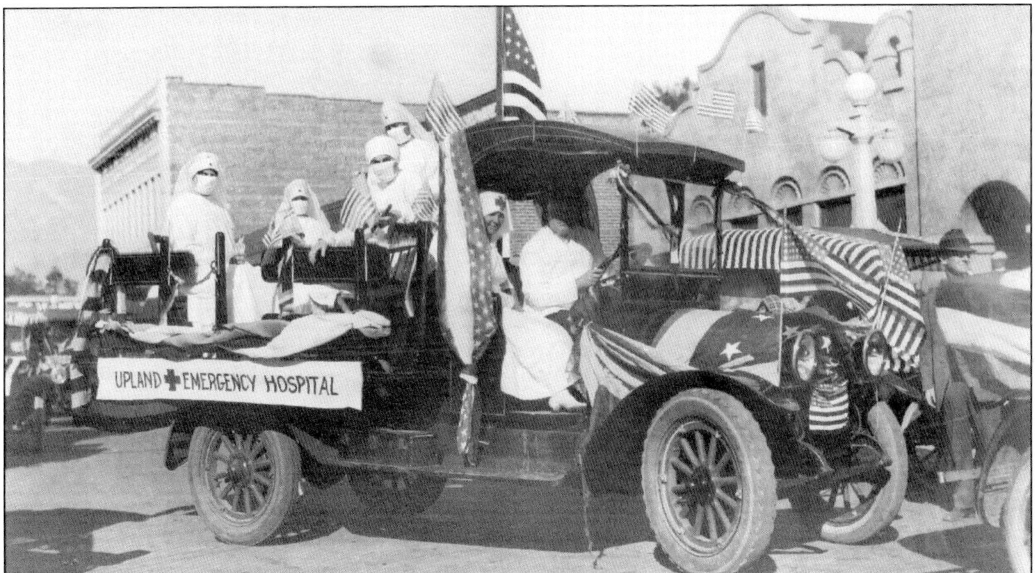


Although the ladies on the bed of this truck may appear to be prepared for an emergency situation, they are actually dressed for some high-spirited fun. It is 1918, and the city of Upland is about to celebrate the end of World War I with a victory parade. (UPL.)

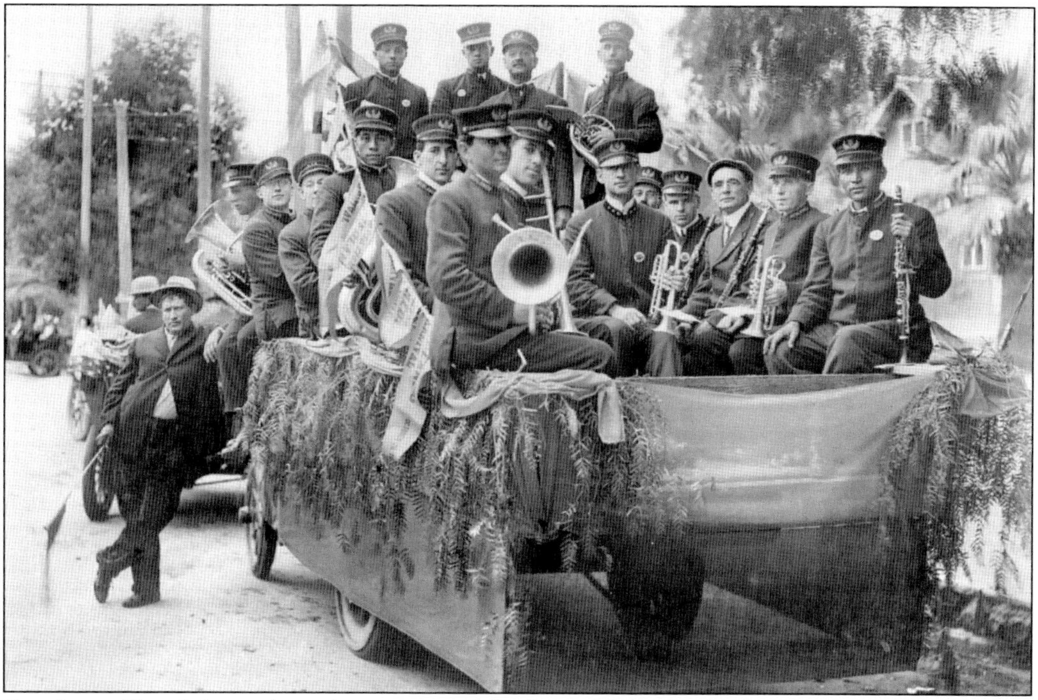

Parades and bands have always been a part of the fun in Upland. This band was one of the parade bands directed by Fred Wilding Jr. in the early 1900s.

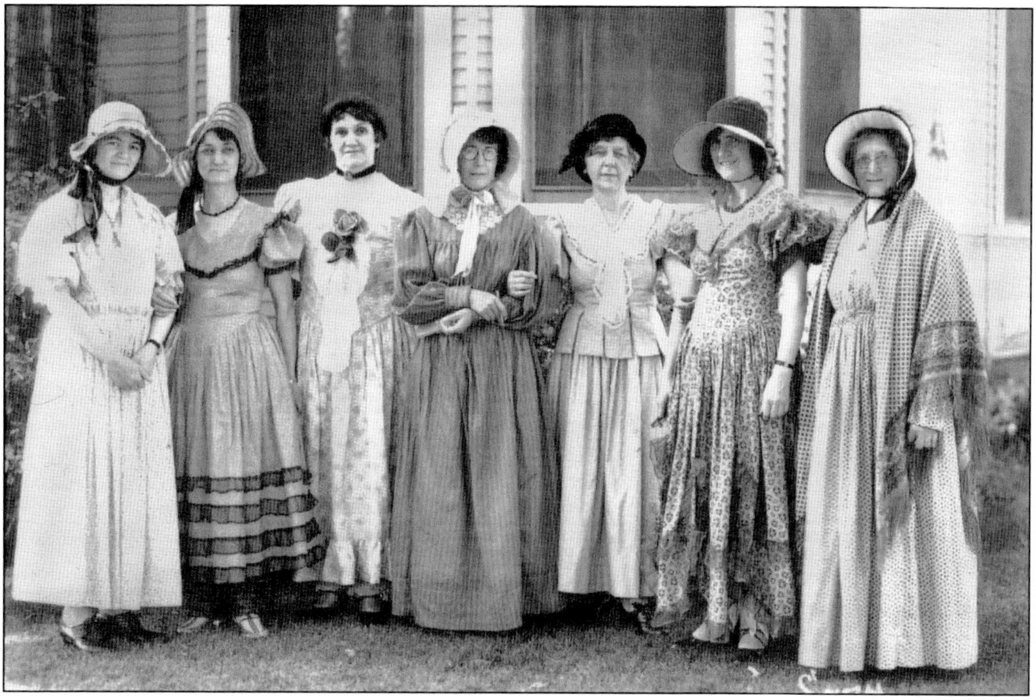

In 1920, these employees of the J. J. Atwood Department Store dressed in their best old-time costumes for the annual Pioneer Days celebration. From left to right are Lulu Schlecht, a Mrs. Samuels, Mary Bailey, Ethel Thrush, Linda Schmidt, Nell Dority, and a Mrs. Williams.

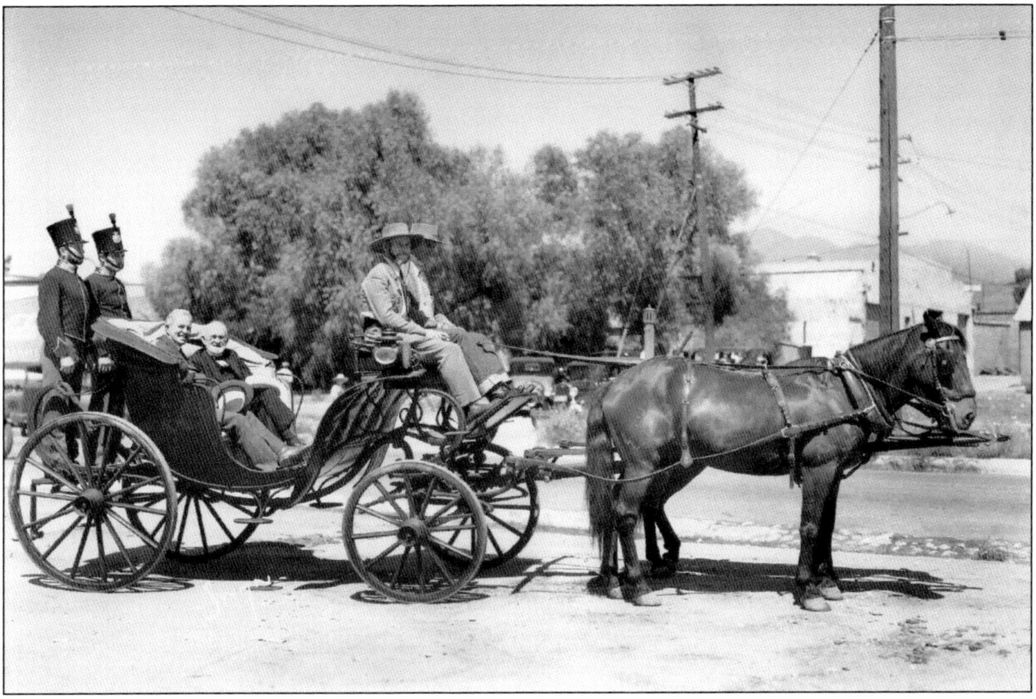

John Steven McGroaty (seated, left) and C. E. Harwood ride in a carriage as part of the parade for the 1930 Pioneer Pilgrimage of the Shrine of the Madonna of the Trail Monument, which was held to celebrate the first anniversary of the dedication of the Madonna.

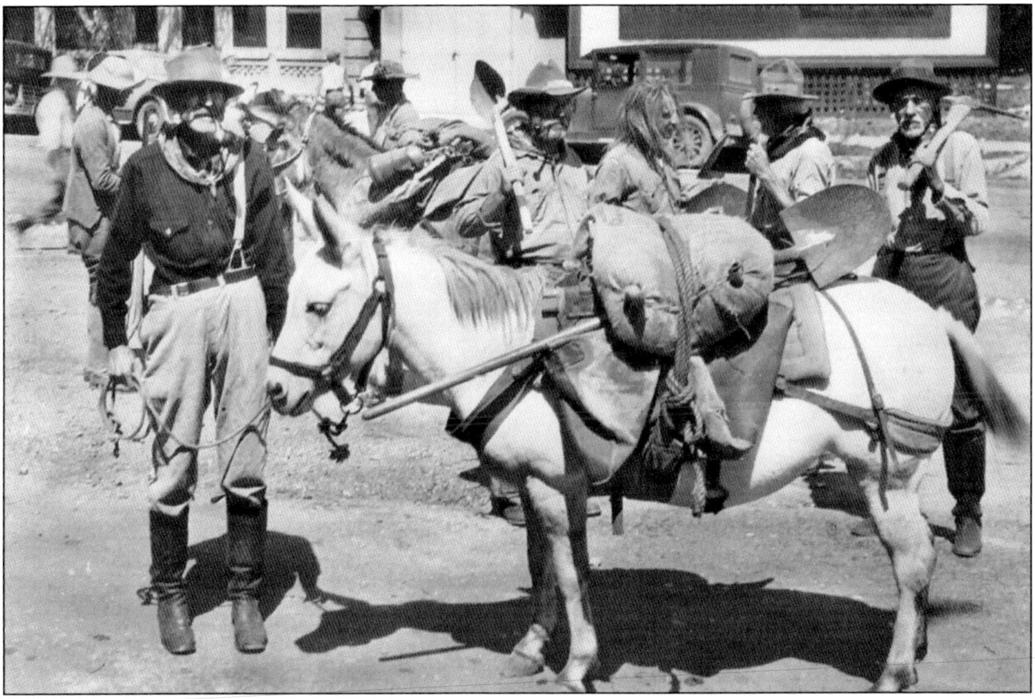

These "forty-niners" and their burro are outfitted and ready to take part in the 1930 Pioneer Pilgrimage.

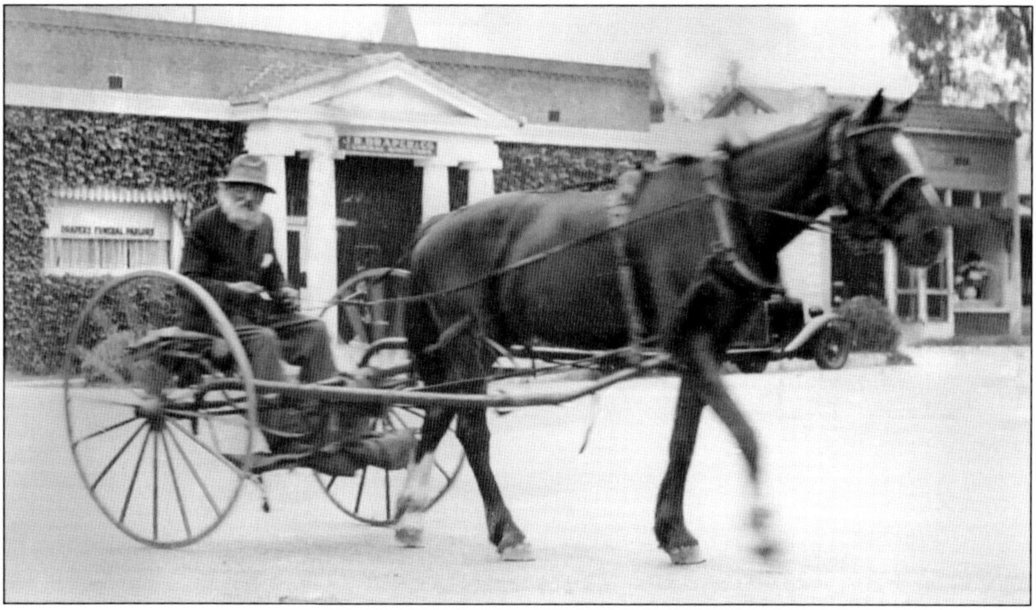

Another participant is heading toward the staging area for the 1930 Pioneer Pilgrimage parade.

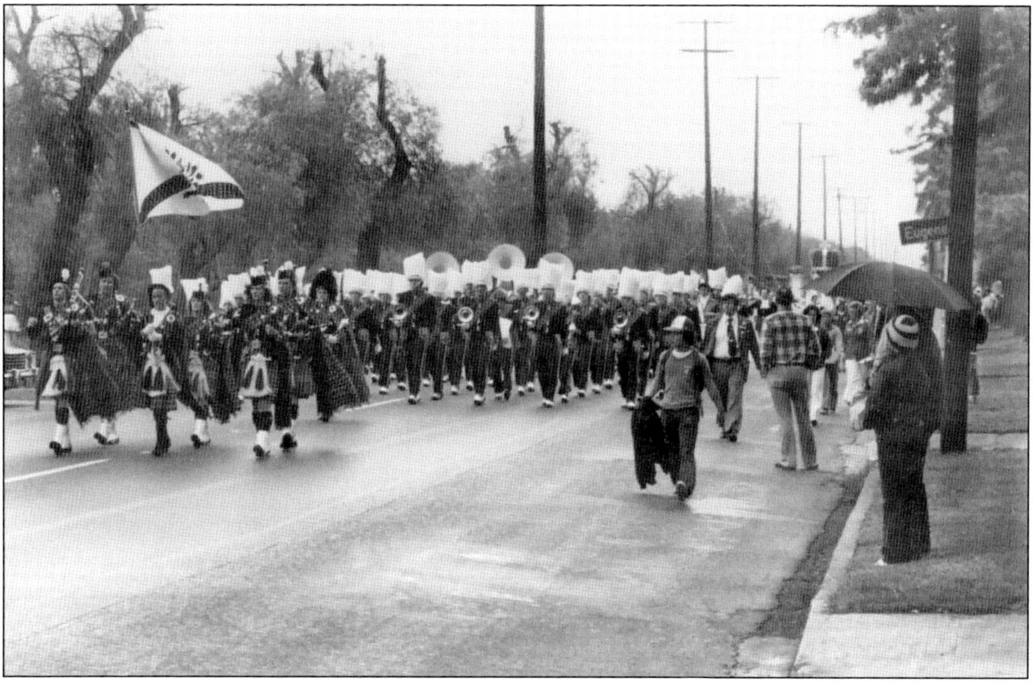

Bands and parades have continued to be an important part of entertainment in Upland, as is shown by this photograph of the Upland High School Highland Regiment taking part in the city's 75th anniversary parade in 1981.

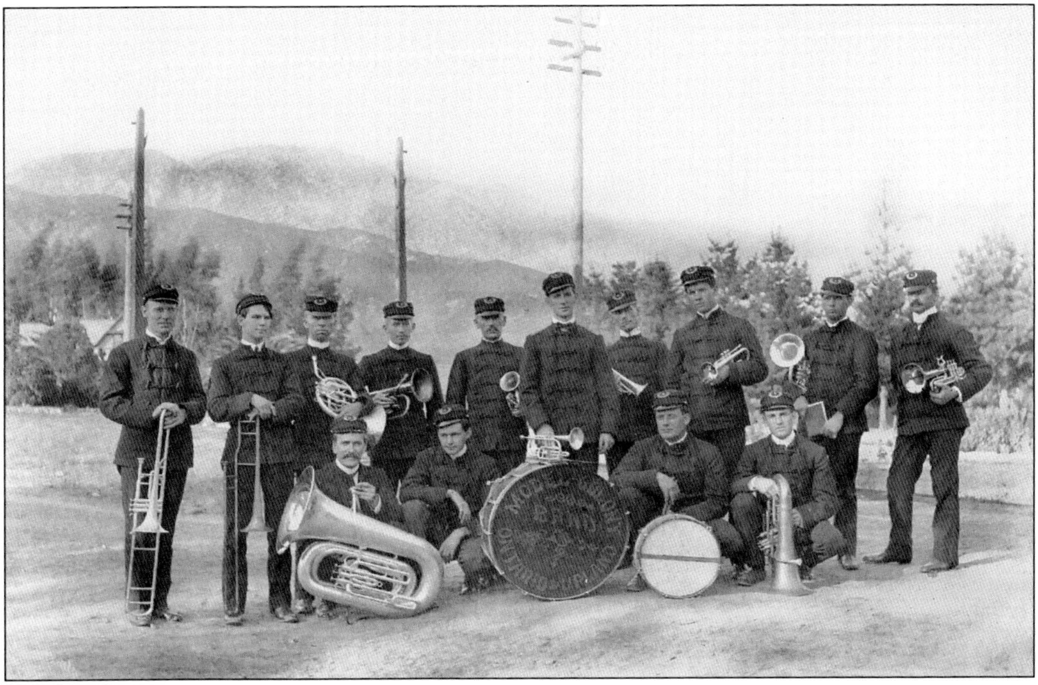

The Model Colony Band, directed by Fred Wilding Jr. in the early 1900s, included members from Upland.

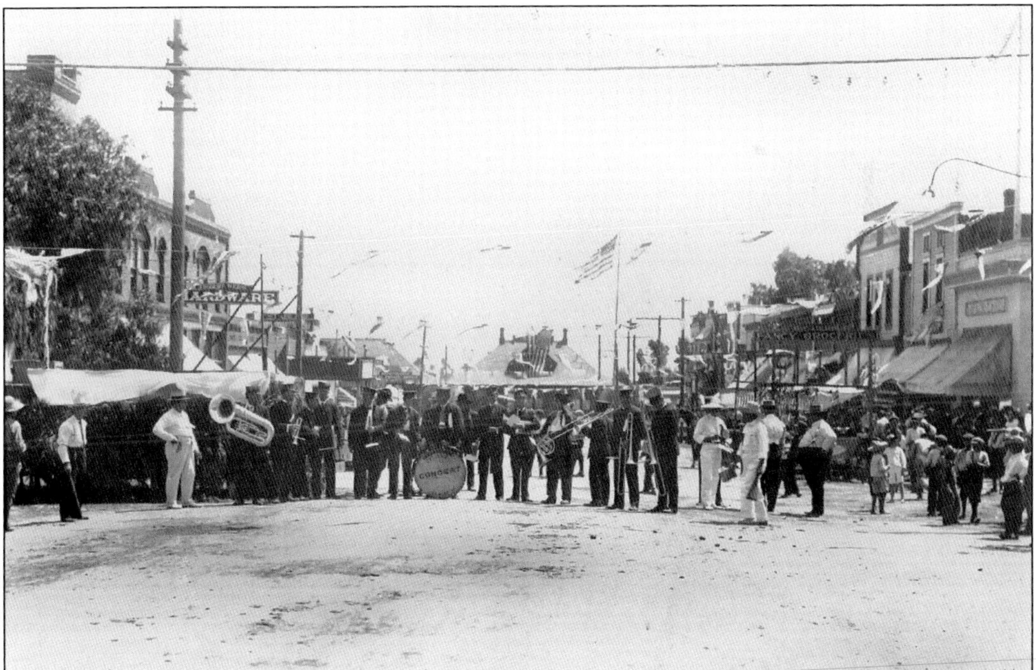

Fred Wilding Jr. also conducted the Upland Concert Band, seen here on Second Avenue in 1910. (UPL.)

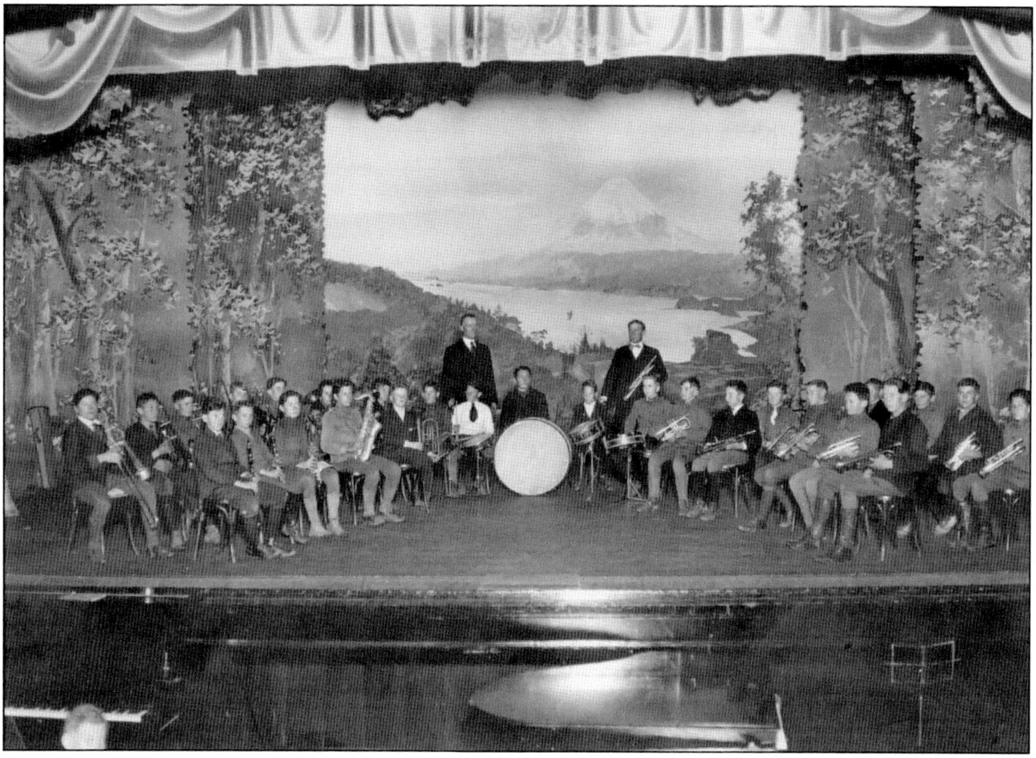

Another of Upland's bands from the past was the Boy Scout Band, seen here in 1920. The group was organized by Rev. R. C. Stone and was conducted by Fred Wilding Jr.

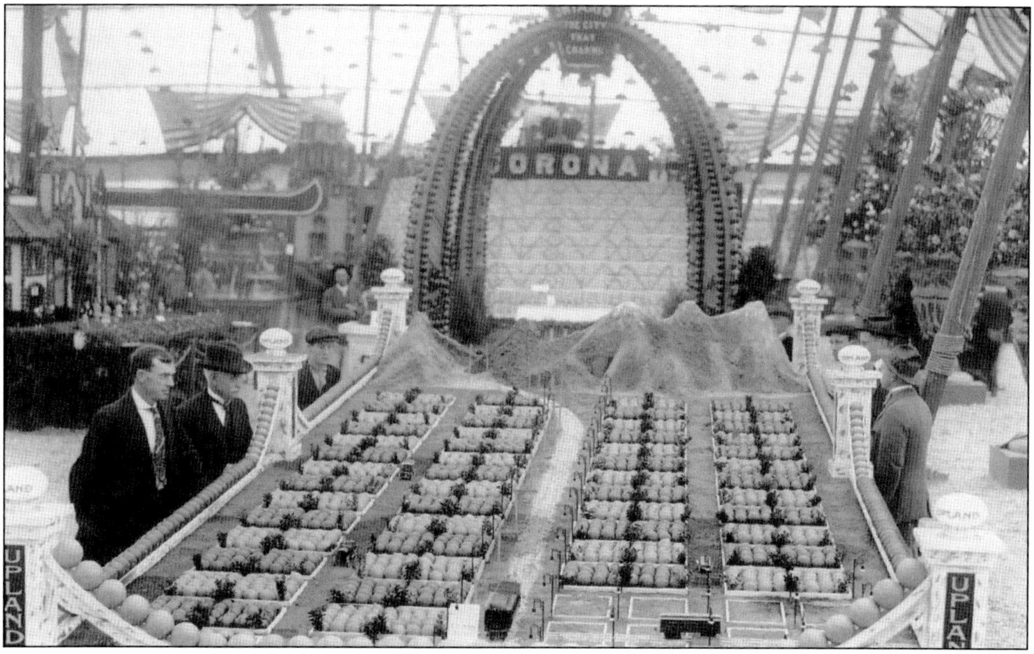


The residents of Upland had a good time helping create this float for an early 1900s celebration at the National Orange Show in San Bernardino.

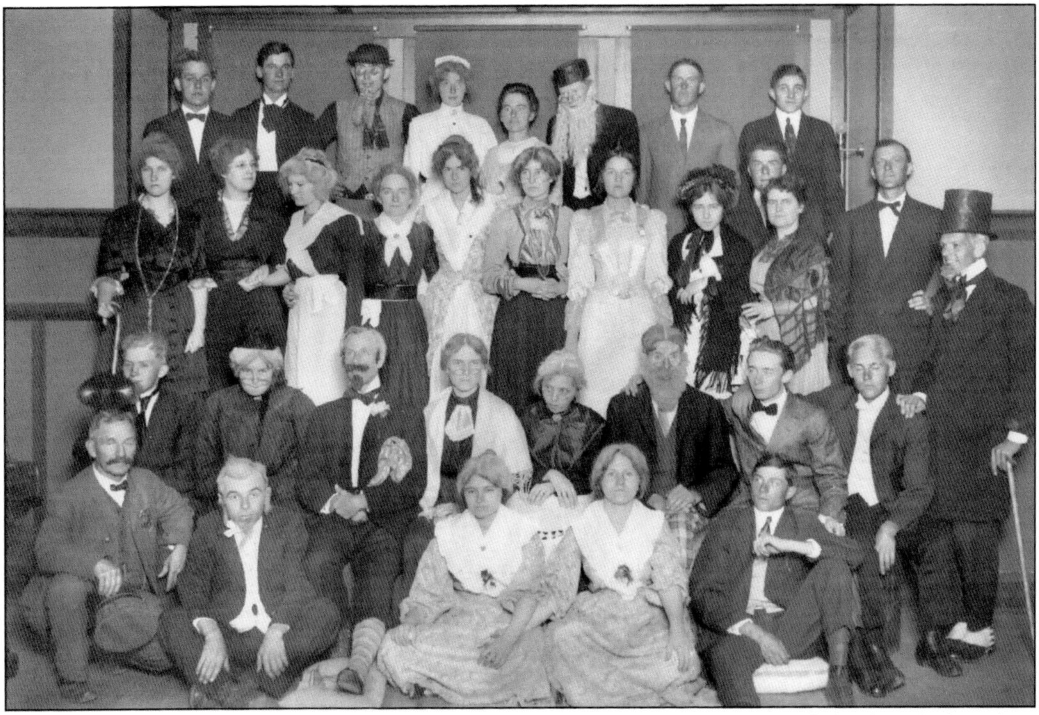

This early-1900s costumed group is ready for a night of fun at one of the local churches in town.

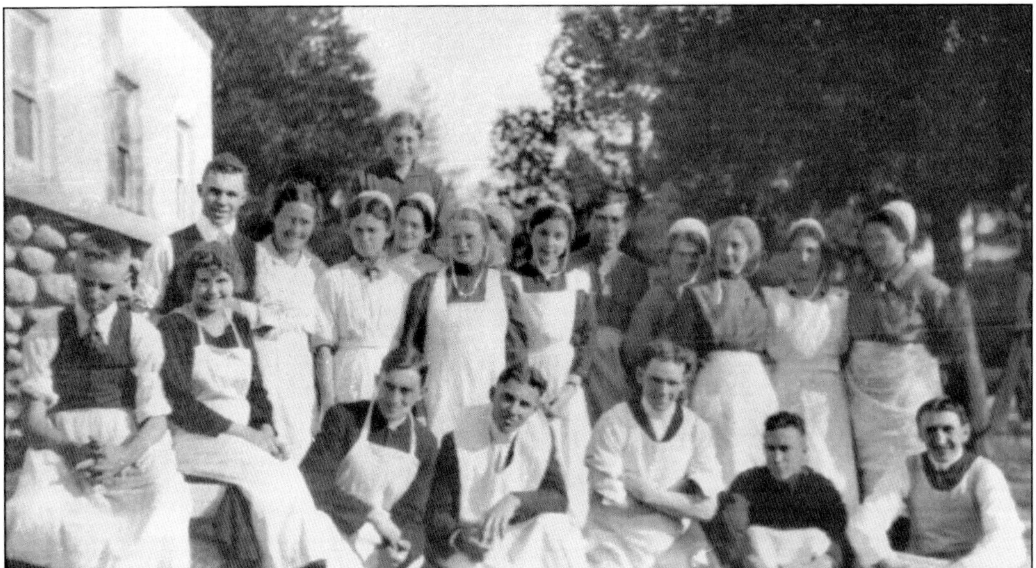

This group of Beulah College students has gathered together for a good time at the old school building on Third Avenue and F Street for the 1919 Brethren in Christ Church General Conference. (UPL.)

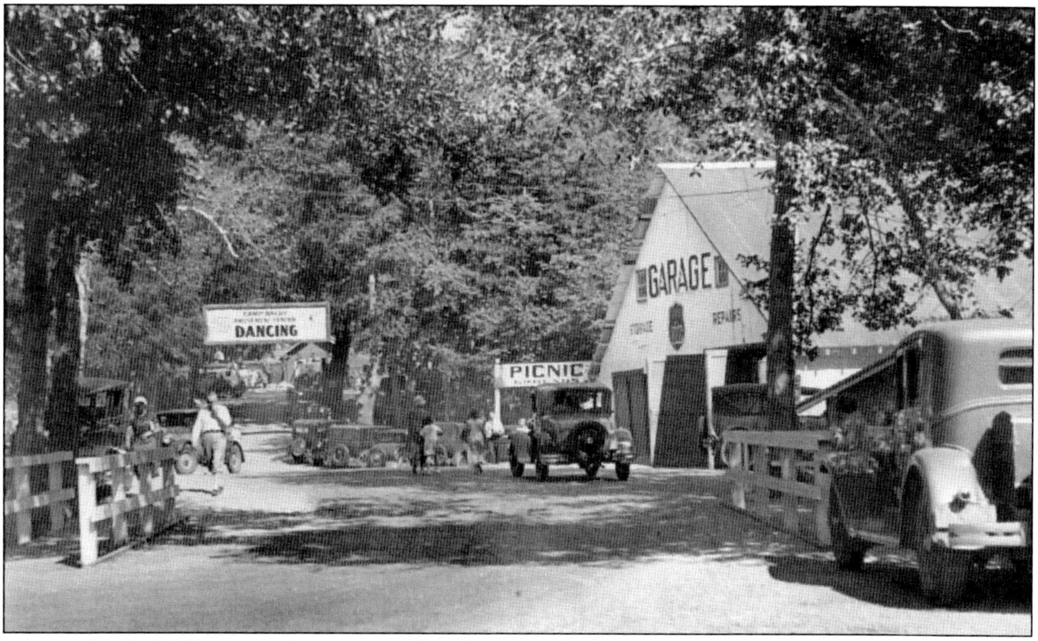


Mount Baldy Village has been a nearby place for Uplanders to spend some leisurely time in the cool mountains above the valley. This view shows Camp Baldy as it appeared before the devastating flood of 1938.

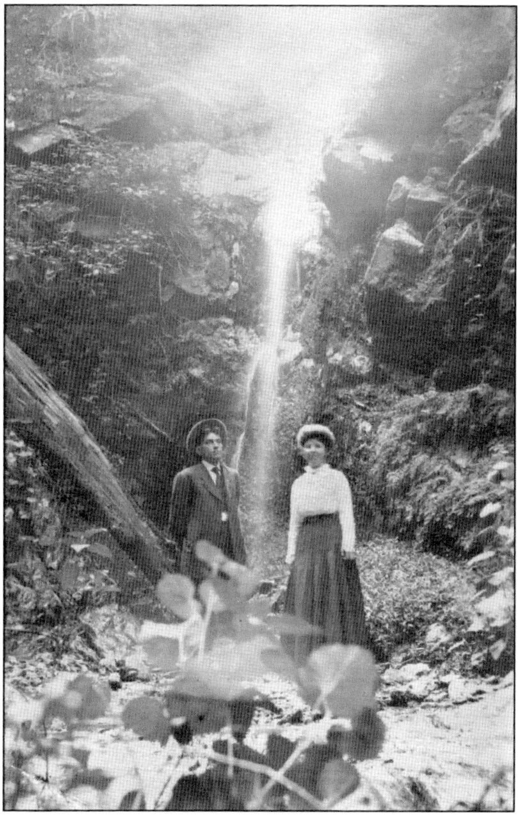

This early-1900s photograph shows a couple near the base of a waterfall in one of the canyons above Upland.

This group of three Upland hikers had a good time hiking to one of the falls in Cucamonga Canyon.

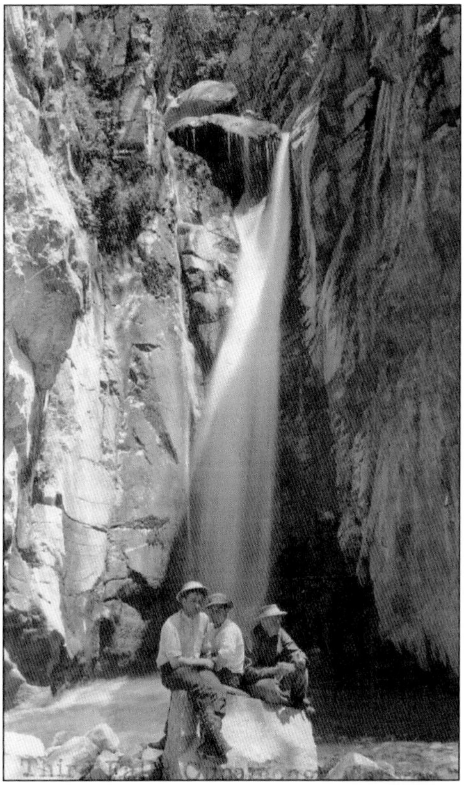

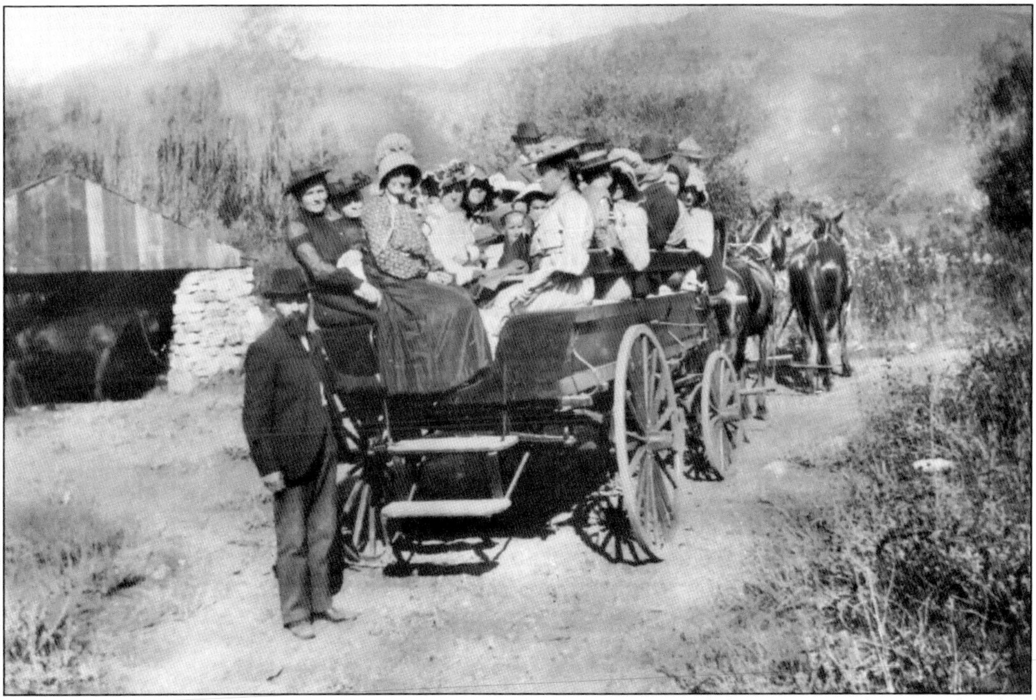

A group of day-trippers is heading out for a good time into one of the canyons above Upland in the 1890s.

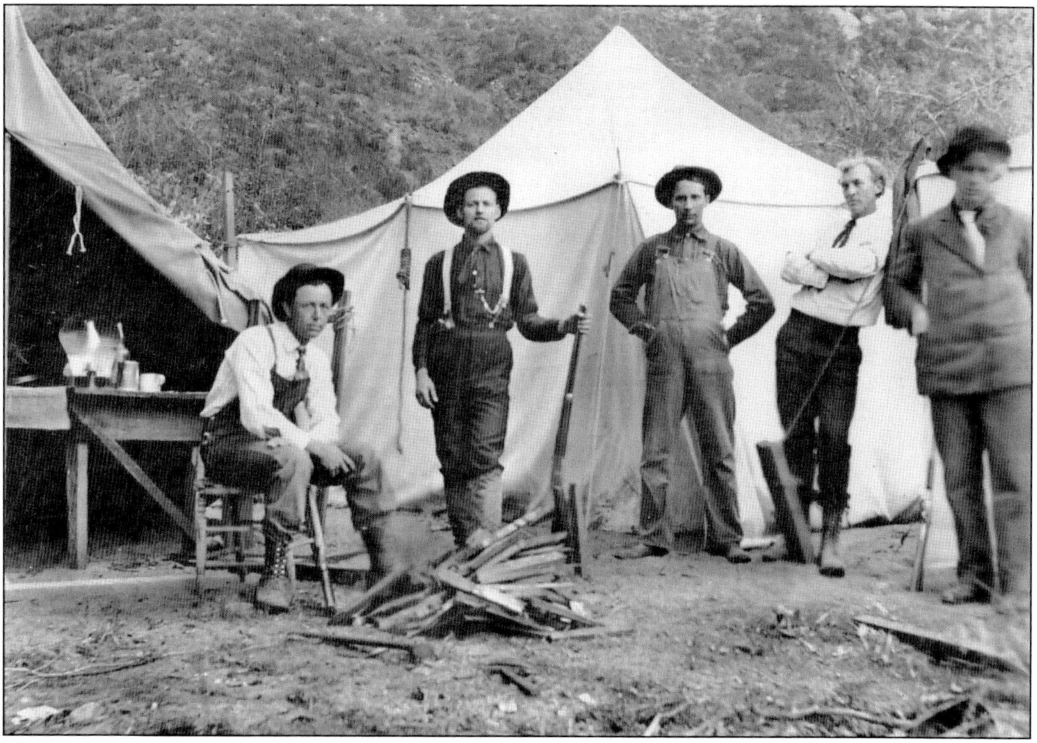

The canyons and mountain areas above Upland have provided numerous places to camp for many years. This group is enjoying a time roughing it during the 1890s. (UPL.)

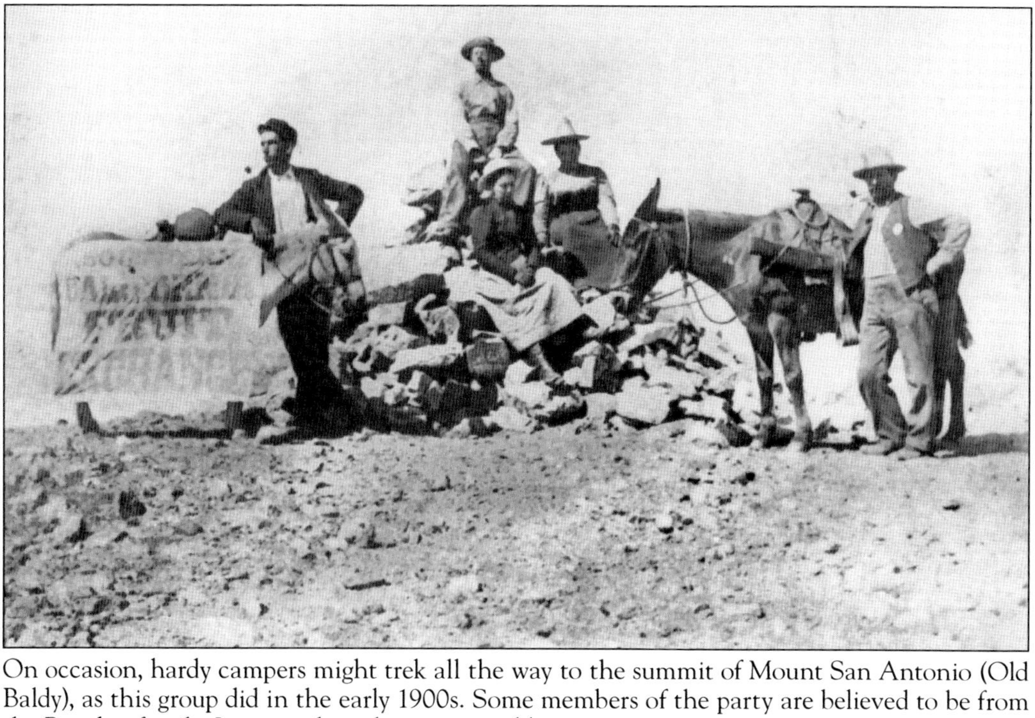

On occasion, hardy campers might trek all the way to the summit of Mount San Antonio (Old Baldy), as this group did in the early 1900s. Some members of the party are believed to be from the Bowden family. It seems they always enjoyed living in tents.

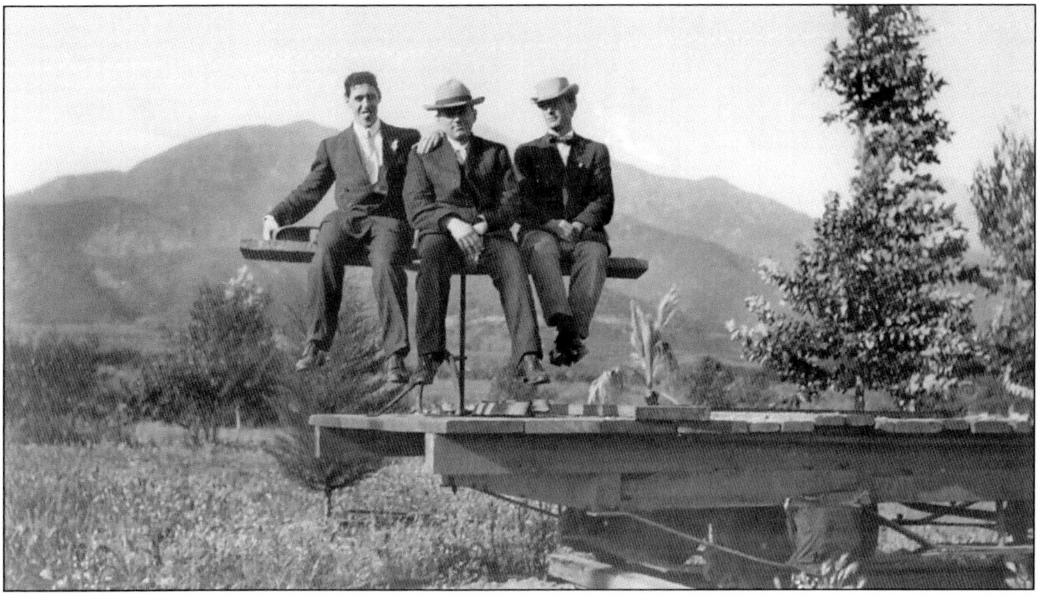

These three gentlemen were apparently out for a good time during the 1920s in the foothills of Upland. The man on the right is believed to be Mac McQuillen.

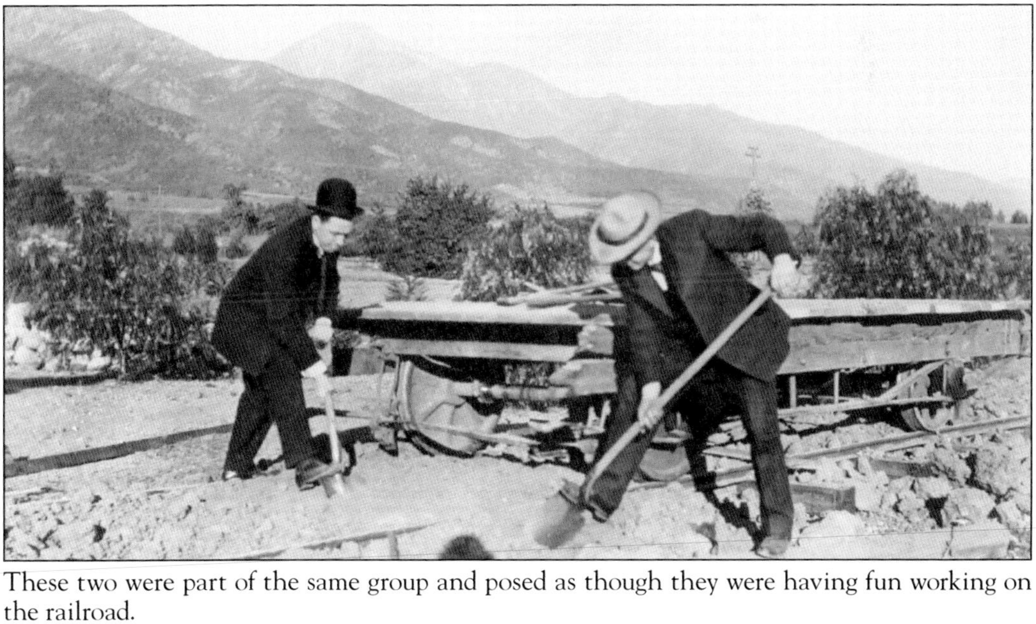

These two were part of the same group and posed as though they were having fun working on the railroad.

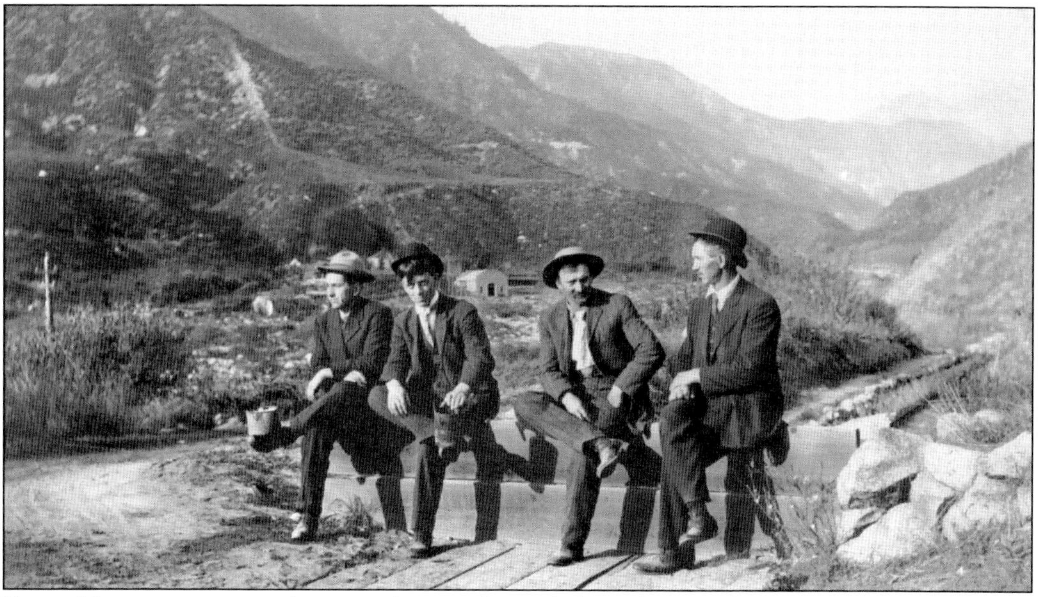

Four of the group apparently stopped to rest for a while at the mouth of San Antonio Canyon.

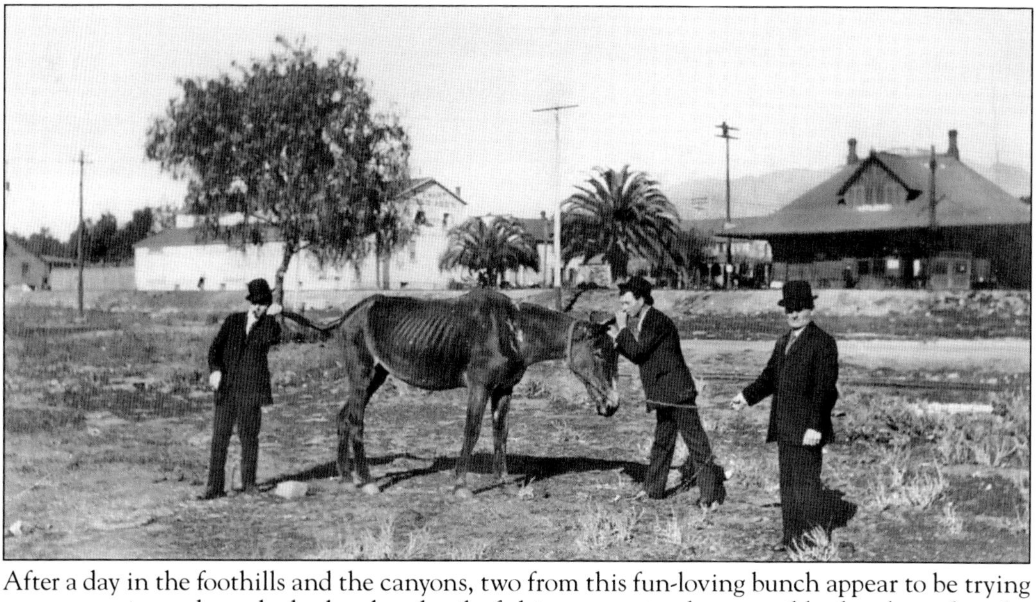

After a day in the foothills and the canyons, two from this fun-loving bunch appear to be trying to communicate through the head and tail of this poor animal, or possibly they have found a long-lost brother they have been looking for.

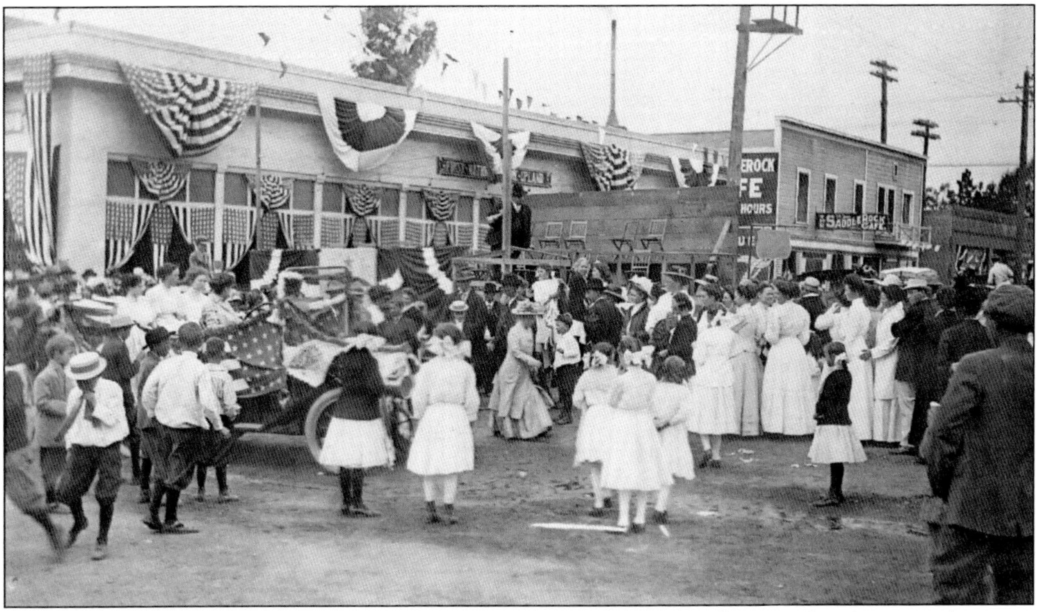

Fourth of July celebrations have been a part of the American way of having fun for more than two centuries. It is no different in Upland. In this early 1900s photograph, a crowd gathers downtown for one of those celebrations. (UPL.)

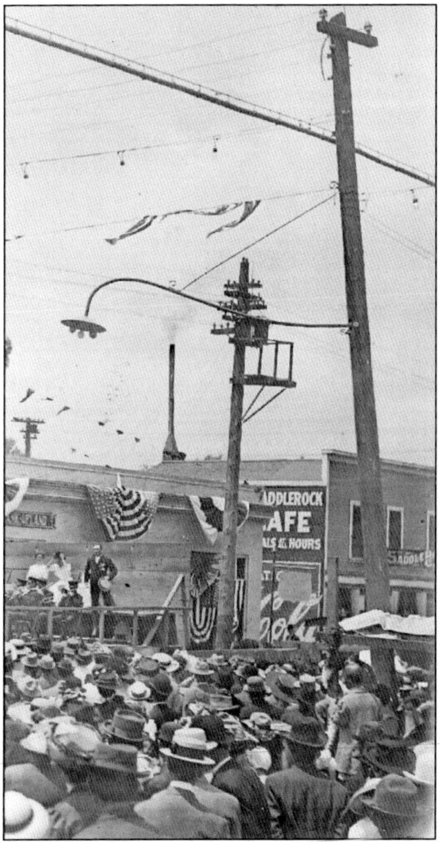

The same Fourth of July crowd continues to gather as dignitaries climb onto a platform in order to deliver patriotic speeches of the day. (UPL.)

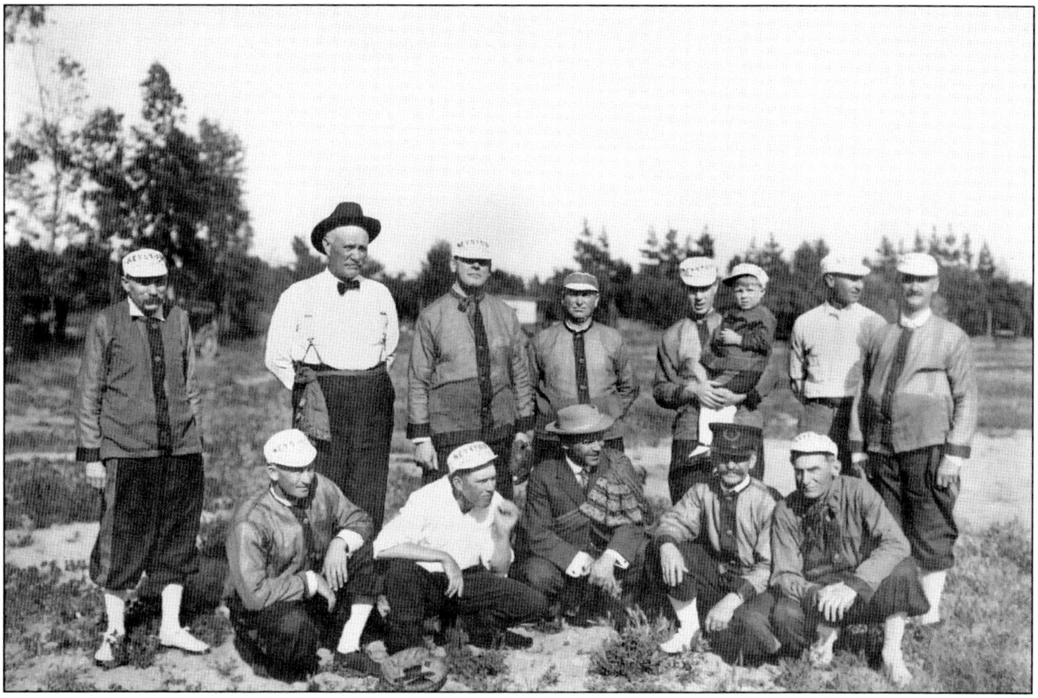

This 1920s baseball team was known as the Keystone Group. Baseball was a favorite pastime in Upland, and several teams were organized by business and civic groups.

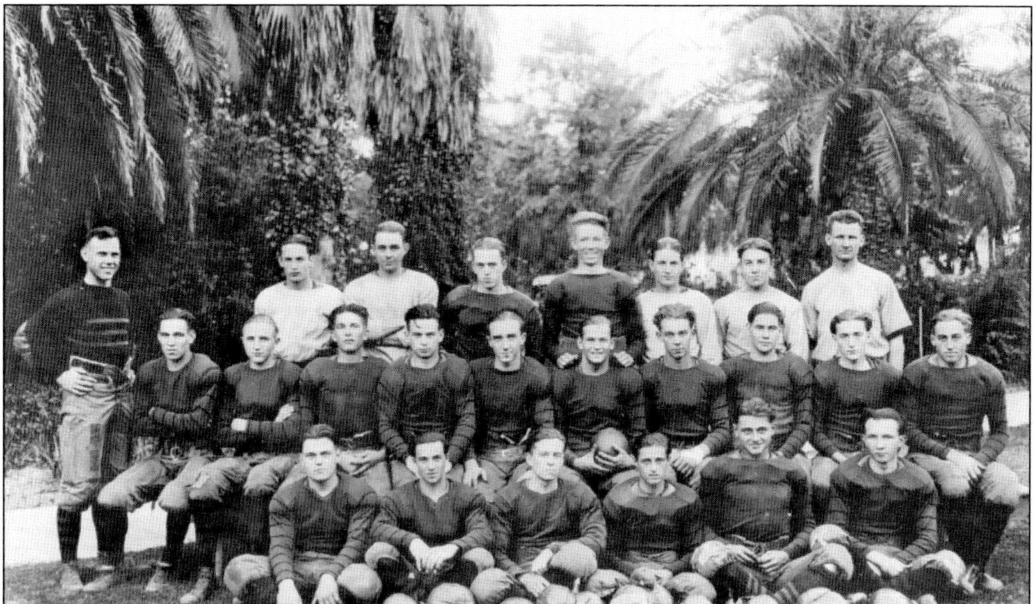

Friday and Saturday night high school football games have been a longtime part of the fun in and around Upland. The 1923–1924 Chaffey Union High School team is pictured with coaches Anson Smally (far left in uniform) and Fred Clapp (far right).

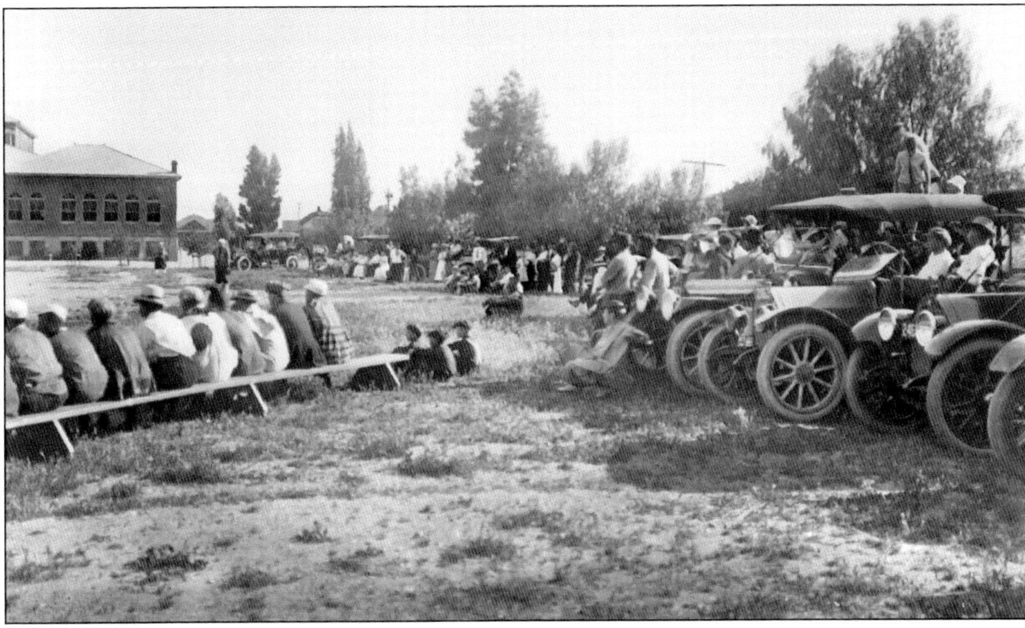

For this baseball game being played at Upland Grammar School in the 1920s, the fans were obviously allowed to drive right up to the field and make use of their automobiles as front-row seats. (UPL.)

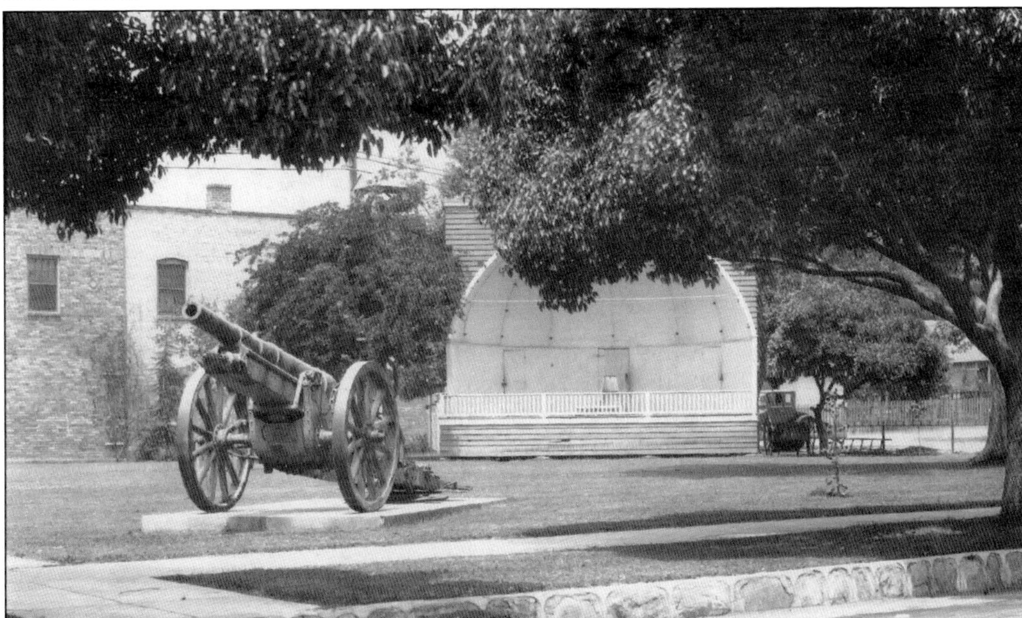

Parks have provided many hours of enjoyment to people throughout the years. Before Upland Memorial Park was established, Municipal Park stood at the corner of Third Avenue and C Street. This had been the gathering place for bond rallies and the victory celebration during World War I. The cannon, a captured German fieldpiece, was acquired as a result of a petition asking Congress to award some type of armament to Upland as a monument to the city's dedicated war efforts. It now sits at Memorial Park as a tribute to all veterans.

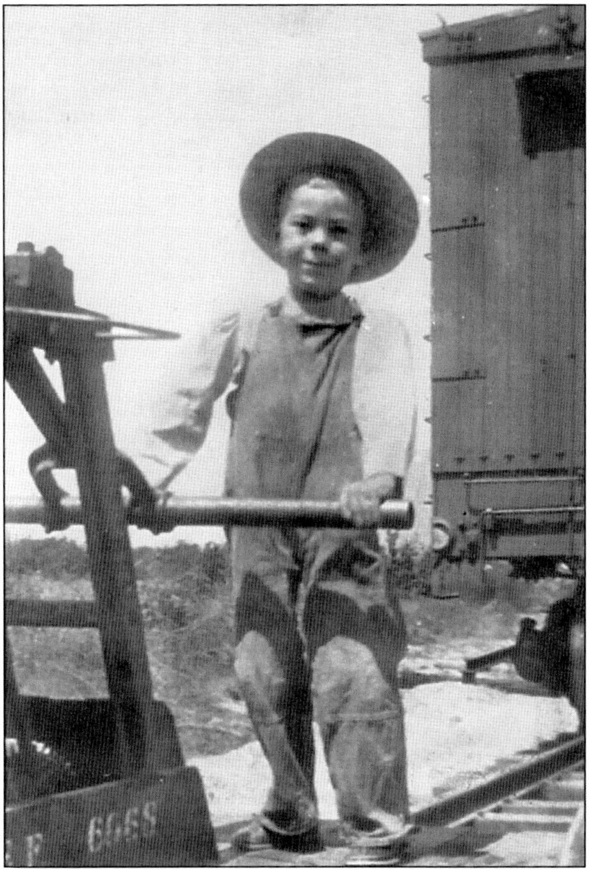

Isaac Studio was an early Upland photography business primarily noted for its outstanding studio portraits. In this photograph, however, the Isaac photographer caught this young boy in a playful mood on board a Santa Fe gandy dancer handcar.

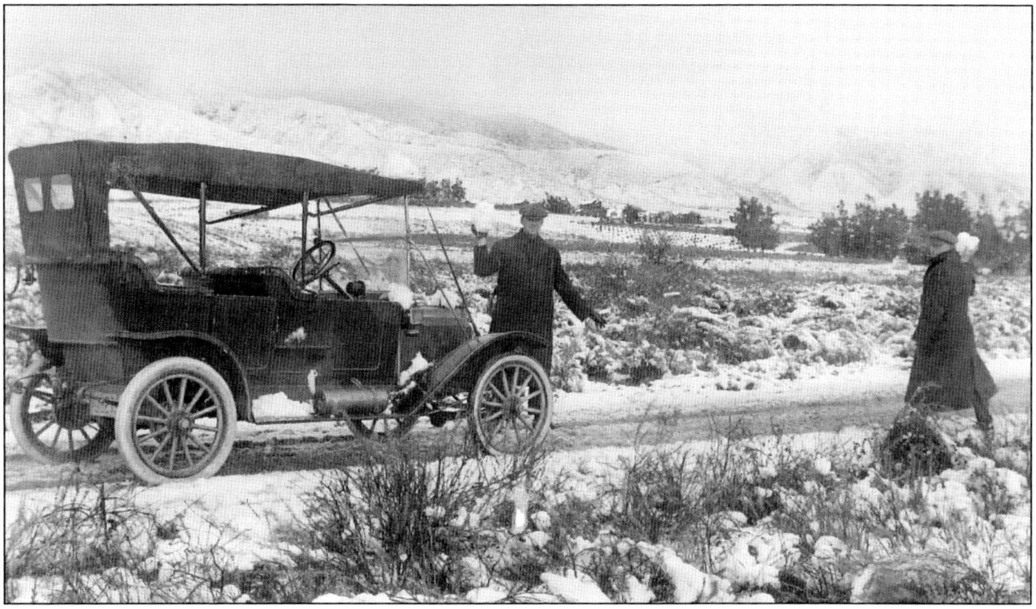

A good romp in the snow is always fun, and that is just what these two men are having in this 1915 photograph, taken at the top of Euclid Avenue.

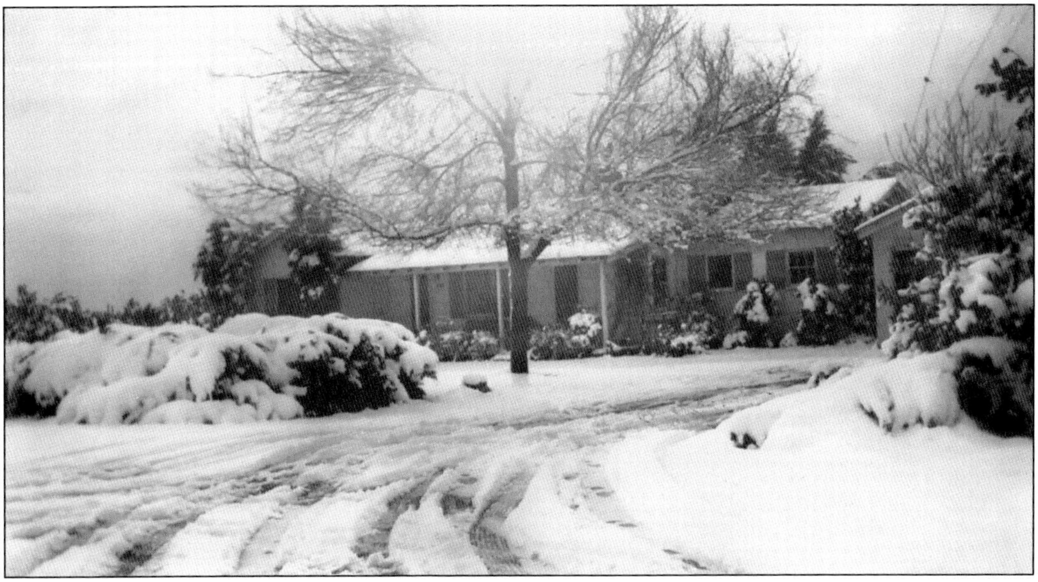

The night of January 11, 1949, brought a freak snowstorm that blanketed Southern California from the San Gabriel Mountains to the Pacific coastline and on to the peaks of Santa Catalina Island. This Upland home was typical of the sight residents awoke to in the morning.

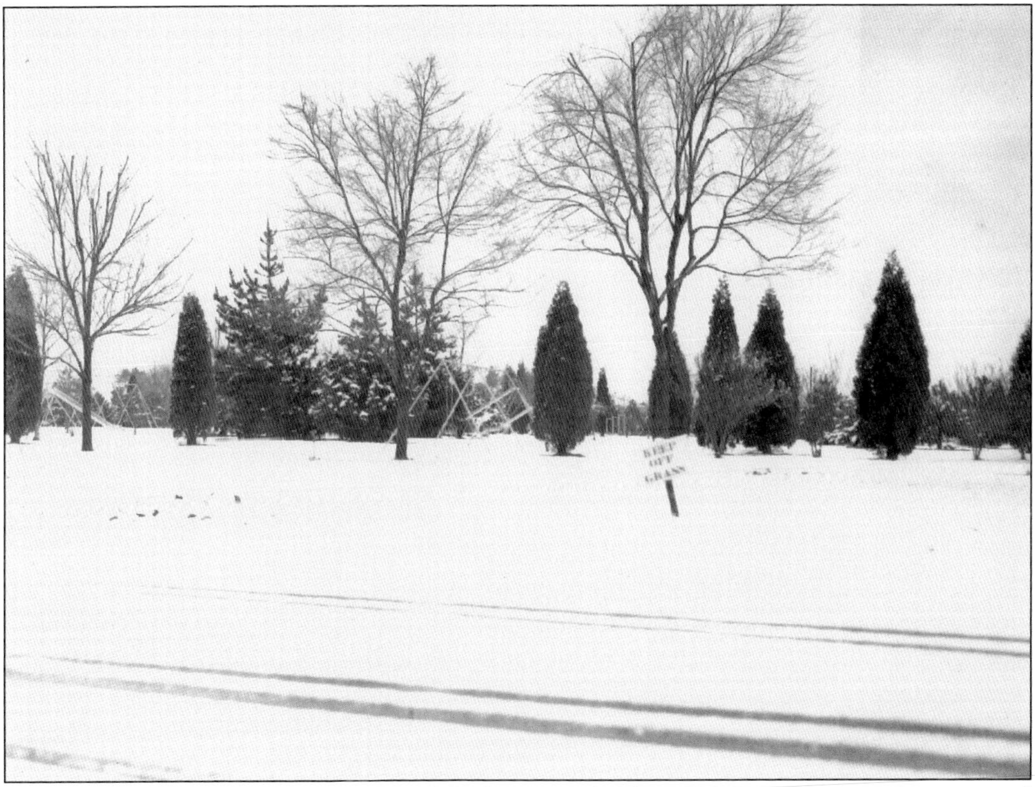

This "keep off grass" sign at Memorial Park was probably given no attention when a grand snowball fight most likely took place directly following the taking of this photograph of the 1949 snowstorm.

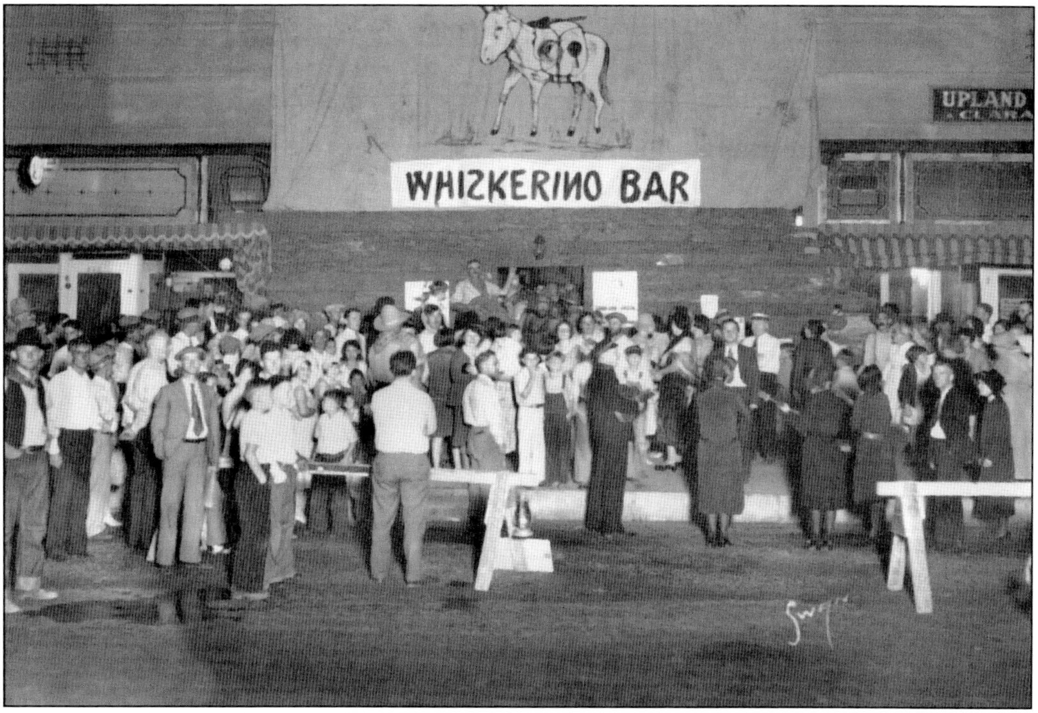

The Pioneer Days celebration of the 1930s brought great fun, especially when the Old Colonial Theater on Second Avenue was transformed into the Whiskerino Bar.

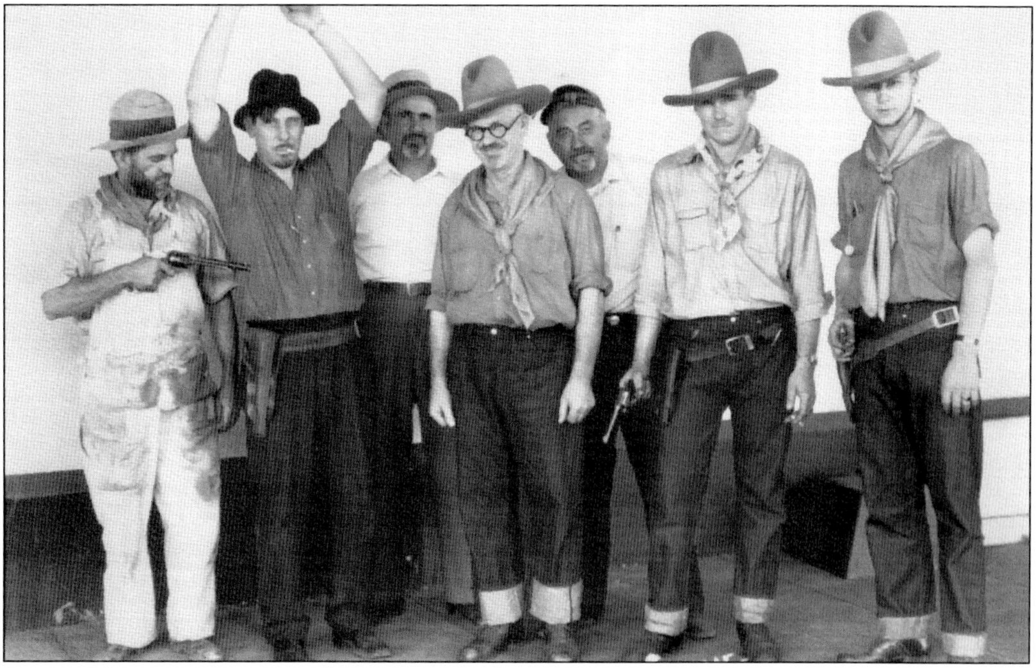
Some of the town's most noted citizens turned into "Whiskerinos" during Pioneer Days.

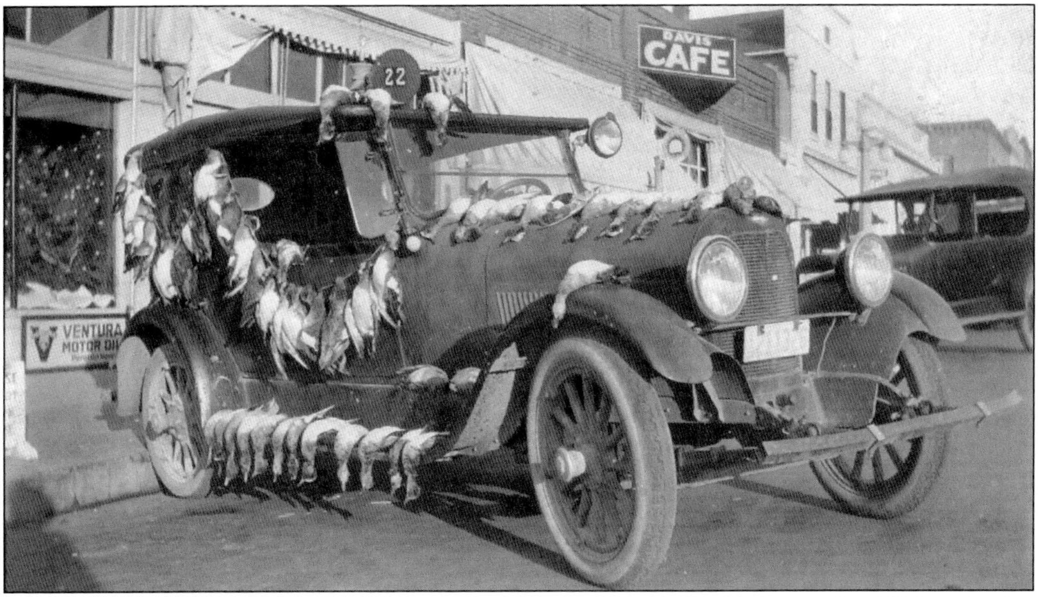

The Upland Red Hill Gun Club apparently participated in a parade during the 1920s with this automobile, as there is the number "22" (a staging number) attached to the top of the vehicle. The club members have adorned the car with some of the birds they bagged on a recent outing in the foothills.

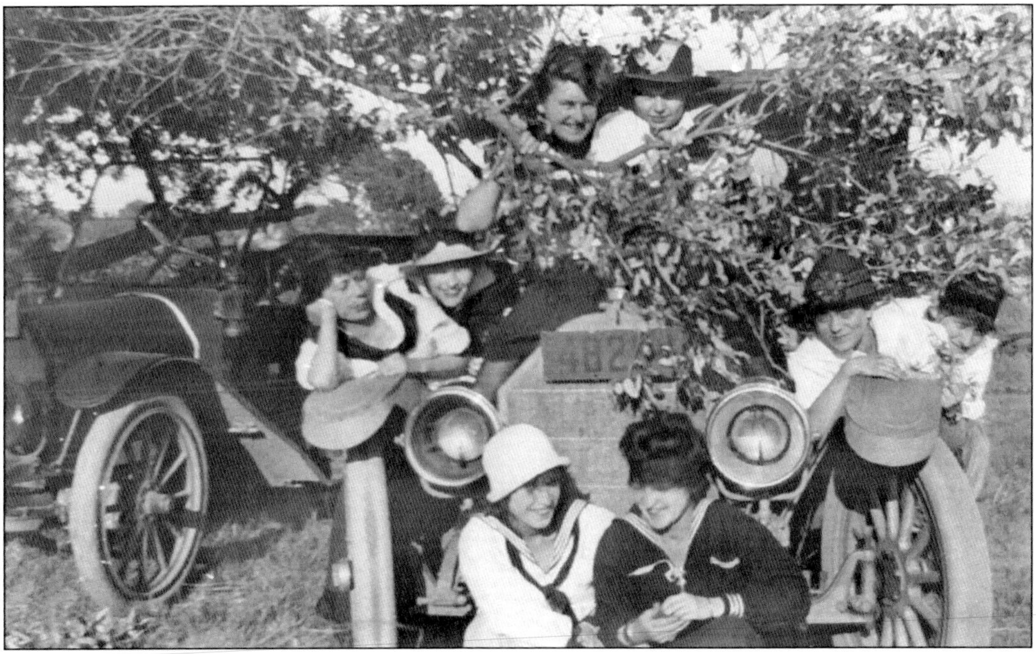
Some of Upland's girls, pictured in 1920, had a good time when they got together. Could that possibly be daddy's car?

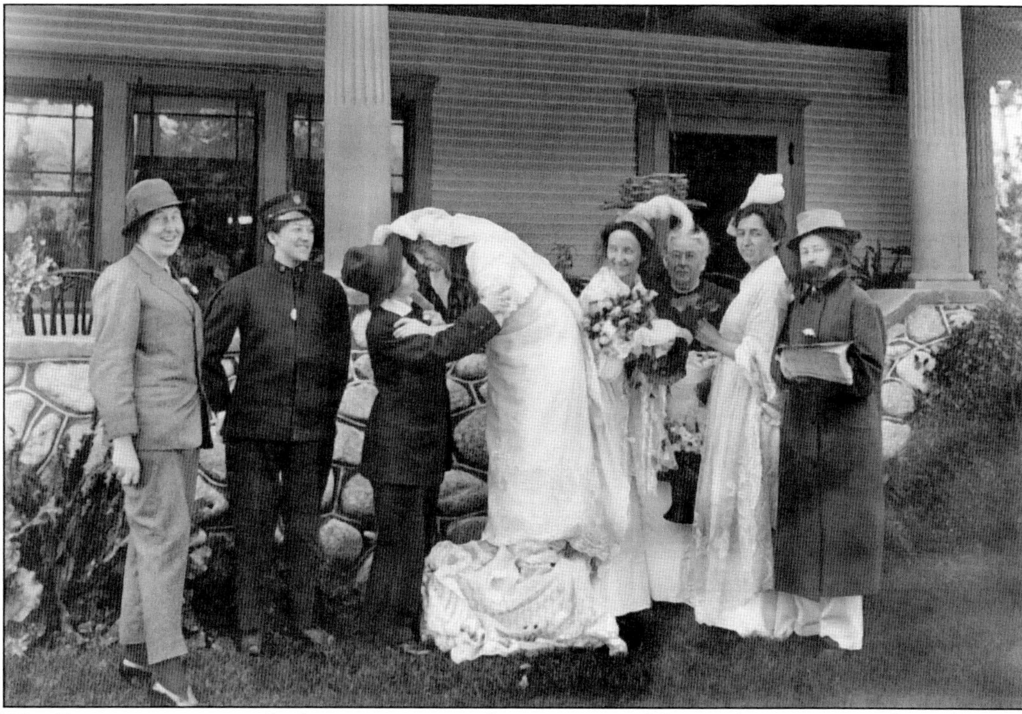

The Eymanns appear to be having a tremendous amount of fun with a 1920s mock wedding at their home on Washington Boulevard.

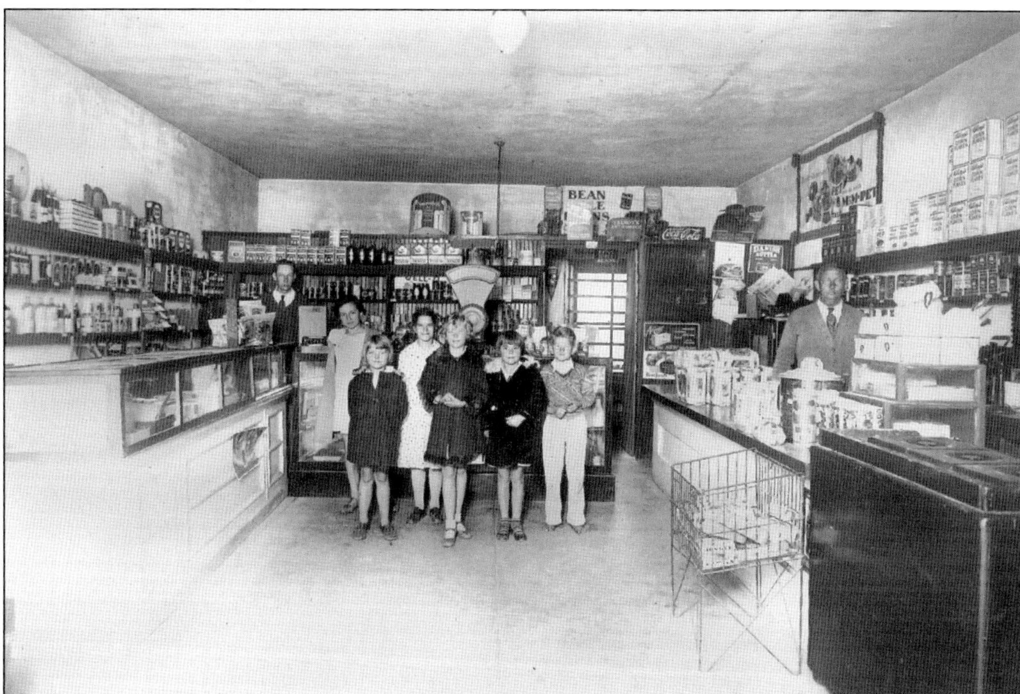

It was always fun to stop by Garoutte's Arrow service station on the way home from school to pick up some penny candy, as this 1932 photograph shows.

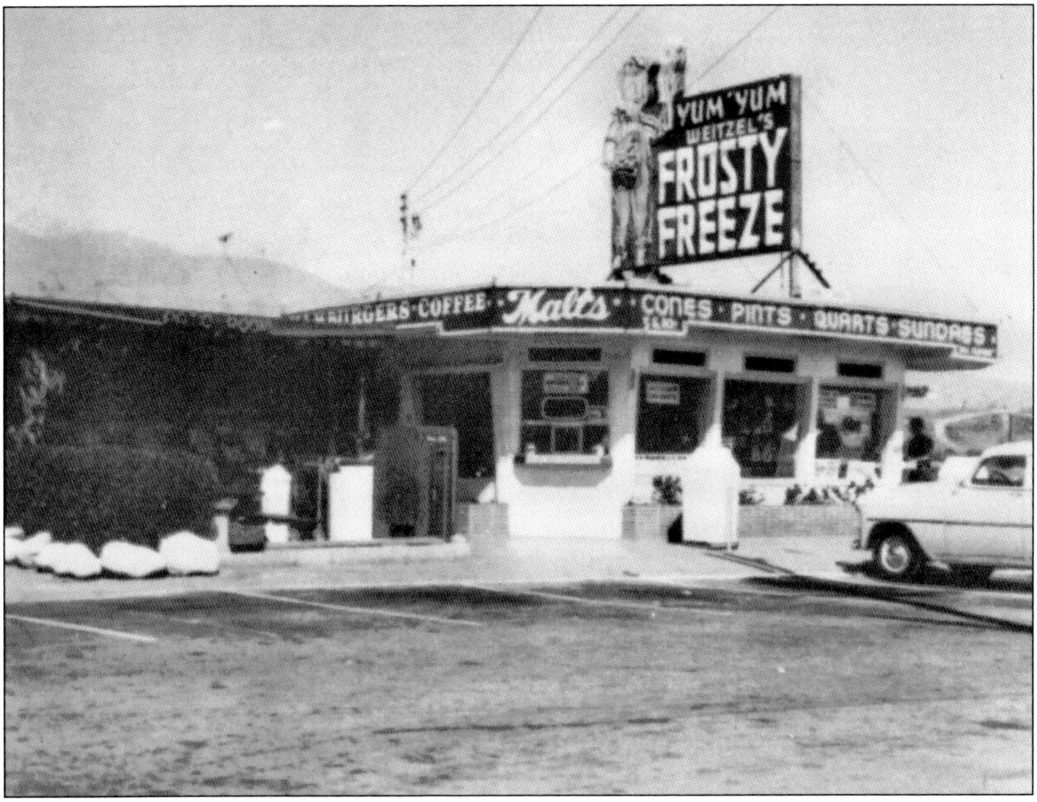


Weitzel's Yum Yum Frosty Freeze on Foothill Boulevard, seen here in 1955, was a favorite place to get a frosty cone or milkshake. (RDX.)

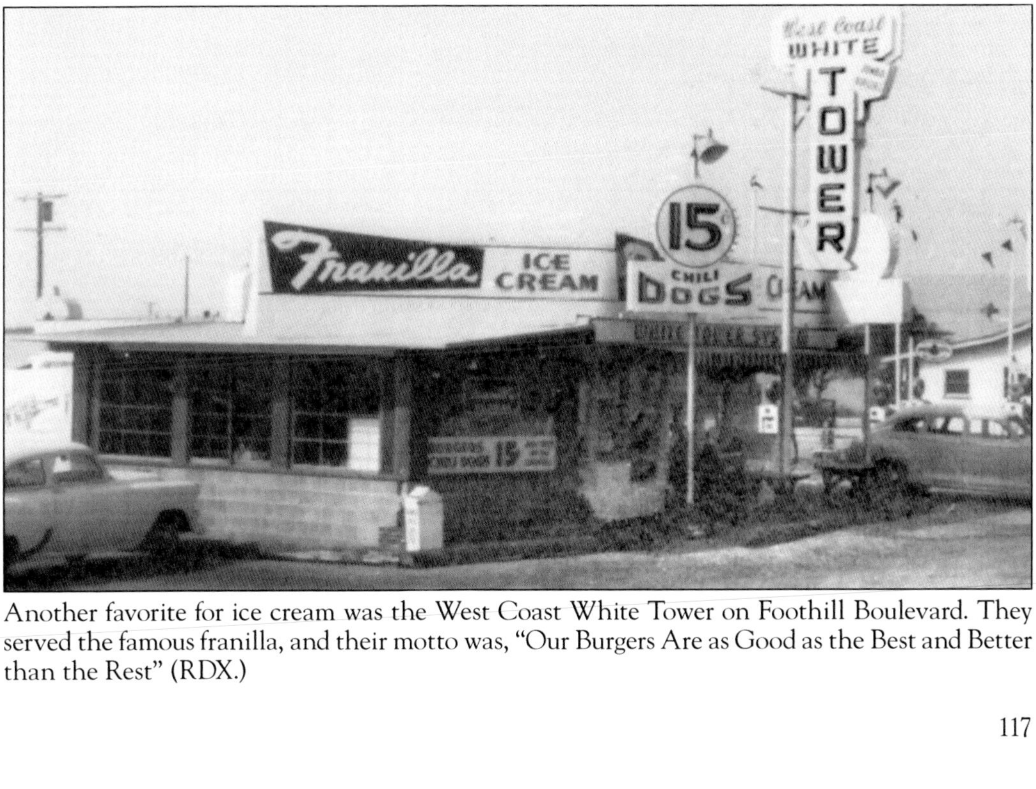


Another favorite for ice cream was the West Coast White Tower on Foothill Boulevard. They served the famous franilla, and their motto was, "Our Burgers Are as Good as the Best and Better than the Rest" (RDX.)

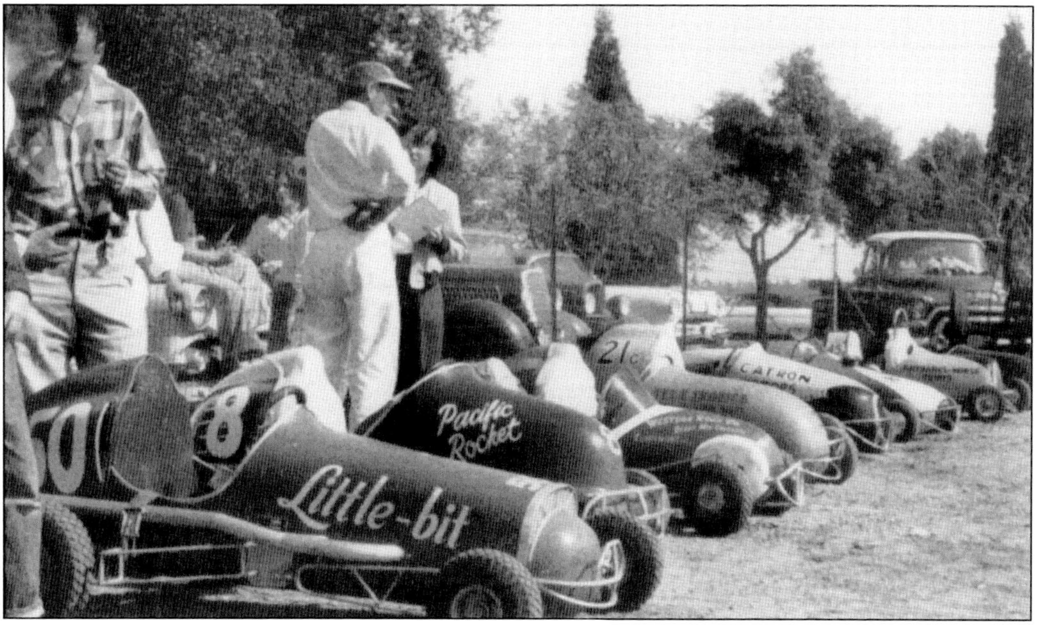


Not many people recall that there was at one time a midget automobile racetrack at Memorial Park. Proof that the races did exist is captured in this 1957 photograph, as would-be Indy drivers lined up for the Junior Midget Auto Races at the park. (UPL.)

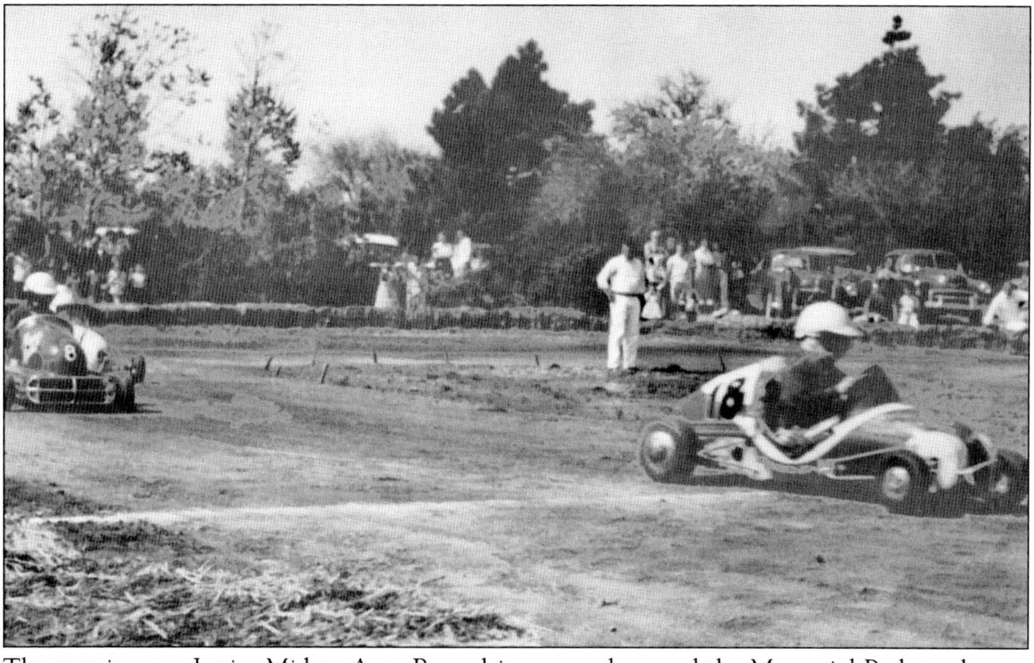

The race is on as Junior Midget Auto Race drivers speed around the Memorial Park track on a summer evening in 1957. Two-year-old Gena Higgins is standing in the white dress slightly to the right and to the rear of the official in the white outfit (center). Gena is now Gena Sizoo, senior library assistant of the Upland Public Library. Gena's father, Gene Higgins (white shirt) is standing to her right. Gena's grandparents, George and Goldie Kurtz, are standing just behind and to Gene's right. (UPL.)

# *Seven*

# Capturing the Image of the Town

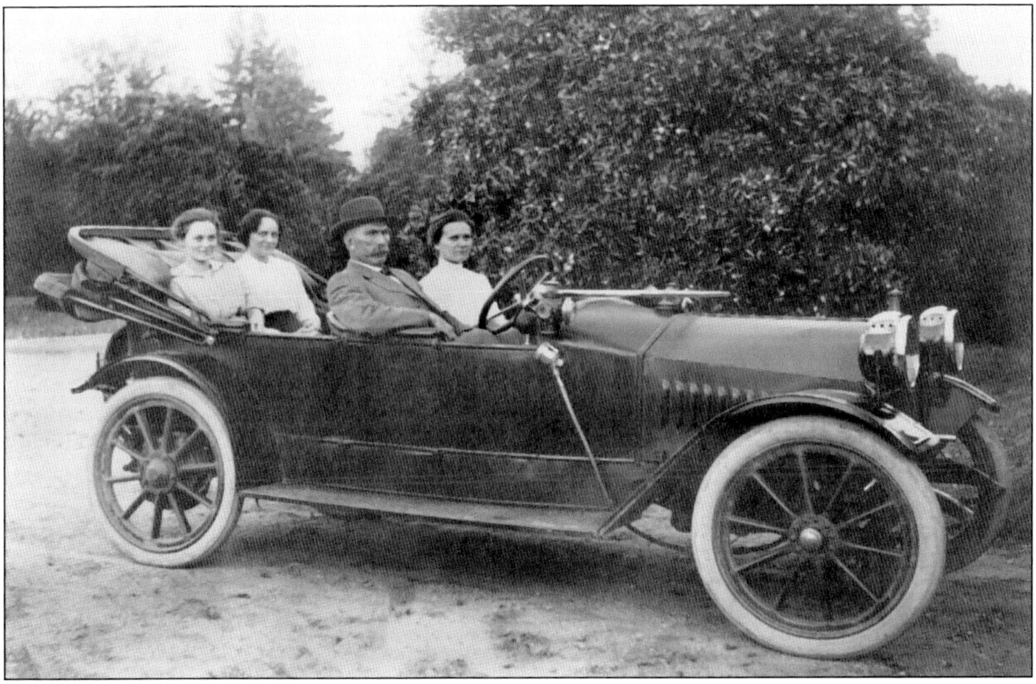

Some of the pictures on the preceding pages were taken by Upland's most noted photographer, Edna Swan. Fortunately for the city, she has provided a valuable photographic record of its history. In this 1912 photograph, Edna (right rear seat) is still a student at Chaffey Union High School. She rides in the family's first automobile, a Hupmobile, with her parents, George and Etta West, and her sister, Ora Dappen.

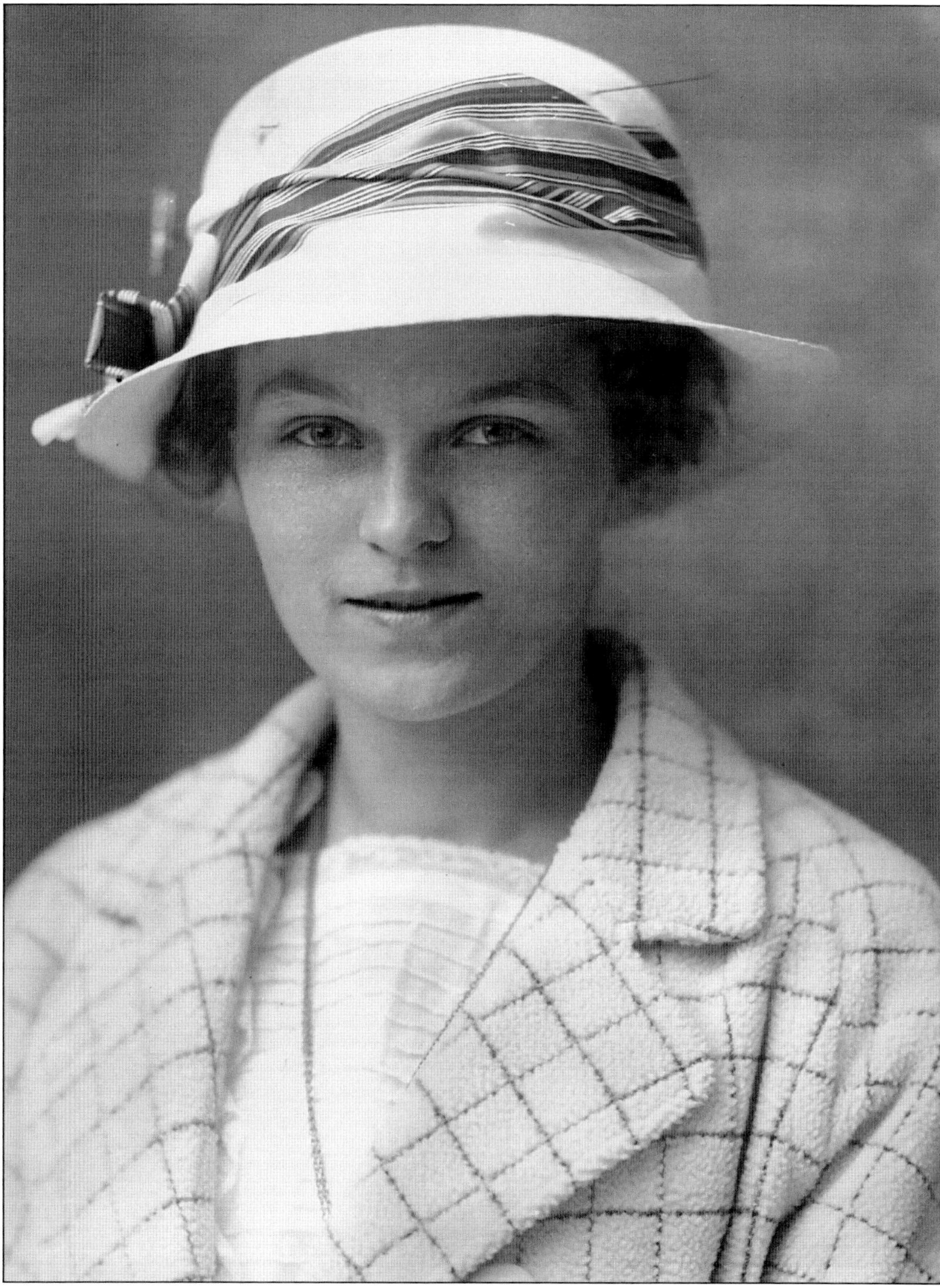

Edna West Swan poses in her honeymoon dress on her wedding day in 1915. Edna was usually on the opposite side of the camera, taking photographs of Upland's townspeople, neighborhoods, and events. On this grand occasion, the photographer was her new groom, Earle Swan. Together the couple operated a photography business until their separation in 1924. Edna continued with the business until her retirement in 1959.

Earle and Edna Swan stand outside the front of their first photography studio, which opened for business in 1915. It was located next to the Old Colonial Arts Theatre on Second Avenue.

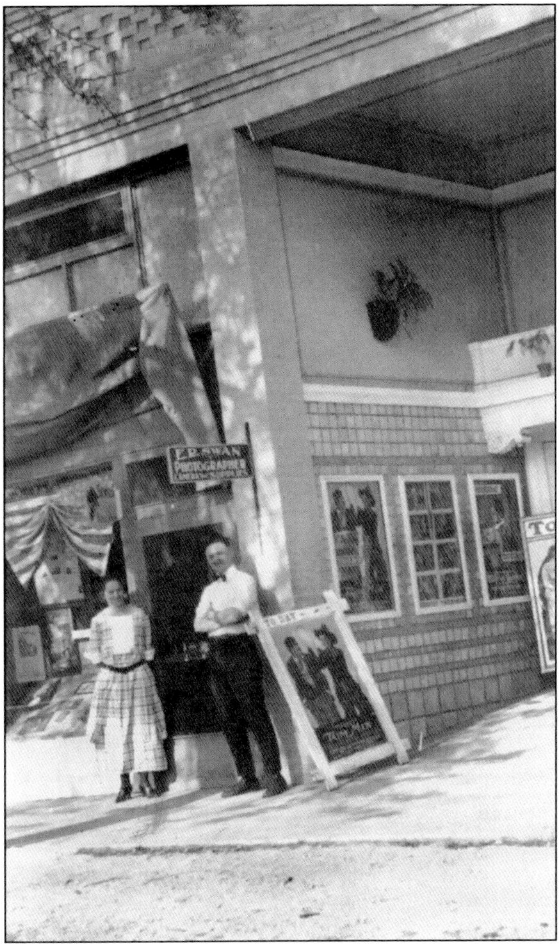


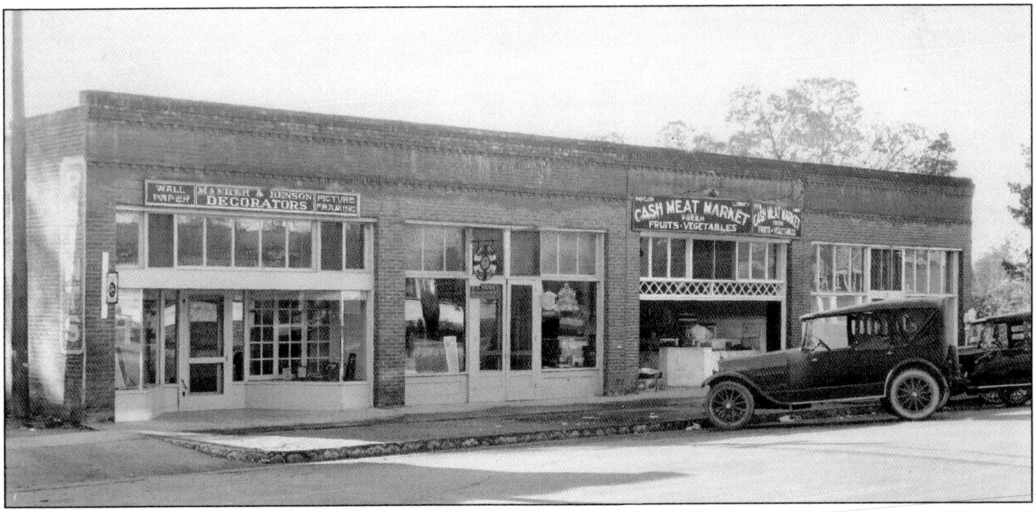


The Swans later moved their business to the south side of Ninth Street between First and Second Avenues. The studio is the second store from the left in this photograph and was renamed Swannie's Music and Art Shop.

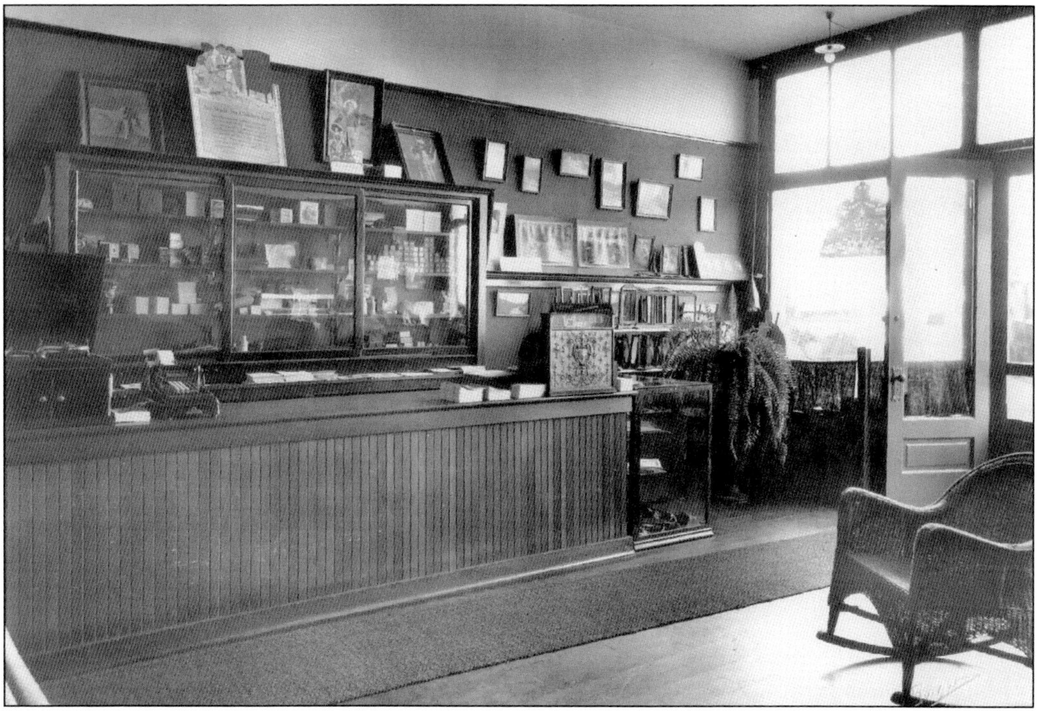

This is an interior view of Swannie's Music and Art Shop on Ninth Street.

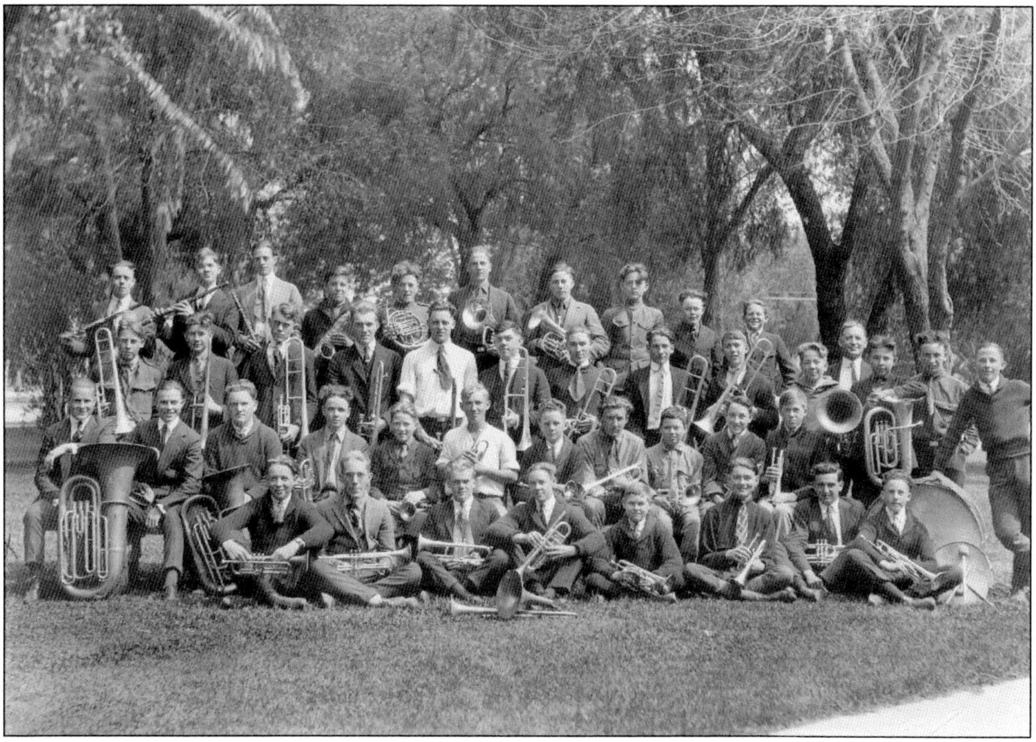

Edna enjoyed photographing anything in town that had something to do with community involvement and entertainment. This 1920s photograph is of the Upland Concert Band. (UPL.)

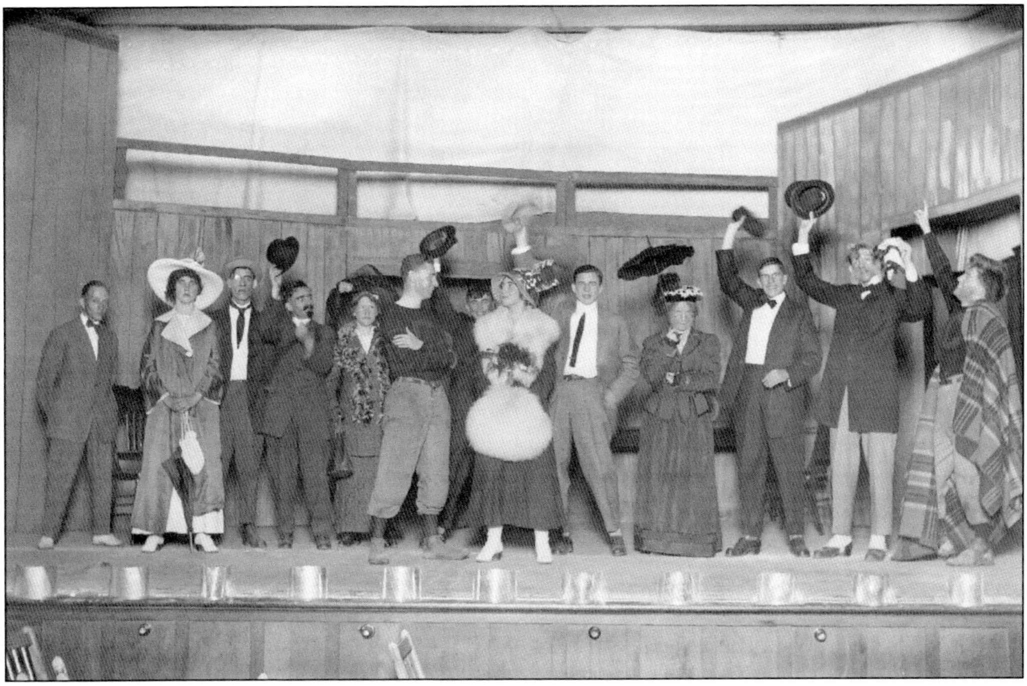

Another of Edna Swan's favorite groups was the Chaffey Union High School Drama team. Here is the cast of the 1914 senior class play.

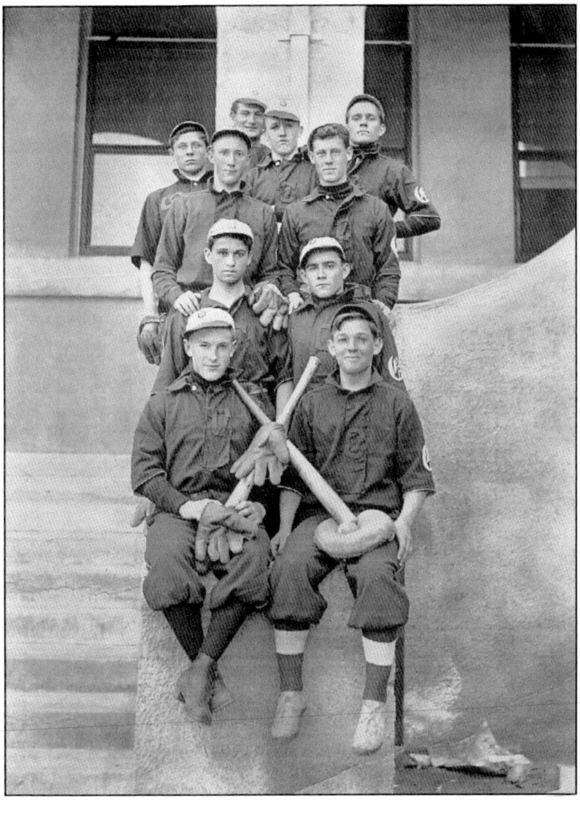

Edna Swan photographed the 1910 Chaffey Union High School baseball team when she was a part of the *Fasti* yearbook staff.

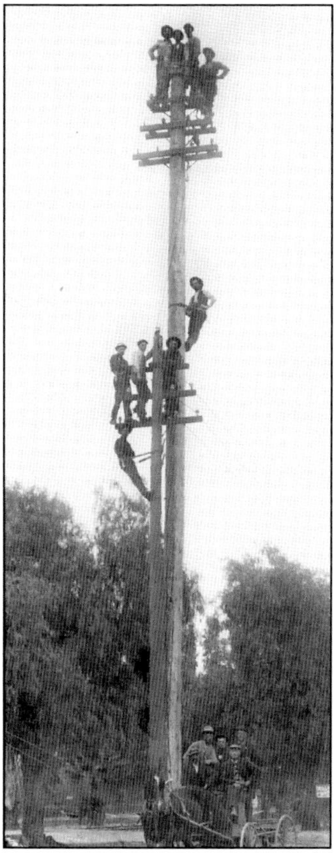

In this early photograph, Edna has captured some of the Ontario Power Company workmen up a pole on Euclid Avenue. (UPL.)

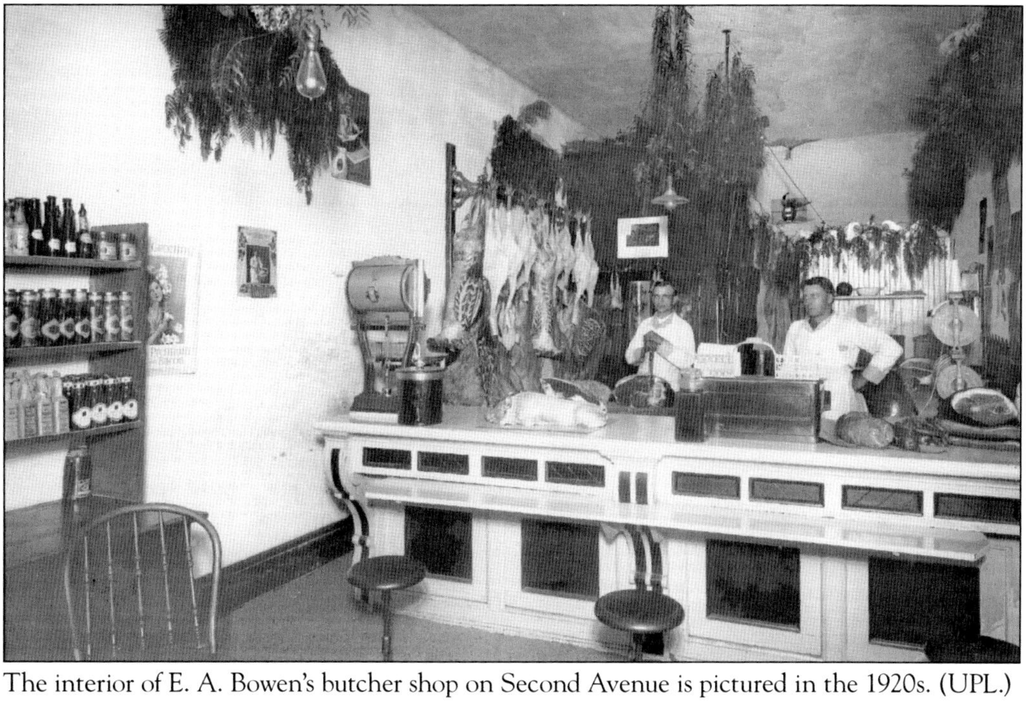

The interior of E. A. Bowen's butcher shop on Second Avenue is pictured in the 1920s. (UPL.)

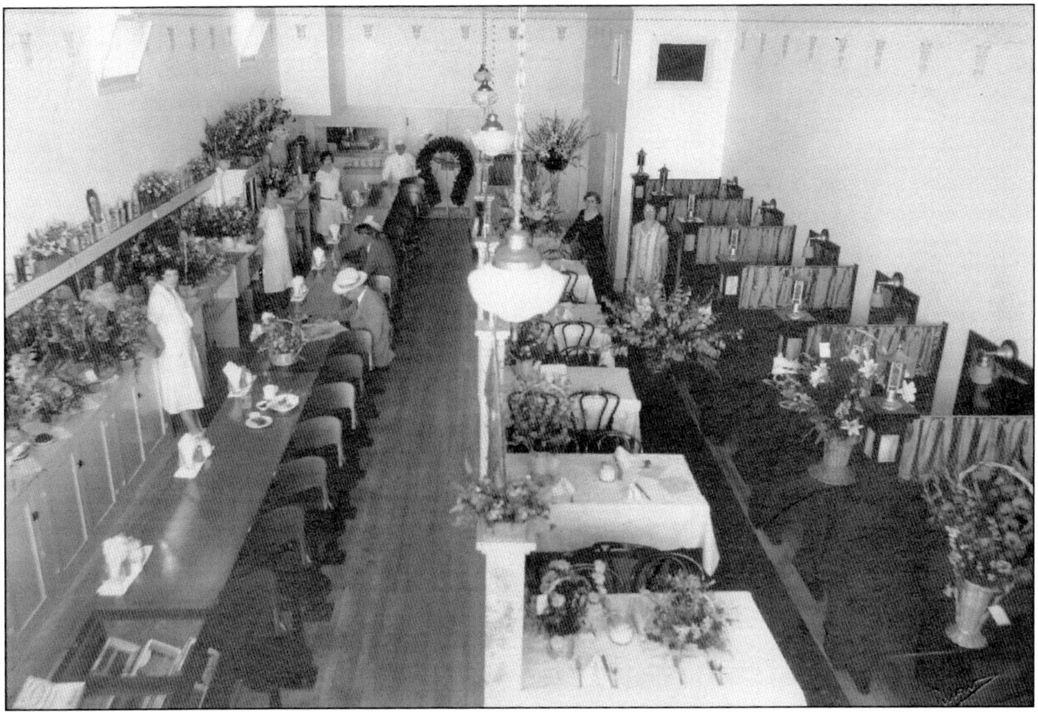

Judging from the numerous floral bouquets, it appears that Edna took this photograph on opening day at the Davis Café on Second Avenue. (UPL.)

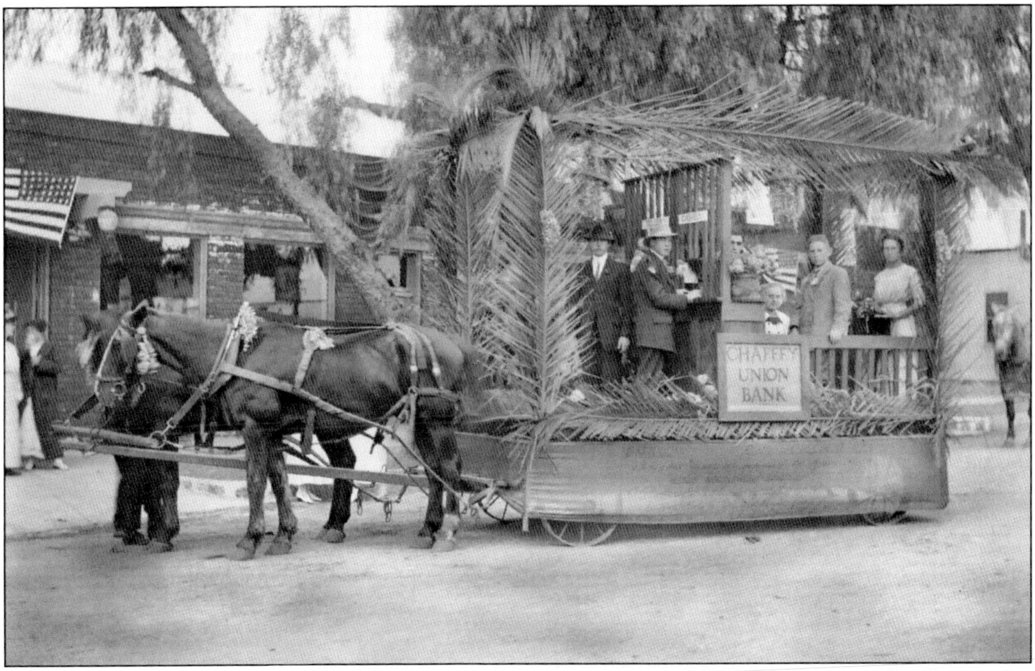


Edna took this photograph of the Chaffey Union Bank's entry in a 1912 parade. The flag in the background is probably a new one, as the canton appears to contain 48 stars. In 1912, Arizona was admitted as the 48th state.

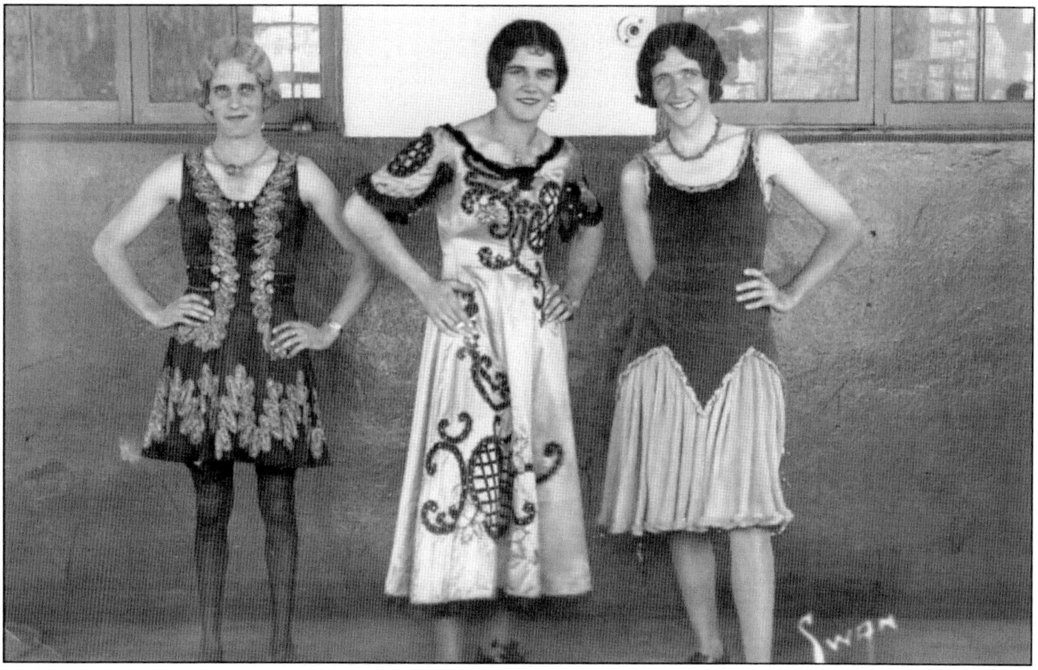


Edna Swan captured these boys getting all dolled up for the 1930 Pioneer Days Pageant. From left to right are Dorsey Glover, Pete Benton, and Ray Flickinger.

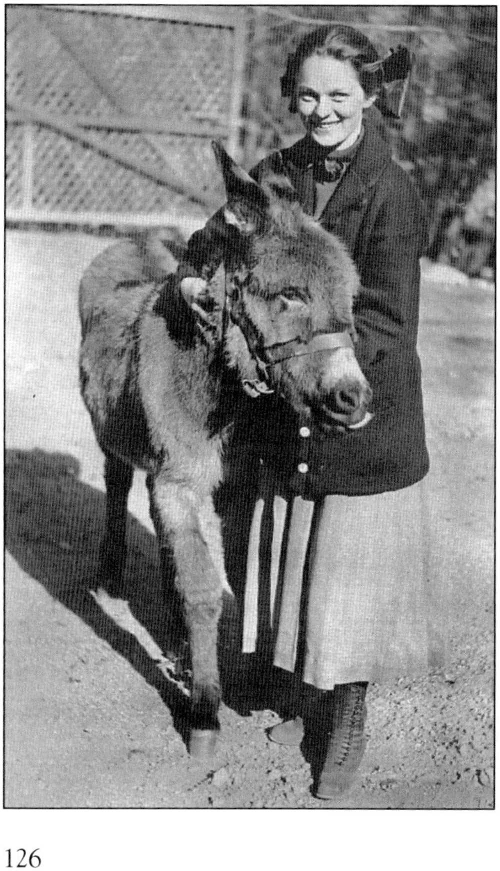

Edna is seen here with a friend at Camp Baldy about 1915.

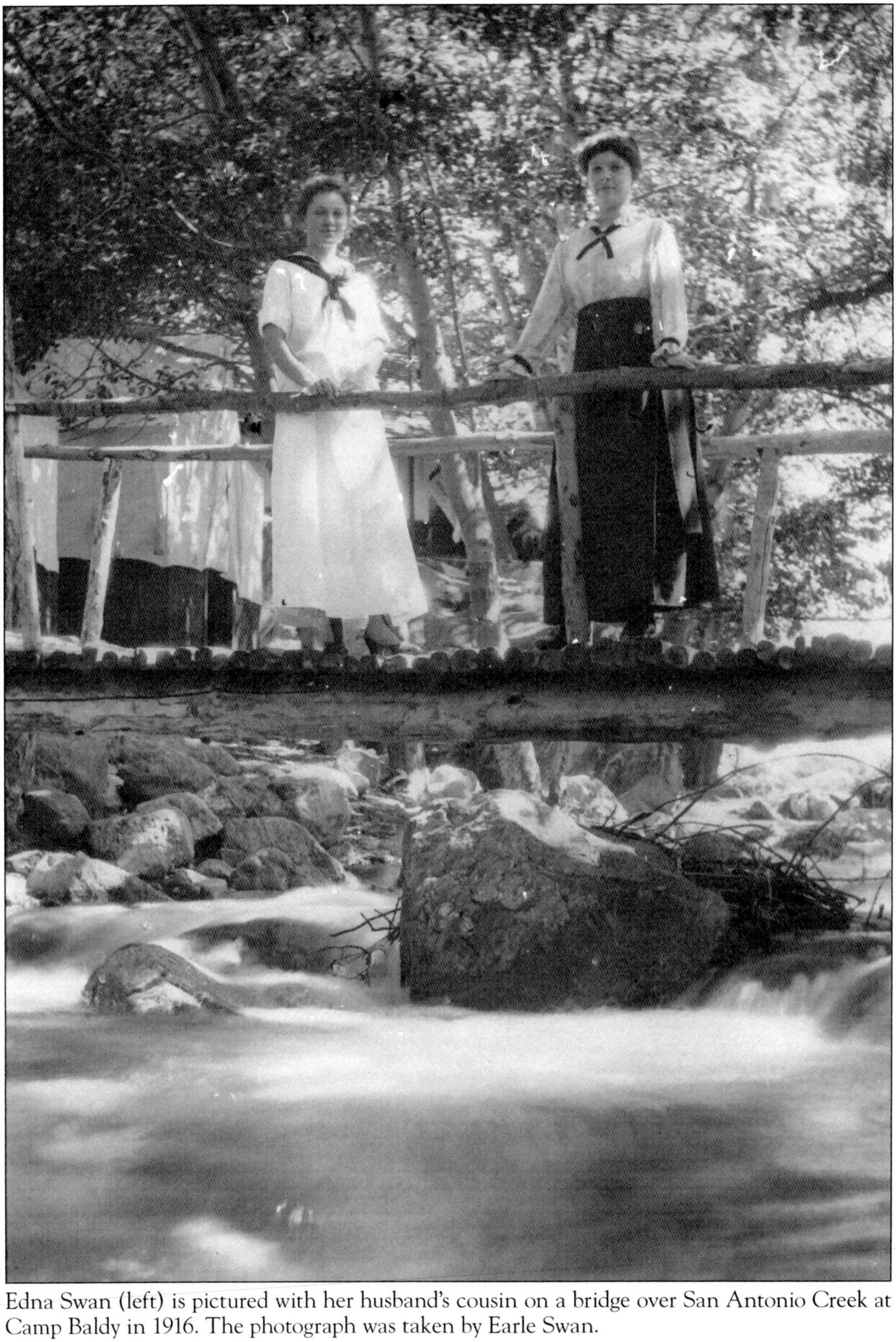

Edna Swan (left) is pictured with her husband's cousin on a bridge over San Antonio Creek at Camp Baldy in 1916. The photograph was taken by Earle Swan.